2

HOUSING DESIGN

An International Perspective

HOUSING

Ian Colquhoun
Peter G. Fauset

DESIGN

An International Perspective

B.T. Batsford Ltd · *London*

Typeset by Graphicraft Typesetters Ltd, Hong Kong
and printed in Great Britain by
The Bath Press, Bath, Avon

Published by B. T. Batsford Ltd
4 Fitzhardinge Street, London W1H 0AH

A catalogue record for this book is
available from the British Library

ISBN 0 7134 6107 1

CONTENTS

ACKNOWLEDGEMENTS

THE aim of this book is to bring together examples of most of the forms of new housing that have been created over the last ten years. The projects included are illustrative of their type. They all have in common the fact that they were designed by architects who were socially and artistically motivated to create housing schemes of real significance. Our thanks go to all the Architects who provided the material and for waiting so long to see their work published. Also to Ms E. M. Wood, Regional Development Manager of North British Housing Association for permission to include The Gables, Hambledon Street, Blyth, to the Birmingham City Council Housing Management Committee for permission to include their housing project at Bristol Road, to Grosvenor Estates for Bowland Yard, and to Jacqueline Johnson of the London Ecology Unit for information on ecological design.

Much of the research was undertaken in the British Architectural Library at the RIBA, 66 Portland Place, London; the friendly help and advice received from the staff there is an important aspect of a unique facility which is frequently under-valued by the architectural profession in Britain. Research was also undertaken in the libraries at Sheffield University and our thanks go to the staff there, particularly to Peter Lathey for developing and printing many photographs and to Elaine Hornbuckle of the Department of Architecture for secretarial assistance.

The support of the Leverhulme Trust was much appreciated. Other special acknowledgements are due to Jo Westgate for redrawing some of the plans, Fiona Colquhoun for her photography in Berlin and to Paul Hibberd and Pam Reaston for photographs from the United States. Particular thanks are due to Christine Colquhoun for her contribution throughout. Also appreciated is the hard work of Elizabeth Holloway and Margaret Mitchell who so patiently typed the numerous drafts of the text and to Tony Seward, Melanie Birdsall and Thelma Nye of B. T. Batsford Limited.

The photographs were taken by the authors, Fiona Colquhoun and Paul Hibberd; or were provided by the architects of the projects illustrated. If advised by the architects, copyright clearance has, wherever possible, been obtained from individual photographers. However, in a few cases, it has proved impossible to trace the copyright holders and the authors wish to convey their apologies to anyone whose rights may have been infringed.

To the best of the authors' knowledge, permission to use the photographs has been given by the following:

Abraham, R. for figures 4.23, 4.25; Ando, T. for 4.16; Annau Associates for 3.4; Baitz, O. Inc for 2.97, 3.16; Bastid, Bazaud and Gravayat for 2.57, 2.58; Bentz, F./Thompson, M./Rietow, R. Inc Architecture and Urban Design for 3.6; Birmingham City Council for 5.57, 5.59; Broadway Malyan for 5.34; Brock, Carmichael and Associates in association with BCA Landscape for 6.1; Cass, J. for 5.31; Charles, M. for 3.24, 3.31, 5.48; Colquhoun, F. for 2.9, 2.10, 2.12, 2.13, 2.14, 2.15, 2.23; Colquhoun, I. for 1.1, 1.3, 1.7, 2.2, 2.3, 2.4, 2.5, 2.6, 2.18, 2.19, 2.20, 2.51, 2.56, 2.64, 2.65, 2.66, 2.69, 2.70, 2.73, 2.74, 2.75, 2.77, 2.78, 2.86, 2.89, 6.4, 6.5, 6.6, 6.29, 6.31, 6.33, 6.34; Correa, C. for 2.21, 2.104; Dahinden, Prof. J. for 2.91, 2.92, 2.94, 2.95; Dahlström, R. for 2.47; Darbyshire Architects for 5.6; Domenig, G. for 6.7; Dupain, M. for 2.16, 2.28, 4.1, 5.51; Ejlers and Graversen for 5.7, 5.8, 5.41, 5.43; Eriksen, P.-J. and Knutsen, B. E. for 2.100, 2.103; Fauset, P. G. for 1.8; Feilden and Mawson for 2.1; Foto/C for 1.5, 6.3, 6.17, 6.22, 6.24; Graf, C. for 6.25, 6.26; Gudmund-Høyer, J. for 6.2; Hecker, Z. for 4.29, 4.31; Hertzberger, H. for 6.9, 6.12, 6.14; Hibberd, P. for 3.9, 3.12, 3.14, 5.1, 5.2; Huth, E. for 6.38, 6.40, 6.41; Jagger, W. for 5.20; Johnson, J. for 1.16; Kalischer, C. for 5.18; Karmi, R. for 4.34, 4.38, 4.39; KLM Aerocarto for 2.52; Knox and Markwell for 2.17; Kramer Group for the cover; Krupp, B. for 5.38, 5.39; Kuva-Ala, K. for 5.44, 5.47; Lenscape Incorporated for 2.31, 2.35, 3.2; Ley, P. de for 3.28; McGrath, N. for 3.17; Mazzuchi, J. for 5.14; Mills, J. for 5.30; Mischcon, P. and Associates for 2.47, 2.49, 2.51; Moore, D. for 2.27; Otte, G. for 2.44, 2.45; Otewell, C. for 5.6; Panda Associates for 2.33, 2.35, 2.41; Pietersen-Davison International for 2.108, 2.109; Regnbuen, Arkitektgruppen for 2.83, 2.84; Reijenga Postma BV for 2.80; Rista, S. for 1.10, 1.13; Robotham, B. for 1.6, 5.4, 5.23, 5.24, 5.25; Rosland Arkitektkontor AS. for 6.36; Scott, S. for 2.30, 2.31; Sexton, R. for 3.23; Sleigh, D. (Wessex Photography and Design) for 5.26; Smith, Hutton, Nichols for 4.3; Solomon, D. for 1.9, 3.10; Spalding Smith, F. for 2.41; Stephens, S. (by courtesy of the English Courtyard Association) for 1.12, 5.12; Summers, R. for 1.4; Szyszkowitz, M. and Kowalski, K. for 6.43, 6.44; Tanaka, K. for 2.62; Telgens Fotoatelier for 6.26; Tsurata, K. for 4.20; Westwood, C. for 5.3, 5.28; Wheeler, N. for 4.10, 4.13; Yamashita, T. for 4.8; Zimbaldi, D. for 3.15.

Ian Colquhoun and *Peter G. Fauset*
1991

1 THE POPULARITY OF GROUPED HOUSING

Principal Influences

OVER three-quarters of the population of the Western world live in town and cities. Most live in housing which was built as part of a group. The group may be along a street, around a cul-de-sac, designed in the form of a square, clustered on a hillside or even designed within one building. Throughout history towns and cities have grown in these ways. History, however, has also shown that grouped housing has been considerably influenced by social ideologies and by particular planning and design concepts, which, whilst they were initially developed in one or two countries, have thereafter become internationally adopted. The attempts in so many countries to create the ideal human habitat, in the form of grouped housing, have also been influenced by factors beyond the control of the designers and the occupants. Of these influences, the lack of proper levels of financial investment and the manipulation of house building by national governments to suit political objectives have been amongst the strongest. The results are all too evident in most countries, but in recent years the approach to the design of grouped housing by architects has shown a new awareness of the factors that make for good design in housing. This book attempts to demonstrate the quality of the new approach by illustrating examples and explaining the principles which make them successful.

The influences that have brought about the new awareness are related to an increase in the general level of expectation by society at large. This concerns not just the functional requirements – space, convenience, accommodation for the motor car, etc. – but also the level of esteem the housing represents for its occupants. Such expectations also mean that new grouped housing has considerable competition. Firstly, there is a wealth of second-hand housing, which is frequently more spacious than housing built today, and which is set in an environment that has matured over many years; such housing may also have larger gardens. However, the second, and perhaps much greater influence, is people's desire for detachment and their preference for individual identity. The greater the individuality of the location and of the form and appearance of the dwelling, the greater the dwelling's acceptability. It is also easy to extend a detached house or bungalow, and noise transference from one dwelling to another is less of a problem. If a detached dwelling is beyond people's means, a semi-detached one is their second choice. The desire for detachment has nowhere expressed itself more vigorously than in the sprawling low density cities that have grown up in countries such as the United States of America, Australia and New Zealand in the last hundred years. The effect of the desire for detachment can now be seen spreading across Britain and parts of

Western Europe, and it can only be countered by the construction of well-designed grouped housing built to reasonable densities and to a reasonable standard.

In Britain over the last ten years around half a million people have left the cities to live in low density housing in red brick estates which encircle or infill existing country towns and villages. By the year 2000 it is estimated by the Office of Population Censuses and Surveys that this trend will not have slowed down, and that another 73,000 hectares (180,000 acres) of land will be required. Polls show that 80 per cent of Britons want to live in country towns and villages but preferably not in large estates. Much of the land that has been identified by planners for new housing development exists in urban areas. If need and land availability are to be balanced there must be a positive policy for investment in the revitalization of the inner cities, which must be preferable to despoiling the countryside.

However, low density housing forms in urban areas raise problems which cannot be easily disposed of. Prominent amongst these is the fact that the detached house and the semi-detached house, with gaps between where garages are located, built at low density, are not really urban. The pattern of layout and housing form is all too familiar: the land around the cul-de-sac road system is divided into more or less equal plots, each of which receives a box-like three-

1.1   Dockside development in Hull.
Architects: Browne, Smith, Baker and Partners.

bedroom house and separate garage. The road is often wide with kerbs, pavements and out-of-scale street-lights. The spaces between the buildings are secondary in every sense to the motor vehicle: no community is envisaged or planned for. This contrasts sharply with the traditional town or city street or square in which housing is inextricably mixed with shops, workshops and community buildings of all kinds. Here patterns of habitation reflect social relationships and the dependence of people on one another. The land take for low density housing can be enormous and, whilst the individual's requirements may be met, it has a considerable effect on the community as a whole, as movement from home to work, school, shops, etc. becomes even more dependent upon the motor vehicle and the quality of the infrastructure of roads. Whether it is more important to meet the

desires and aspirations of the individual, as opposed to those of the community as a whole, is a much debated issue. What is clear in all western countries is that the spread of low density housing into the countryside is taking up valuable agricultural land and absorbing physical and financial resources which would be better if channelled into urban regeneration. It is to the credit of city authorities, developers and architects in many countries that this reality is now beginning to be expressed in programmes of new housing in inner urban location, on land formerly devoted to industrial and commercial uses. Dockland sites (Fig 1.1), riverside sites and infill sites within existing residential areas are all benefiting from a new realism. Architects have traditionally sought this ideal and opposed suburban sprawl. However, what they must not overlook today is that to attract people to such development it must offer more than the occupant could obtain from a detached or semi-detached

dwelling in a suburban location. The new grouped housing must allow for individual expression and possess high esteem value: the environment and the quality of architecture must be beyond normal expectation.

1.2   Urban design proposals for the Kingswood area of Warrington New Town, Cheshire, prepared by Warrington and Runcorn Development Corporation.
Chief Architect and Planner: Hugh Cannings.

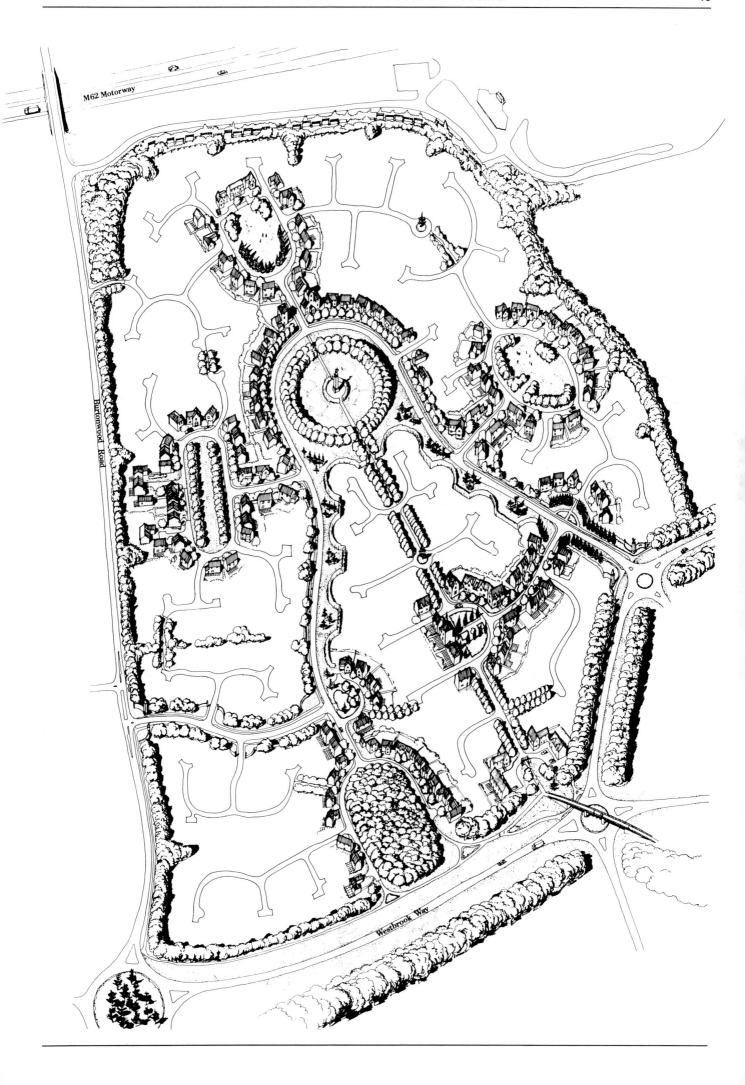

Design principles

In recent years architects have risen
to the new challenges and have
produced highly imaginative design
solutions. Not all the schemes
illustrated in this book may be liked by
everybody but most of them adhere to
some or all of the following principles,
which should be adopted if good
design is to be achieved.

1   They are either small in scale or
     designed to create a sense of
     security and local belonging.
2   The roads and footpaths are not
     segregated from each other or
     from the buildings they serve.
3   They are appropriate to the site.
4   They relate to the surroundings
     in terms of the built form and the
     hierarchy of spaces created,
     whilst being of human scale and
     recognizable as such by the
     occupants.
5   The image of the development
     compensates for any loss of
     detachment.
6   The amount and division of the
     space within the dwellings, and
     any ancillary accommodation,
     relate to the particular pattern
     of living of the occupants; in
     addition, the spaces within the
     dwellings have been designed
     as pleasant, workable interiors
     and have been carefully made
     to complement the external
     environment, aspect, orientation,
     etc.
7   The future residents have been
     involved in the design process in
     one form or another.

These principles are further explained
below.

1   Size of development

The projects are of such a size that it
was possible for each of them to have
been designed by one architect or,
at most, by a very small team of
architects. Their size also allowed
construction methods that do
not require large-scale building
operations. These points are not
without significance, for perhaps part
of the failure of the mass housing
programmes of the 1960s can be

**1.3   Hillside housing in Givors, near Lyons,
France.**
Architect: Jean Renaudie.

1.4 Executive housing in Esher, Surrey, preserves all the existing features of a beautiful site.
Architects: Royston Summers.

attributed to the sheer size of the developments. However, large scale development will always take place and architects and planners need to come to terms with the problem of creating development strategies for them which ensure that individual projects are of a sufficiently small size within an overall co-ordinated urban design policy. This means the production of broad-based development plans which are not to be seen as master plans but as a set of urban design principles which provide common design objectives (Fig 1.2). Such objectives are achieved most satisfactorily when they relate new housing to, either the nature of the site, its topography, orientation and aspect, or to a strong pattern of social events such as community facilities, parks, open spaces, etc.

2 Roads and footpaths
The plan should create a pattern of roads and footpaths which relate to the buildings. Whilst the size and scale of development in the 1960s was a major reason for its failure, the segregation of traffic and pedestrian ways from each other, and from the buildings they served, was also a significant contributory factor. The loss of the relationship between front door and street, with its bustle of cars and people, will never be acceptable without other compensatory attractions such as a convenient location, an extremely attractive site, a good view or a very high quality product. Likewise, a large length of road which has no direct relationship to housing is undesirable. This is perhaps the greatest area of failure in the new towns built after the Second World War, where highly engineered road systems actually divide the residential areas they were intended to link.

3 Appropriateness to the site
Almost every site, by virtue of its location, shape, gradient or character, will influence the form of the new housing development. Some sites exert a stronger influence than others. Infill sites, for instance, call for solutions which harmonize with the surroundings (chapter 3); hillside sites frequently inspire unique and innovative solutions (Fig 1.3 and chapter 4). In some instances the choice of sites may dictate a high density solution, whilst others may point to a low density development complementing preserved landscape features such as existing trees, hedgerows or rock outcrops (Fig 1.4)

**1.5   An architecture that reflects its
Danish heritage: Hedelyngen, Herlev.**
Architects: Tegnestuen Vandkunsten.

4 Relationship to the surroundings

Within urban areas, the relationships of dwellings to the scale and character of their surroundings is important. This does not mean a rigid adherence to the existing architectural style of the area, more a respect for its layout and proportions in terms of space and height of buildings. The pattern of the existing streets should not be lost. The new schemes built as part of Berlin's Internationale Bauausstellung (IBA) best illustrate this principle, with new housing designed around the perimeter of the city blocks leaving the opportunity for open space within (Fig 2.8). The project at Fécamp in northern France (Figs 2.55 to 2.59) illustrates an approach appropriate for the centre of a medieval town or city.

5 Image

Image is a major requirement of satisfaction. It is made up of a number of factors: layout, density, degree of openness, appearance of the dwelling, and quality of planting. The most critical factor of image is the appearance of the dwellings themselves.

The overriding trend today is for architects and their patrons to seek refuge in nostalgia. Faced with the public outcry from the last 20 years for the rush to build large numbers of houses quickly in the 1960s, architects all over the world have now come to believe that a vernacular image is the only viable solution. Gabled roofs, windows with shutters, wood and brick predominate, and the results are tremendously popular. Their gentility and folksiness correspond to the universal ideal of a house. These cute houses are what people want and only a highly sophisticated urban and well-off society, as in New York or London for instance, will accept different concepts, and even there the longing for suburbia is strong. (Pallasma 1988)

In urban locations, the trend is for housing to look like the buildings which formerly stood on the site. The 'warehouse' image, the 'boat yard', the 'mock-dock' or 'seaside front' provides the nostalgia. This does not mean that everything reflecting the local vernacular of an area or a country is essentially wrong. For instance, the Danish architects, Tegnestuen Vandkunsten, have pursued and developed an approach to architecture which reflects Danishness (Fig 1.5). Their architecture is essentially domestic but they use twentieth-century materials, including sheet metal roofing, in a thoroughly present-day manner. British architects, Mathew Robotham Associates, adopt a similar approach to their work but use traditional local materials (Fig 1.6). Their approach to the design and the detailing gives the new dwellings an air of permanence without copying the

1.6 Housing for elderly people at Lynn Road, Wisbech, Cambridgeshire.
Architects: Mathew Robotham Associates.

past. In Australia, architects Philip Cox and Partners and Allen, Jack and Cottier also reflect tradition in a modern way. Their urban regeneration at Woolloomooloo, Sydney, creates an architecture that owes as much to Australia as to America or Europe (Figs 2.16 and 2.25 to 2.29). It is authentic and not reproduction. In the USA traditionalism has strong roots but nevertheless modernism flourishes, particularly in the cities. White painted boarding and cedar shingles are still very much in evidence but contrasting with this are schemes such as those in San Francisco – Macondray Terrace Condominiums by architects Hood Miller Associates, and Castro Common by Daniel Solomon and Associates (Figs 3.9 and 3.23) – which are very much of the twentieth century.

1.7   The crescent at Les Espaces d'Abraxes, Marne-la-Vallée.
Architect: Taller de Arquitectura: Ricardo Bofill.

century. Designs such as these need no labelling as to their architectural style. They are amongst a wealth of schemes in many countries offering an alternative to nostalgia and suburban sprawl.

Style and fashion are important to the French, but in France traditionalism exists side by side with modernism. In northern France the housing scene is clearly influenced by Britain and many of the new schemes built in recent years have an 'Anglo-Saxon' feel – low rise in form with comfortable tiled roofs and brick or white-painted walls. The dwellings are laid out in small clusters or are grouped around traditional culs-de-sac or loop roads. In contrast to this is the high density housing in Paris (Fig 2.2) and in the new towns around Paris. Constructed in concrete – either precast or in situ – with flat roofs and walls clad in a variety of materials, including render, brickwork and ceramic tiles, the housing is very distinctive. The ultimate expression of French

modernity is the classicism of Ricardo Bofill's housing in St Quentin-en-Yvelines and Marne-la-Vallée (Figs 1.7, 2.5, 2.63 to 2.67).

The form and architectural style of these schemes would be totally unacceptable in Britain but so too might much of the more simple and admirable, but still modern, designs of other French architects and their counterparts in Germany, the Netherlands and elsewhere – such as those by Alain Sarfarti and Rob Krier. In Britain society has strongly resisted all attempts by the architectural profession to persuade them of the merits of anything other than what they are familiar with. The more the housing design incorporates the essential amenities of the detached or the semi-detached house, the more acceptable it will be to the residents. This does not mean, however, that a dogmatic adherence to popular taste should be adopted, but more that design should, at least, follow some of the criteria set out below.

1.8 Span Housing in Cambridge.
Architect: Eric Lyons Cunningham Partnership.

a) A degree of aesthetic complexity should be provided that enables people to identify their own dwelling within the group (Fig 3.2).

b) Individual entrances at ground level to as many dwellings as possible: even those on upper levels should be highly attractive (Figs 3.24, 3.25). (Figs 3.24, 3.24).

c) Care should be taken in the choice of materials, colours, etc, if they are other than those with which people are familiar.

d) Opportunity should be provided for the residents to personalize the land around their dwelling and particularly their front doors.

e) Exploit the design of corner houses and ends of terraces by placing doors and windows in the gable ends.

f) In large developments exploit differences of appearance and character through the use of a variety of building materials and colours. A sensitive urban design policy is essential to create variety but it should be applied in a structured way which takes account of the fact that contrast in itself becomes monotonous.

g) Avant-garde solutions should be attempted on a small scale initially and their success proved before being developed further.

British architects frequently lament the lack of innovative modern design in housing and many argue that as a nation the British are architecturally illiterate. It is indeed a fact that good innovative modern domestic architecture has few patrons even amongst the highest levels of society. If change is to happen, it must come about as a result of different aspirations on the part of the consumer who must be educated to realize and appreciate the possibilities. It also requires a spark of imagination. As in any artistic sphere, innovation starts with a small number of creative designers whose ideas filter down to the mass market. Eric Lyons and Span Developments achieved this in the 1960s. They saw that good design pays and this principle is no less important in today's highly competitive market (Fig 1.8).

6   Internal design

In Britain the design of the individual dwelling has always been synonymous with standards, yet most new dwellings are smaller than their European and American counterparts. Moreover, the space provided is seldom used as imaginatively. Even within a tight budget it is possible to design internal spaces, not merely as a series of rooms for cooking, eating, sleeping and sitting, but as spaces which create an atmosphere of warmth and security, pleasure and enjoyment, and in which the occupants can express themselves. Some of the means by which this can be achieved are demonstrated in the projects illustrated and are as follows:

a) The creation of privacy and an opportunity for personalization of internal spaces by the design of the dwellings. The function of rooms should be as inter-changeable as possible to cater for the more varied households and life-styles of the future. Dwelling types that offer the maximum acoustic separation from adjoining dwellings should be used. Wide frontage dwellings are preferred for this reason but also because they allow opportunity for the construction of add-on sun rooms, bay windows, and other extensions.

b) Sensitive location and design of windows, rooflights, skylights and other openings, related to the interior as well as the external appearance of the dwellings. Windows with low cills can allow people to look into their garden whilst sitting. The use of bay and oriel windows can help to create intimate areas internally for sitting, eating and working, whilst enhancing the appearance of the exterior (Figs 1.9, 3.17, 3.28). This can be a most significant feature in housing for the elderly where people with mobility difficulties may spend much time sitting indoors. It is essential to ensure that the location of radiators does not prohibit the full use of such features. It is important also to consider the arrangement of windows and other openings in relationship to orientation. The penetration of the sun can be either a benefit or a disadvantage but good design can maximize its potential (Figs 1.14, 1.15, 2.83).

c) Staircases should be designed to provide a visual link between floors rather than merely a means of access (Fig 1.10, 6.10). The natural lighting of stairs is an important factor, not merely from the safety point of view, but also for the opportunities windows and skylights can offer for upper level views of the outside and points of interest which enhance the interior (Fig 4.12).

1.9   Oriel windows enhance the quality of the interior as well as the exterior: Pacific Heights town houses, San Francisco, USA.
Architect: Daniel Solomon and Associates.

1.10 Mezzanine level and sloping ceilings make full use of the volume: Kartanonkari housing, Malminkartano, Helsinki.
Architect: A Konsultit.

d) Roofs should be designed to maximize the use of the volume of dwellings. (Figs 2.99, 2.109).

e) A positive relationship should be established between internal and private or semi-private outdoor spaces. Even the smallest private garden or balcony should be considered as an external extension of the dwelling (Figs 2.15, 4,7, 6.12, 6.14, 6.16) and be clearly visible from as much of the interior as possible. Movement from the inside to these areas should flow naturally (Figs 2.27, 6.10, 6.12).

f) A fireplace should be installed in the main living area despite the provision of full central heating. The 'hearth' is a most important design feature in the USA where it is seen as an important focal point for the household, contributing considerably to the atmosphere and character of the home.

g) Sensitively designed communal areas, including staircases and corridors, should be created (Figs 2.41, 4.39, 5.39, 5.59, 6.15).

7 Resident participation in design

One reason for the success of recent grouped housing design in many countries has been the involvement of the future occupants in the design of the dwellings and their grouping. Traditionally, consumer influence is expressed only when the occupants select or are allocated their dwelling but as many people find themselves with more leisure time on their hands and greater affluence, it is only natural that they should become more aware of their environment. In Denmark, the Netherlands, Switzerland and, more lately, in the USA, Great Britain and elsewhere, this has resulted in numerous projects of high quality (chapter 6). Experience from these examples shows that ordinary people – i.e. consumers/residents – are much more aware of housing matters than is, perhaps, usually recognized.

If the users are given the chance to influence their housing situation from the earliest planning stages to the point where they move to their dwellings, they really do make use of that influence and the final utility value of the product is enhanced. On the other hand, users clearly have to acknowledge the special insight and experience of experts and, in a mutual relationship, must learn that at all levels there are limits to the influence they can exert. Users cannot and must not decide the size of beams or the proportions of the spatial and external appearance. There are specialists who have been trained to do the job better. But the work of the specialist attains greater quality. If they can be provoked into defending their choice and keeping an open mind towards the opinion of others. (Hansen and Larsen 1981:18)

Other Influences

There are other factors which influence the form and appearance of grouped housing. These are:
1 The move back to town.
2 The need to cater adequately for needs previously overlooked, such as those of elderly people,

disabled people, the young and other new tenure groups who desire independent housing and new patterns of living.

3   Energy and ecology issues which are becoming an increasingly dominant influences on new housing design.

1   The move back to town

The move back to town is a new and important opportunity for architects to create urban housing. The cost of travel on congested roads and the increasing quality of the centres of large towns and cities as places in which to live, together with social and cultural opportunities now available, make urban living an attractive alternative to living in the suburbs and other out-of-town locations. In the large, sprawling cities of the USA, Australia and elsewhere experience points to serious social problems arising from a public transport service that could never operate without huge subsidies. This is a particular difficulty in households where both partners work but cannot afford two cars, in single parent families and for elderly people who become isolated. The lack of transport is also a difficulty for adolescents, who at a much earlier age are seeking more and more independence from their parents. In a low density environment in an out-of-town location, meeting up with friends and getting to facilities can be almost impossible without great support from parents.

For these reasons households are beginning to move back to the city to be closer to work opportunities, public transport and facilities. However, this trend is taking off more slowly in Britain and there is still immense prejudice against living an an urban environment, both because of a fundamental desire to live in the country and because of the legacy of the 1960s when utilitarian post-war developments, put up everywhere to house the needy, left many inner urban areas characterless. However, in recent years there has been a concentration of effort in Britain and many other countries to restore old

1.11   New infill housing relates to the historic architecture of Wetter Freiheit, Germany.
Architect: Karl Friedrich Getise.

buildings in the centre of towns and cities and to inject new developments back into the older urban areas. The approach differs: in some countries the authorities are guided by the demands of the market; in some housing design is an instrument of social policy, whilst in others it is dictated by a desire to beautify. The result, regardless of the motives, is either small scale, sensitive infill (Fig 1.11) or large scale urban renewal projects in run down, largely cleared sites, previously used for industrial purposes (Fig 2.20). Both are producing popular design solutions which are entirely different from semi-detached suburban housing.

2   Housing the whole community

Housing for elderly people
The social structure of most of the western world has altered significantly over the past few years. The proportion of elderly people in society has increased dramatically and will continue to do so. The number of very elderly in particular – i.e. those over 80 years old – is increasing at a considerable rate. Most elderly people are quite happy to remain in their family home with some support from the community. Some, however, prefer to move to new housing designed to meet the needs of old age. In the United States this has led to the development of large, privately funded retirement villages but also to a wealth of small projects (Figs 5.1, 5.2,

5.13 to 5.20) similar to those built in Great Britain (Figs 1.12, 5.3 to 5.6, 5.10 to 5.12, 5.21 to 5.35 and Scandinavia (Fig 5.40 to 5.47). The quality of these designs is very high; the overriding problem, however, is the shortage of such suitably designed housing for the large number of people who need it.

Housing for disabled people
The desire of most disabled people for a normal life brings with it the need to integrate their homes within the community (Figs 5.54 to 5.59). However, so far only countries such as Denmark and Finland have effective national policies which have been reflected in some highly imaginative projects. Most housing for disabled people has been financed by public bodies and charitable organizations through the provision of subsidized housing. In Britain 94 per cent of housing designed specifically for disabled people has been provided by the public sector. A similar percentage is applicable to the provision of special housing for elderly people.

1.12 Lyfield Court, designed for the English Courtyard Association.
Architects: Sidell Gibson Partnership.

Housing for young people

The numbers of young people establishing their own home is increasing rapidly in most countries in the Western world, yet the percentage of new housing specially designed to meet their needs is extremely low. Large numbers of young people therefore turn to the private rented sector which in Britain is totally inadequate to cope with demand. In addition the marriage rate has fallen whilst the divorce rate has risen. The Department of the Environment estimates that in Britain by 2001, two million new, if smaller households, will need to be accommodated: much of this should be for young people.

1.13   Scandinavian expertise in low energy design is illustrated by the Ylatuvanpolku housing at Torpparinmäki, Helsinki.
Architects: Helin and Siitonen Bernhardinkatu.

3   Energy conservation

The energy crisis has brought about the development of new forms of housing (Figs 1.13 to 1.15) but in many countries the technology has yet to filter down to the mass market. The Scandinavians have responded most significantly.Denmark and Finland have developed large district heating schemes many of which take advantage of the combined generation of heating and power. The target in Denmark is for 55% of the country's heating requirements in 1995 to be met this way, which could result in over £2000 million in energy savings per year. District heating schemes require new dwellings to be close together in order to obtain maximum efficiency from the cost of installing the pipework and the subsequent running costs. High density/low-rise housing schemes developed since the early 1970s in Denmark offer design solutions to the energy

problem, as illustrated in the 'Sol og Vind' project (Figs 2.82 to 2.85).

The cost of energy for personal transport could encourage more people to live in urban areas. It is not beyond reason that the cost of commuting will eventually affect income groups that can currently afford the cost of travel from their homes in country towns or villages to their places of work and recreation in the city. A more rational approach to accommodating people must be to locate new housing in inner urban areas at higher density than in the suburbs. However, energy costs will have to rise still more significantly than in recent years to force people away from their single family house in its own plot. Good design will be an essential ingredient for the alternative to succeed.

1.14 Energy conscious housing at Tiergarten, Berlin. The use of conservatories add to the external appearance of the project as well as saving energy.

Architects: Pysall/Jensen.

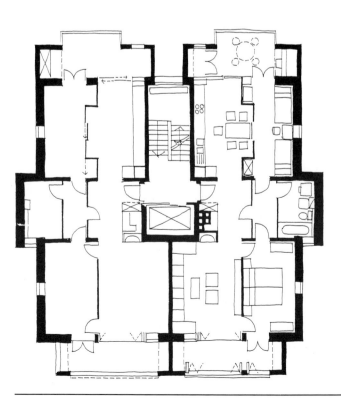

1.15 Floor plans of apartment block in Berlin: note the 'winter gardens' on either side of the dwelling.

Architects: Manfred Schiedhelm and Karen Axelrad.

Ecological design

As towns and cities have expanded, people have become increasingly alienated from nature: most people need regular contact with nature for their spiritual refreshment and well being. It is this that generated the Garden City movement at the turn of the century and it has remained a principal influence on the design of human habitat ever since.

Housing development in urban areas would therefore benefit greatly if an ecological approach to its design were to be adopted. The key design principle is to create 'sustainable' development. This can be defined as development which meets present day needs without compromising the ability of future generations to achieve their needs. Architects therefore need to think of how new housing development affects the air, water, soil, vegetation and people: an ecological approach means looking at a multitude of issues from energy use, waste, water run off, transport, to, most significantly, green space. Here nature should be the back-cloth to housing development and not merely the add-on or the greening which softens the hard built forms. In her paper presented at the Royal Institute of British Architects in June 1991, Jacklyn Johnson of the London Ecology Unit explained the benefits of this approach:

- greenspace can help to clear the air — one hectare of trees will filter 4 tonnes of particulates out of the air each year
- green areas will take in carbon dioxide and thereby bring cooler, fresher air to urban areas
- there are obvious benefits to wildlife by providing natural habitats
- green areas are attractive and even soothing: they provide an escape from the hard environment of urban areas. They provide places for recreation and for reinforcing the relationship between people and nature
- green environments enhance

development value and can therefore be attractive to investors.

Greenspace can be incorporated into development in a number of ways: firstly through taking maximum advantage of existing open space, woodland, water or any other natural feature: secondly greenspace can be incorporated by creating new green areas: thirdly opportunities also exist in the spaces between the buildings and on the buildings themselves (Fig 1.16).

Greening values can also be achieved by sensible detailing and selection of materials. Minimizing the use of hard surfaces, tarmac, concrete, etc, can achieve a high degree of local recycling of water and improve the permeability of the ground. Building products should be selected on the basis of the

replacement of the raw materials. Softwoods should be used instead of hardwoods wherever possible but where hardwoods have to be used they should come from sustainable sources only.

The chapters which follow expand on some of these influences. Each commences with an explanation of the main design principles for the particular type of housing. This is followed with descriptions and illustrations of built examples. It is hoped that this format will make clear what is required of architects if their grouped housing projects are to be acceptable to society in the future.

1.16   The greening of housing in Kreuzberg, Berlin.

2 URBAN HOUSING

IT is not the location that makes housing urban but more often its form. Village housing can be just as urban as housing built in large towns and cities (Fig 2.1). Urban housing is essentially terraced housing, built along streets and around squares, or housing that is clustered around small spaces. There are often only small areas of private open space. It is often common for car parking provision to be lower than in suburban housing, and sometimes integral or even underground garaging may be provided. The housing may be mixed with other uses, such as shopping or offices on the ground floor.

From Victorian times urban housing in Britain has been associated with the apparent evils of the Industrial Revolution. Despite the existence of Bath, Edinburgh new town, Cheltenham, Buxton and other examples of pre-Industrial Revolution towns, the generally held concept of an urban environment is still that of the northern industrial city with its 'by-law' street housing accompanied by the tower blocks and deck access developments of the 1960s. Housing of this kind has been deplored in many countries, but urban housing as such has always been more acceptable to other nationalities than to the British.

2.1 Urban housing in a village setting: Rialton Heights, Cornwall.
Architects: Feilden and Mawson.

This attitude might be attributable to the climate, in that warmer weather encourages people in other countries to live more of their lives outside – in the street, along the promenade and in the square. Perhaps more significantly, it can be put down to a difference in cultural legacies. Prior to the Industrial Revolution the vast majority of people in Britain lived in rural communities; the city-state, that predominated elsewhere in Europe, did not exist in Britain. The rigours of the Industrial Revolution were disliked to such an extent that both the rich and the poor in Britain never lost the longing for their rural roots, whereas in the rest of Europe the impact of the Industrial Revolution was far less significant. This cultural difference expresses itself in attitudes towards 'home'. The Anglo-Saxon ideal of a country cottage on its own plot is strong, whereas the urban European ideal is of city living.

However, this difference had no effect on the almost universal dislike in all countries of the international housing built in the 1960s, which was based on the theories of Le Corbusier and others. When Le Corbusier replaced the traditional street with the skyscraper out in the middle of nowhere, in the 1920s, he claimed to be a socially engaged architect. Along with an entire generation of architects in the 1960s, he genuinely meant to improve the increasingly run-down housing in the large towns and cities. He justified his ideas by producing a picture depicting a strong and hard-working individual bathed in sunlight amidst the green of nature between the blocks. The concept failed because it had no understanding of the past. However, such an understanding is not enough on its own: the cultural, social, economic and political realities of the present day must not be ignored either. Society as a whole, as well as architects, is discovering that urban cultures and the built forms of pre-industrial towns and cities can be seen as memorials to intelligence and pleasure. The task for architects is to resolve today's design problems in a way that offers, in current terms, new interpretations of

past experiences. What architects create must, however, be devoid of the currently fashionable affection for past images: the design itself must be the style.

Design principles

The principles of designing urban housing are straightforward. The most important design criterion is to relate the development to the existing pattern of streets, squares and open

2.2   The new urbanism in Paris at Rue Baudricot.
Architects: Georgia Benamo and Christian de Portzamparc.

spaces, whilst at the same time creating identifiable places and a sense of belonging and security.

In his search for urban forms Rob Krier's research and designs are of fundamental importance. His main goals are the creation of streets and squares for people. In his book *Stadtraum in Theorie und Praxis*, he tries to establish a methodical typology of urban space systems. He is against land use zoning and the division of towns and cities into areas of different functions, as proposed by Le Corbusier and planners thereafter. He believes that it is the complexity of urban space, with its multiple and changing functions, not the restriction of space to one function only, that creates life

2.3 These apartments in the Quartier des Epinettes, Evry New Town, near Paris, are typical of the French approach to housing in urban areas.

Architects: A. Peritore and J. Duval.

and harmony in cities (Krier, R. 1979). His ideas have been manifested in several projects, of which, the culmination is, perhaps, his work for the Internationale Bauasstellung (IBA) in Berlin. (Figs 2.8 to 2.13) His brother, Leon, shares the same conviction but goes on to advocate that:

> Architecture must be refounded in the intelligence of history. This it must take as its concern, the understanding, adoption and evolution of building types which express human needs and experience. (in Morgan and Naylor 1987:500)

The principles of the design of urban housing can best be demonstrated by referring to the approach in a number of countries.

France

In France, the architectural form and appearance of much of the country's new housing is highly distinctive as architects seek to create an urban identity in their work. Le Corbusier's theories of town planning, which epitomized housing design in the 1950s and 1960s, have given way to a preference for re-creating urban forms: the street, the traditional urban city block with dwellings lining the back edge of the pavement (Fig 2.2) and enclosing a landscaped courtyard within. The urban ideal is also echoed in the appearance of the dwelling blocks themselves. The French construction industry became highly centralized by the late 1960s when it was geared up to build public sector housing fast. This influence on French housing still remains and today much is built using in situ concrete construction clad in render, brickwork or tiling (Fig 2.3). Pre-cast concrete panel construction is also extensively used. There is little consensus on architectural style but there is clearly an intention to concentrate on creating specific urban images.

This intention is illustrated in new housing at Rue Baudricot, Paris (Fig 2.2) designed by Georgia Benamo and Christian de Portzamparc. Roland Simounet's town houses grouped

2.5   Form triumphs over function at the Palacio d'Abraxas, Marne-la-Vallée, near Paris.
Architect: Taller de Arquitectura: Ricardo Bofill.

2.4   Town houses overlooking the Cathedral of Saint-Denis, Paris.
Architect: Roland Simounet.

size and type is closely tailored to predetermined price ranges, while their form and appearance are more closely in tune with the policies of marketing men than the preferences of architectural purists. (Ellis 1986)

Germany – Berlin

The principal aim of the IBA was to rebuild the city of streets within a three dimensional urban framework established by the nineteenth-century pattern of streets, squares, parks and public buildings. It has been the single most important influence on building in Berlin: everywhere schemes have arisen from the architects' intention to hand the city back to the people. Whatever its shortcomings, there is no doubt that in its scope and enthusiasm the IBA has had no equal in any European city. Its findings and its errors will have a far-reaching influence on city planning all over the world.

Much of the recent housing in western Germany has been constructed to meet social needs with rents fixed according to earnings: with rising earnings occupants are allowed to stay, but they must pay higher rents. The IBA may have been about social housing, but it is not the housing of the 1950s and 1960s. New policies of refurbishment ('Altbau') and sensitive infill ('Neubau') were adopted. The IBA had no grand overall plan nor all-embracing solution such as had previously marked urban planning and architecture. Each individual project was carefully judged on its merits and potential; variety was considered the essential criterion. Resident participation was an important element of the design process. People were asked to join in the planning, and the result was an environment much less dominated by the architecture and one which left enough room for the individual. In every scheme there is evidence of the residents' self-expression and their spontaneous response to the architects' creations. Perhaps the scale of the developments – rarely more than 150 dwellings in each project – has something to do with

around two hard-paved squares close to the Cathedral of Saint-Denis in Paris (Fig 2.4) relate in modern terms to the Gothic architecture of the cathedral. Ricardo Bofill adds a new dimension: his aim is to develop a new typology of urban tissue based on the ambience of Medieval, Renaissance and Baroque examples of street, square and open space. His recent work in Marne-la-Vallée (Fig 2.5) and St Quentin-en-Yvelines shows his total reliance on classical models treated in a monumental manner.

A totally different kind of French urbanism is illustrated at Le Haut de l'Echelotte at Paron, near Sens, Yonne. Here architect J. Fatosme

has created, in a very rural setting, housing, which in its total grouping, takes on the form of a chateau, even down to the small towers, turrets and gatehouses (Figs 2.6, 2.7). Is this urbanism or is it a protest against the housing scene in and around the large cities? Charlotte Ellis makes the suggestion that the French do actually like low density housing of a domestic appearance 'in a very Anglo-Saxon sense'. New estates of detached, semi-detached and terraced houses are sprouting up everywhere.

Their architectural pretensions rarely stretch beyond a grouping sufficiently 'urban' to please the town planning authorities; house

2.6   Towers and turrets at Le Haut de l'Echelotte.

Architect: J. Fatosme.

their success. Money is clearly being spent on the maintenance of the dwellings, but everywhere there is evidence of people's imagination, love and pride in their homes and a total absence of neglect – so different from the attitude to much social housing in Britain. (See Clelland 1984; Clelland and Davey 1987; Gough 1984; Hannay 1986; *Techniques et Architecture* 1983)

Ritterstrasse Nord

The principles of the approach are best illustrated in the working-class district of Ritterstrasse Nord, where Rob Krier and six other architectural practices designed prototypes for urban social housing.

Rob Krier's 23 apartment houses are grouped around three courtyards, each with a distinctively different character (Fig 2.8). The central

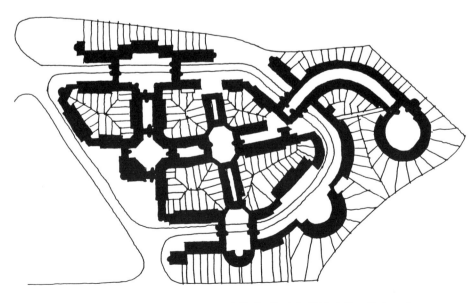

2.7   Le Haut de l'Echelotte: site layout.

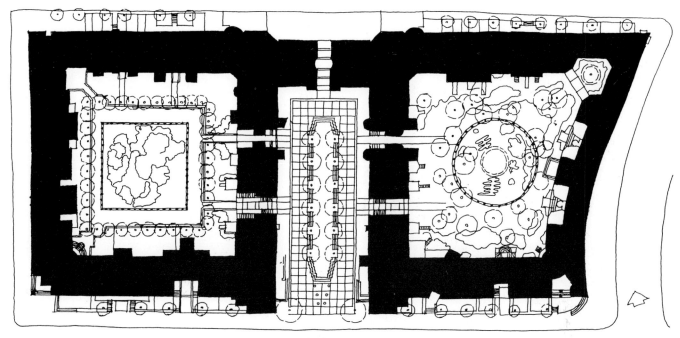

site layout

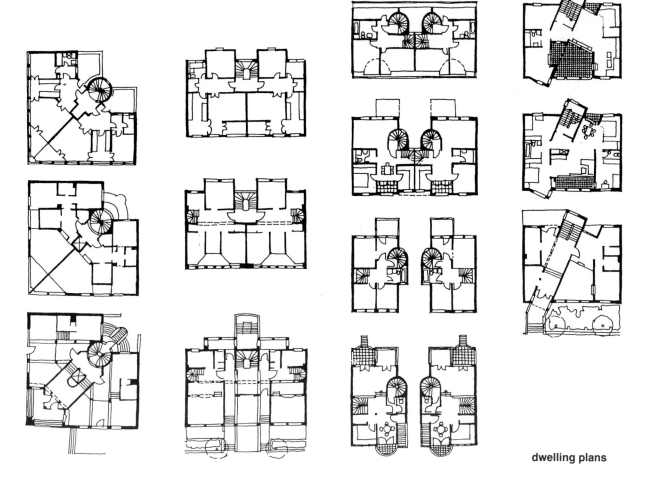

dwelling plans

2.8   Ritterstrasse Nord, Berlin.

Architect: Rob Krier.

2.9   Ritterstrasse Nord, the grand archway.

courtyard is intended to be public and
serve as the grand entrance to the
project (Fig 2.9). The other two are
residential: one is designed with an
emphasis on private use and has
private gardens; the other has a large
communal space (Fig 2.10).

Rob Krier firmly believes in this
design approach and said in the BBC
TV programme, *Architecture at the
Crossroads*:

> You need the block as a basic urban
> unit and in that block the house as a
> cell . . . a neighbourhood of some
> 10, 12, 15, 18 families in one house
> with the block as a basic urban unit
> to build up a city structure . . .

between blocks you can find streets
and a composition of streets and
squares.

The architecture is clearly of the
post-modern school, with columns and
colourful windows, and façades of
great variety. An environment has
been created which is full of incident.
By grouping this architecture around
courtyards which are familiar to the
local people, Rob Krier hopes that he
will promote a feeling of belonging and
that the residents will accept the
scheme all the more readily.

Tiergarten

A somewhat different approach to
the design of urban housing was
developed in the Tiergarten area of

Berlin which was once one of the most
prestigious districts in the city,
containing a number of embassies and
grand villas for wealthy citizens.

The IBA decided to revitalize this
building type but within the framework
of new social conditions. The
open competition for the site at
Rauchstrasse was won by Rob Krier
who thereafter supervised six
international architects in the building
of eight town houses with a total of
239 flats (Fig 2.11). Each Architect
was given the same amount of money
in accordance with the standard
German provision for social housing.
Rob Krier himself designed one of the
houses and the building at the end of
the group (Fig 2.12) which closes off
the central green. His house is a

**2.10 Landscaping has taken over the two
large communal spaces.**

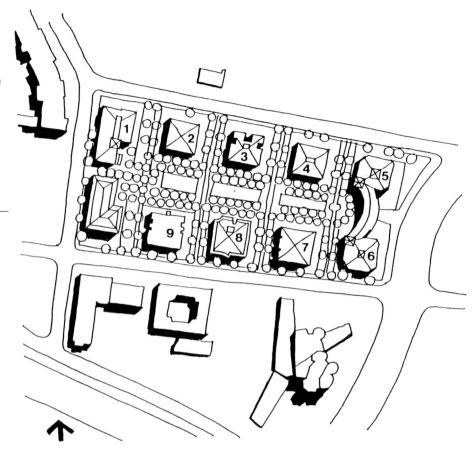

2.11   Urban villas at Tiergarten, Berlin: site layout.

Architects:
1   *Aldo Rossi*
2   *Nielebock and Partner*
3   *Giorgio Grassi*
4   *Brenner and Tonon*
5/6 *Rob Krier*
7   *Herman and Valentiny*
8   *Hans Hollein*
9   *Rob Krier*

2.12   Rob Krier has produced a stunning visual stop at the end of the group of villas.

typical post-modern building, with columns and a variety of different openings covering the façade.

The variety of approach to the design of all these blocks of dwellings is stimulating. (Figs 2.13, 2.14). In *Architecture at the Crossroads*, Krier said that they are buildings people can associate with. They are not anonymous or interchangeable. They are a form of development that would be acceptable in most countries in the western world.

Herman Hertzberger's project in Berlin (Fig 2.15) adds a further dimension to the design of urban housing. The development takes its form from the corner created by the intersection of Lindenstrasse and Markgrafenstrasse. It is three and four storeys in height, curves around a central courtyard and links with an existing courtyard to the north. Subsequent to his earlier developments at Houttuinen and Kassel (chapter 6 and Figs 6.8 to 6.16), Hertzberger develops his ideas about communal stairs, making them not merely a means of gaining access to upper floors, but designing them to create a social contact. Children playing on the stairs can be overlooked from the kitchen and, in addition, the stairs lead to terraces on the roof which can be used by anyone whose door opens onto the staircase. Most of the rooms open onto private external spaces of generous proportions in a manner which is typical of Hertzberger's work – 'openness, respect for tradition, and humane ingenuity make Hertzberger's building one of the most important in the IBA' (Clelland 1987).

Australia

Australia is not renowned for its urban housing, but in the historic areas of Woolloomooloo, Sydney, several architects have shown considerable skill in designing urban forms. A 'townscape' approach was adopted by the team, which entailed the retention of existing street patterns and ensuring that developments of no more than two and three storeys would be built to avoid overpowering the remaining older housing. It was

2.13 General view along the Rauchstrasse showing villas by Rob Krier, Hans Hollein and Herman and Valentiny.

2.14 Contrasting design by Italian architect Aldo Rossi.

2.15 Hertzberger's ingenuity with balconies.

recognized that it was essential to create the diversity of architectural interest that had existed before demolition took place. To achieve this it was decided to break up the area into a number of small projects to limit the impact of any single architect.

Today, this 13-acre site is a splendid mixture of old and new housing, the latter expressly designed to be in harmony with its surroundings, complemented by good landscaping in the form of paved and planted areas. Materials were carefully chosen to match or blend with the old. The new houses in Forbes Street (Figs 2.16, 2.25 to 2.29) are typical of such harmony. The new town houses and flats were built alongside the refurbished old houses with cream-rendered concrete blockwork to fit in with the paintwork on the old façades and with projecting balconies, sometimes with curved corrugated iron roofs in the best Australian tradition (see Browne 1979; Devenish 1981; Perkins 1986:18,19).

Britain

The opportunity for architects in Britain to create urban housing is rare but there are good examples, even amongst private sector developments (Fig 2.17). The redevelopment in recent years of derelict sites in former docklands has provided the major opportunity. Most of the new housing has been constructed by private developers or housing associations, sometimes with the benefit of government grants, to refurbish dock and riverside walls, to repair roads and sewers, and to carry out landscaping and ground consolidation.

London possesses the world's largest area of redundant dockland and the opportunity for good design is immense. Central government established the London Docklands Development Corporation to achieve regeneration by attracting private investment. To do this the Corporation has the power to assemble land and to control development but until recently developers have been relatively unrestricted in their approach to design. Their *laissez-faire* non-

**2.16 Dormers and projecting balconies
reflect the colonial architecture of the old
area of Woolloomooloo.**

Architects: Philip Cox and Partners.

planning policies have produced
nothing more urban than mock-village,
neo-vernacular suburban estates, few
of which create a 'sense of city'.

Now the London Dockland
Development Corporation is
attempting to inject more appropriate
housing design into the programme,
which is evident in schemes that
suggest urbanism (Figs 2.18, 2.19).
Peter Davey likens the new schemes
to housing in Berlin produced for the
IBA. He considers the approaches to
housing in the two cities to be similar
in

> trying to reinterpret the urban weave
> of eighteenth and nineteenth
> century [developments] . . . in terms
> that will work in the late twentieth
> century, so creating architectural

resonances between life today and
the patterns from the past that to
some extent determine it'. (Davey
1989)

However, he considers that there is no
tradition in Britain for relating housing
to water and British architects have no
'tradition of the courtyard apartment
block to draw on'. Nevertheless, these
schemes begin to demonstrate a
coherent type of high density urban
housing which either relates to the
scale of the spaces it surrounds, or
makes a suitable wall to the adjacent
water.

The project at Greenland Passage,
Surrey Docks, by Danish architects
Kjaer and Richter, goes a step further
in its creation of large semi-private
planted spaces in the manner of the
traditional London Georgian Square
(Fig 2.18).

The popularity of such developments dispels the myth that the
British will never accept anything

2.18 Housing at Greenland Passage, Surrey Docks, London.
Architects: Kjaer and Richter.

2.17 Balmoral Mews, Belfast: private sector housing in an urban form.
Architects: Knox and Markwell.

other than detachment; their commercial success clearly demonstrates that in the right situation genuine urban housing is popular. The myth of detachment is also dispelled in other towns and cities where urban regeneration associated with waterside sites is taking place (Fig 1.1). Maritime Village in Swansea, started in 1981 was the first such development and won a Welsh Housing Design Award in 1987. Although the scheme is referred to as a 'village', there is no rural connotation: it is essentially an urban

development, designed around a large dock and outer basin with a sea frontage. The spectacle of the old Swansea docks, now full of vitality, ships and colour, is exciting. Many of the elements associated with dockland development have been used – small pedestrian spaces, semi-public squares, steel balconies, cast iron bollards – all juxtaposed in a wide selection of claddings, brick and blockwork. The development is predominantly made up of dwelling blocks three and four storeys high and contains mainly flats. Part of the development overlooks a newly created promenade and seafront where the housing takes on a distinctly 'sea-side' appearance (Fig 2.20). (See Perkins 1986:34–8; Williams 1988)

The principles of urban housing are further illustrated in the examples described and illustrated later in the chapter. The Canadian projects (Figs 2.30 to 2.47) demonstrate how it is possible to create individuality for dwellings within high density monolithic building forms. The Oaklands apartments in Toronto illustrate how internal corridors are humanized by creating a light-filled atrium (Fig 2.41). Elm Village in London (Figs 2.48 to 2.51) is an excellent example of mixed tenure housing in Britain designed in an urban form. Kurhausplein in Den Haag (Figs 2.52, 2.53) and the central area redevelopment in Fécamp, northern France (Figs 2.54 to 2.59), are both designed to re-create traditional urban spaces – at Kurhausplein, the city square and at Fécamp, the organic street pattern of a medieval town.

New residential districts

Unlike new development within existing built-up areas of towns and

2.19 Octagonal Towers at Wolfe Crescent, Surrey Quays, overlook London Dockland Development Corporation's new infra-structure canal linking Surrey water with Canada water.

Architects: Campbell, Zogolovitch, Wilkinson and Gough.

2.20 Sea-front housing at Maritime Village, Swansea.

Architects: Halliday Meecham Partnership.

cities where the design should relate to the surroundings, the design of complete new residential districts may have no such influences. The planning of new towns in many countries has provided the opportunity to create organizational forms for new communities which offer the advantages of living in both the city and the countryside. This was Ebenezer Howard's vision which inspired him to establish the first garden cities in England. Since then successive attempts have been made to create urban housing forms in new town situations with varying degrees of success.

Most of the French new towns illustrated here are distinctively of that country. Only Alain Sarfati's work in Evry (Figs 2.68 to 2.71) and Cergy Pontoise (Figs 2.72 to 2.75) genuinely create urban form. Of the examples from other countries, the District Centre at Waterland (Figs 2.79 to 2.81) perhaps comes closest to creating a wholly urban atmosphere, with buildings grouped along streets and squares.

The projects from Denmark (Figs 2.82 to 2.85) and Britain (Figs 2.86 to 2.90) all illustrate a common approach: most are high density/low-rise in form with development up to three storeys in height. The projects are grouped around winding culs-de-sac and loop roads and are landscaped to a very high standard. The use of shared pedestrian and vehicular roads (Fig 2.87) is common throughout. The results are not urban in the same way as a neighbourhood in a city or large town, nor are they suburban, rather they have quality of their own. The significance of the Warrington schemes is that they were amongst the last to be designed by the new town teams of architects who have had such a great influence on housing design since the Second World War. Warrington New Town has also in recent years endeavoured to achieve a similar quality from private housing development. The approach there is to produce guidelines in a highly positive form (an example of a typical neighbourhood plan is shown in Figs 1.2, 2.86) and this has had some considerable success.

Cluster and courtyard housing

A contrasting form of urban housing to that which involves the creation of streets and squares, is the clustering of housing in high density/low-rise form which aims to combine the benefits of the detached dwelling built at low

2.21   Courtyard housing at Belapur, Bombay, India

Architect: Charles Correa.

Charles Correa's projects in India are perhaps its ultimate form (Figs 2.21, 2.104 to 2.106).

The private housing at Dalkey, near Dublin (Figs 2.107 to 2.109) would not normally be classified as urban. Yet the manner in which the housing is linked creates an urban form. Professor Dahinden's 'House of Symbols' (Figs 2.91 to 2.95) is simply unique and would grace any town or city.

The chapter now continues with a more detailed description of the projects.

density with the high density of the multi-storey unit yet eliminate the disadvantages of both. Often the form of development comprises a cluster of tightly knit dwellings usually not more than three storeys high, with direct access to a garden area from each dwelling (Figs 2.96 to 2.106). Intimate interaction with outdoor areas is combined with close contact between dwelling units in the group. An important criterion is to achieve maximum privacy and a high level of sound insulation between the dwellings and their garden areas. Housing developments of this nature are not new and they have many representatives all over the world, including idyllic, small medieval towns and homogeneous fishing villages, etc, in which people in the Western world clamour to live. Such housing is very common in Eastern cultures and

Town Houses, Lutzowstrasse, Berlin

Architects:	Manfred Schiedhelm and Karen Axelrad; Von Gerkan, Marg and Partners; Oefelein and Fruend; Otto Steidle; Brandt, Heiss, Leipe; Steigelmann

No. of dwellings:	78
Site area:	0.71 hectares (1.75 acres)
Density:	110 dwellings per hectare (44.5 dwellings per acre)

Housing by Manfred Schiedhelm:

Size of dwellings:

Lower maisonettes	126 sq m (1336 sq ft) (+ 83 sq m basement – 893 sq ft);
Upper maisonettes	100.6 sq m (1083 sq ft)

Five architects were chosen in a competition in 1979 to develop a site where the basic street and garden pattern was already laid out. The architects had to design individual houses within the same terraces (Fig 2.22) to a common brief: each house was to comprise two dwellings and had to allow for the provision of a rental unit with an independent entrance. Split-level dwellings (Fig 2.24) were produced by Manfred Schiedhelm in his houses, which have three storeys fronting onto the street and four storeys on the garden side. His apartments were designed so that they could be converted into one large house if required. The housing is considerably enhanced by the provision of bay windows, which allow

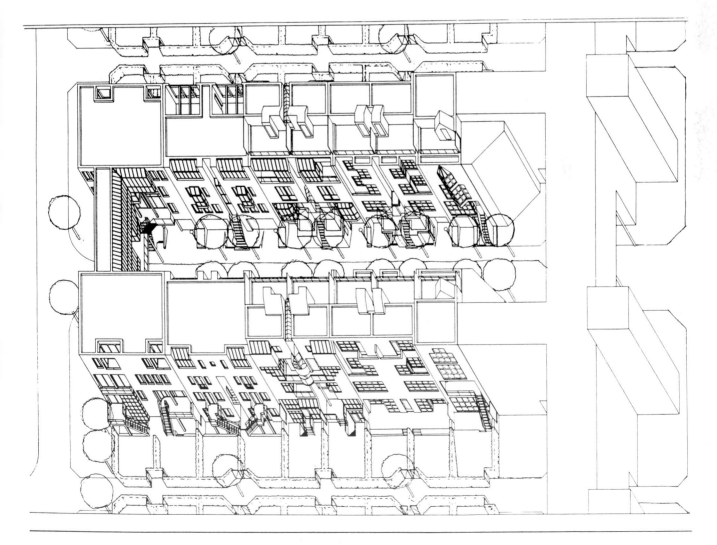

2.22 Axonometric of the whole group of dwellings at Lutzowstrasse, Berlin.

diagonal views, balconies at the front
of the dwellings, garden areas at the
rear, planting areas and winter gardens
for the conservation of energy
(Figs 2.23, 2.24).

Further reading

CLELLAND, D., 'Town-houses, Tiergarten',
The Architectural Review, September 1984,
vol. CLXXVI, no. 1051, pp. 45, 46.

'Pour une nouvelle architecture urbaine à
Berlin', *Techniques et Architecture*,
December 1983/January 1984, p. 119.

**2.23 Considerable variety has been
achieved within a uniform terrace: Professor
Schiedhelm's flats have a spiral staircase
from the third to the fourth floors.**

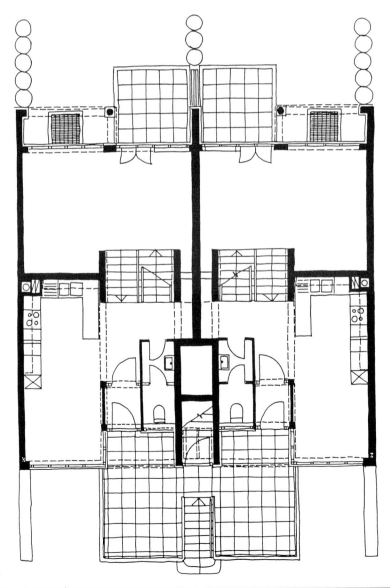

**2.24 Plans of dwellings designed by
Professor Manfred Schiedhelm and Karen
Axelrad.**

Infill Town Houses, Forbes Street, Woolloomooloo, Sydney, Australia

Architects:	Allen, Jack and Cottier
No. of dwellings:	9
Site area:	0.14 hectares (0.34 acres)
Density:	64.3 dwellings per hectare (26 dwellings per acre)
Type of accommodation:	3-bedroom, 2-storey houses
Size of dwellings:	106.6 sq m (1141 sq ft)
Parking/Garages:	6 car parking spaces in a group off Judge Street.

The aim of the development was to provide family accommodation with private open spaces and group car parking adjacent to the housing, all within the townscape requirement of being in keeping with the surrounding buildings and environment (Fig 2.29). By creating a row of houses at right angles to their neighbours, the architects have provided enclosed rear courtyard areas for car parking and communal open space (Figs 2.26, 2.28).

Every house has a full width living-room opening through double doors into a large family dining-room and open kitchen. These double doors enable the two rooms to be used as one large space or separately as

2.25 Elevations, Forbes Street, Woolloomooloo, Sydney.

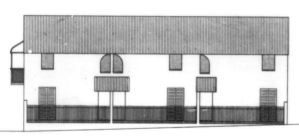

WALKWAY ELEVATION

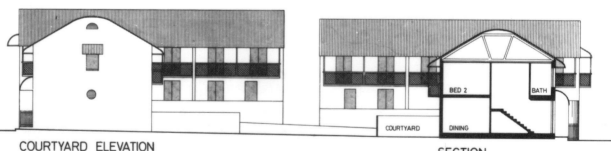

COURTYARD ELEVATION

SECTION
THREE BEDROOM HOUSE

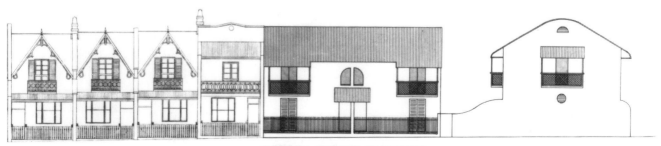

FORBES STREET ELEVATION

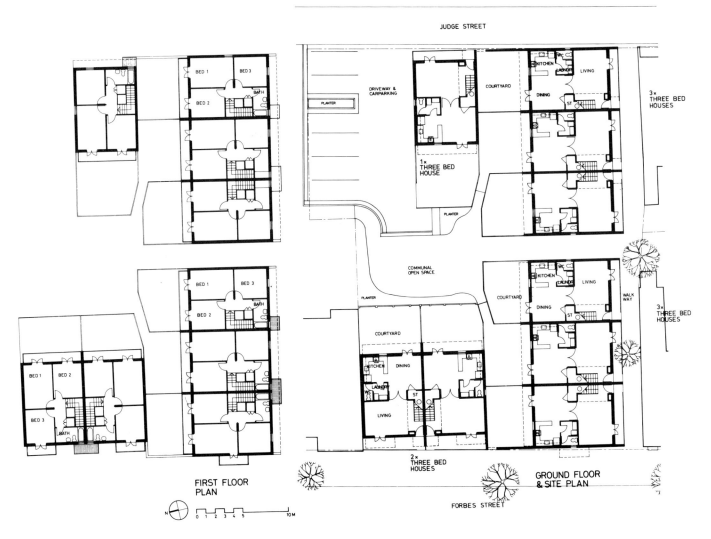

FIRST FLOOR
PLAN

JUDGE STREET

DRIVEWAY &
CARPARKING

PLANTER

COURTYARD

KITCHEN
LAUNDRY
LIVING

WC

DINING

ST

3 x
THREE BED
HOUSES

1 x
THREE BED
HOUSE

PLANTER

COMMUNAL
OPEN SPACE

PLANTER

COURTYARD

COURTYARD

KITCHEN
LAUNDRY
LIVING

WC

DINING

ST

WALK
WAY

3 x
THREE BED
HOUSES

KITCHEN
DINING

LAUNDRY
WC
LIVING

ST

2 x
THREE BED
HOUSES

GROUND FLOOR
& SITE PLAN

FORBES STREET

N

0 1 2 3 4 5   10 M

2.26   Grouping of dwellings and dwelling plans.

2.27   Verandas designed in the tradition of the Australian vernacular.

2.28 View of communal open space.

required (Fig 2.26). All three bedrooms were designed to be usable by two people and most open onto verandas in the tradition of the Australian vernacular.

The Victorian architectural spirit has been evoked by the use of applied elements such as hoods, balcony balustrades, and circular and quadrant windows (Figs 2.25, 2.27).

Further reading

DEVENISH, J., 'Wooloomooloo', *Architecture Australia*, September 1981, vol. 70, no. 4, pp. 54–63.

'Attached houses, Forbes Street, Wooloomooloo', *Architecture Australia*, December 1981, vol. 70, no. 6, pp. 30–3.

2.29 The new houses blend into their surroundings.

False Creek Co-operative Housing, Vancouver, Canada

Architect:	Henriquez Architects Urban Designers
No. of dwellings:	170
Density (two separate areas):	86 and 111 units per hectare (35 and 45 units per acre)
Size of dwellings: 1 to 3–person flats	60–79 sq m (647–851 sq ft)
3 to 5–person maisonettes	97.5–130 sq m (1051–1401 sq ft)
Parking/garages:	170 (under cover)
Construction:	timber-framed construction, stucco externally; sloping sheet metal roof.

2.30   Aerial view of False Creek co-operative housing.

2.31   Elevations.

The programme for the scheme (Fig 2.30) called for 170 units of from one to four bedrooms, but mainly larger units for families. The members of the co-operative came from all walks of life and were known to the architect at the outset of the design process. This enabled the preferences of the users to be solicited by the architect through the use of questionnaires and several design meetings. In addition the members were encouraged to drop in to the architect's office at any time during the design process to see at first hand what was happening and to make comments as well as to choose their houses.

Four types of town house unit were developed, all with a frontage of 4.3 m (14 ft) (Fig 2.32). The plan of two house types are illustrated. One is 'L' shaped to fit into corners and to break down the scale at the end of each block. It provides three and four-bedroom accommodation with an unfinished attic giving access to a private roof deck. The second is 3-storey in form and is incorporated into a 24-suite apartment building which was designed to relate to the architecture of the town houses. (Fig 2.31)

The central spaces, 'plazas', are focal points for pedestrians and children playing. Car parking is accommodated in car ports under the walkways. The scheme also incorporates communal facilities including meeting rooms, an office, craft rooms, photography room, workshop and lockers.

Further reading
BUGDEN, M., 'Eyesore to Showcase – Vancouver's False Creek', *Habitat* (Ottawa), April 1980, vol. 23, no. 4, pp. 20–7.

KEMBLE, R., 'False Creek: decline and rebirth', *The Canadian Architect*, vol. 25, no. 7, pp. 14–39.

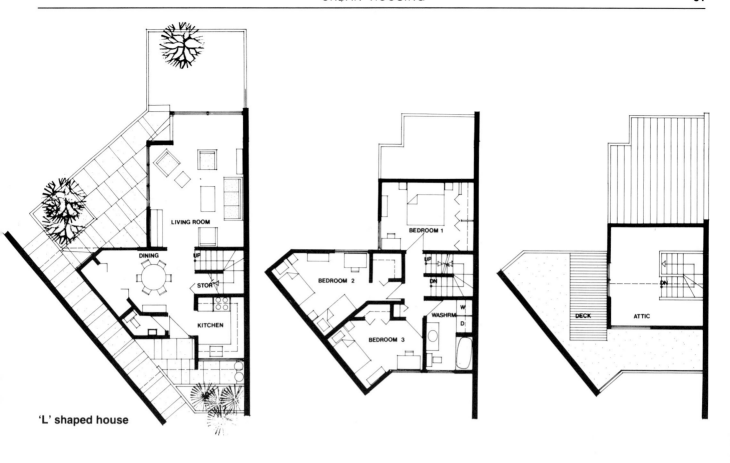

'L' shaped house

2.32 Dwelling plans.

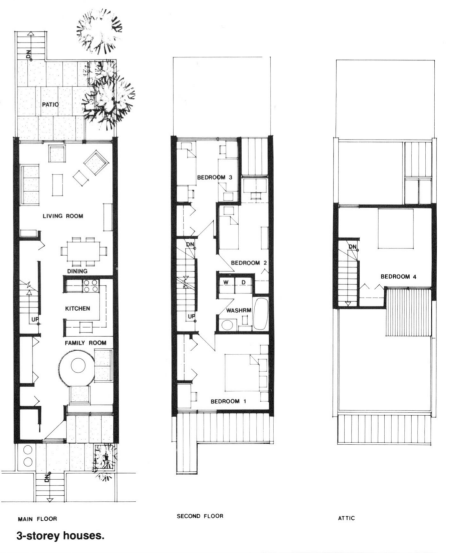

MAIN FLOOR   SECOND FLOOR   ATTIC

3-storey houses.

Bedford Glen Terraced Condominiums, Bedford Park, Toronto, Canada

Architect:	Ernest Annau Associates
No. of dwellings:	207
Site area:	2.27 hectares (5.6 acres)
Density:	overall scheme, 91.4 dwellings per hectare (36 dwellings per acre)
	terraced area, 123.5 dwellings per hectare (50 dwellings per acre)
	311 persons per hectare (125 persons per acre)

Type of accommodation:

3-storey town houses	49
1-bedroom apartments	27
2-storey apartments	59
1-storey 2/3 -bedroom apartments	71

Size of dwellings:

houses (4-person)	190 sq m (2045 sq ft)
flats (2-person)	62 sq m (667 sq ft)
2-storey 2/3 bedroom apartments (3/4-person)	130–145 sq m (1400–1561 sq ft)
1-storey 2/3 bedroom apartments (3 to 4-person)	99.5–120 sq m (1071–1292 sq ft)

Parking/garages:	303 car parking spaces for terraced apartments
	underground garaging provided for the apartment blocks and integral garages for the town houses
Construction:	reinforced concrete structure with brick cladding.

The Bedford Park neighbourhood in North Toronto, where Bedford Glen was built, is a well established single-family residential area comprising mainly two-storey housing lining the streets. When the neighbourhood was originally developed in the 1920s, a deep ravine along Avenue Road was left undeveloped. The development takes the form of six and seven-storey apartment blocks rising from the ravine with three-storey town houses on the remaining part of the site (Fig 2.33). Access from the street to the apartment blocks takes full advantage of the natural topography of the site by being designed at a mid-floor level leading to a central corridor and entrance to the individual dwellings (Fig 2.34). The floors recede at each upper level allowing deep private balconies to be provided. The ravine is beautifully landscaped to provide a pleasant communal 'park'. A laminated timber bridge spans the space linking the apartment blocks on either side.

The three-storey town houses front directly onto the existing Woburn Avenue and the new street constructed within the site. Integral garages are provided together with walled patios which are the major open spaces. The town houses all have a large recreation room on the ground floor. Most apartments have either a 'den' or a loft situated away from the bedrooms and entrances, allowing for their use as work-rooms. The kitchens are all quickly accessible from the main entrance. In the town houses, the kitchens face onto the street but in the apartment blocks they open into the living/dining rooms so that the main rooms enjoy the maximum window frontage. The living-room and dining-room are always adjacent to one another to allow the space to be adjusted according to the owner's needs. The living-rooms of apartment units without balconies have double height spaces (Fig 2.34). Community participation in the design and approval process lead to success in sales, as well as satisfaction for the existing neighbouring residents.

Further reading
'Award of Excellence' *The Canadian Architect*, December 1980, vol. 25, no. 12, pp. 18–23.

2.33 Bedford Glen, Toronto: looking into the landscaped ravine towards the bridge.

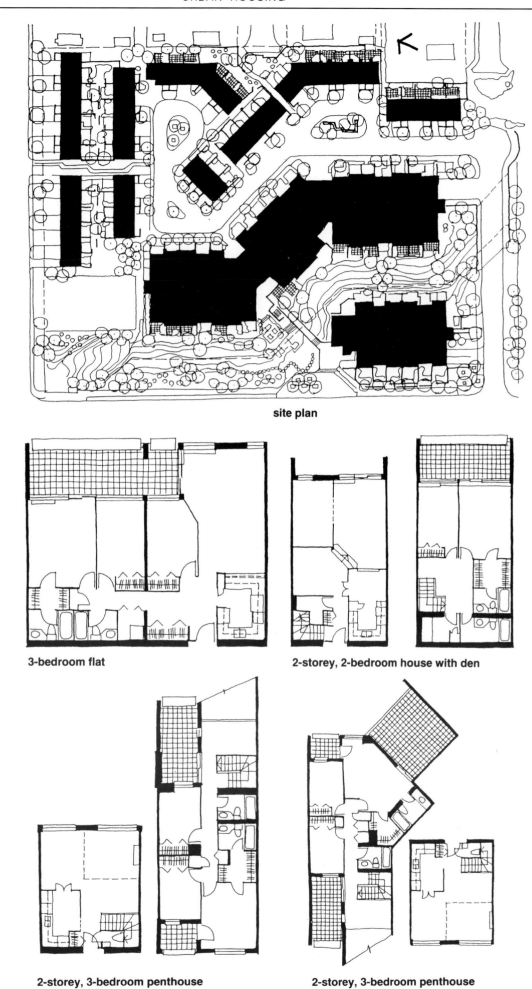

site plan

3-bedroom flat

2-storey, 2-bedroom house with den

2-storey, 3-bedroom penthouse

2-storey, 3-bedroom penthouse

2.34 Site layout and dwelling plans.

Rosegarden Mews Condominium Town Houses, Toronto, Canada

Architect:	Ernest Annau Associates
No. of units:	35
Site Area:	0.53 hectares (1.3 acres)
Density:	66 units per hectare (27 units per acre)
Type of accommodation:	Town houses
Size of dwellings:	sizes range from 125 sq m (1346 sq ft) for the smallest 2-bedroom type to 163 sq m (1775 sq ft) for the largest 3-bedroom type
Parking/garaging:	underground
Construction:	traditional construction materials of brick veneer on wood frame with cedar shingles on the roofs.

The 35 clustered town houses are located in a quiet tree-lined street near a fashionable downtown shopping area in Toronto.

Four different town houses make up a basic cluster which reflects the height and character of the mansions that once stood on the site and, with minor changes, this pattern is repeated throughout the development (Fig 2.36). All buildings are set at a 12.5° angle to the street to increase the distance between the buildings and maximize privacy. The street takes the form of a landscaped inner courtyard, off which the main entrances are located. Each dwelling can also be entered directly from the underground garage. The dwellings are built in warm coloured brick. The rounded stair towers reflect the bay windows and steep gables of the older housing in the vicinity (Fig 2.35). Each

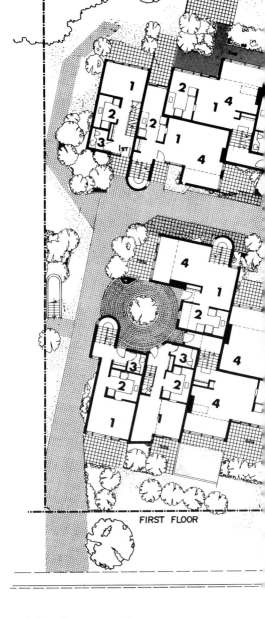

FIRST FLOOR

unit has features such as two-storey dining rooms and fire places forming focal points. Dwellings with northern exposure have breakfast rooms and studios facing north, and master bedrooms have clerestory windows. Each dwelling has a private patio leading to communal landscaped gardens.

2.35   The rounded stair towers echo the architecture of the older housing in the vicinity.

SECOND FLOOR   THIRD FLOOR   ROOF

0   20

**2.36   Site layout of Rosegarden Mews,
Toronto. Key to units:**

1 dining room   6 gallery/study
2 kitchen   7 bedroom
3 washroom   8 bathroom
4 living room   9 master bedroom
5 void

Oaklands Atrium Apartments and Town Houses, Toronto, Canada

Architects:	Dubois Plumb Associates
No. of dwellings:	51
Site area:	0.54 hectares (1.33 acres)
Density:	95 dwellings per hectare (38.4 dwellings per acre)

Type of accommodation:

houses	8
flats (condominiums)	48 (multi-storey) 3 (single storey)
professional suites (i.e. offices)	9

Size of dwellings:

4-person houses	175 sq m (1884 sq ft);
2 to 4-person flats	72–180 sq m (775–1938 sq ft);
Professional suites	95 sq m (1023 sq ft)

Parking/garages:	109 parking spaces in a common garage plus 8 garages provided with the town houses
Construction:	the condominium apartment block has a reinforced concrete structure, brick clad externally.

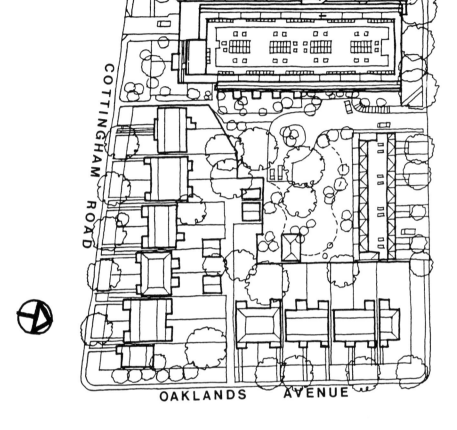

2.37   Site layout.

The site is bordered on one side by a major arterial road, Avenue Road, and by quieter residential streets, Oaklands Avenue and Cottingham Road. The 'condominium' apartment building, with ground-level professional offices on Avenue Road, is arranged north-south. The town houses front onto Oaklands Avenue and Cottingham Road. This arrangement creates a pleasant open area within the development which the apartments overlook (Figs 2.37, 2.38).

There are two main unit types in the condominium apartment building: ground-floor courtyard units on the

2.38   Oaklands atrium apartments and town houses, Toronto.

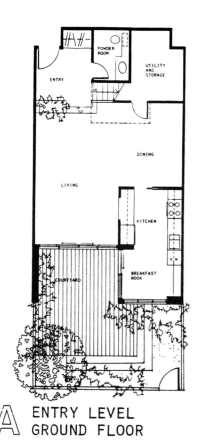

A ENTRY LEVEL
GROUND FLOOR

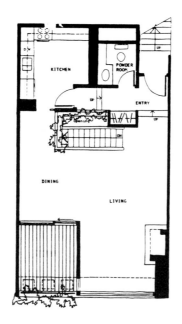

B ENTRY LEVEL DOWN
FROM ATRIUM WAY

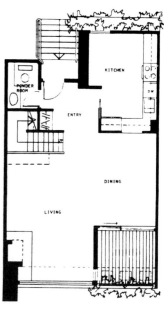

C ENTRY LEVEL UP
FROM ATRIUM WAY

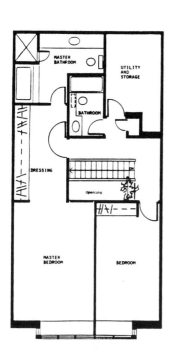

A BEDROOM LEVEL
UPPER FLOOR

0   5'   20'

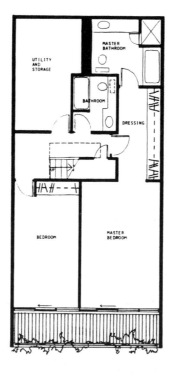

B BEDROOM LEVEL
LOWER FLOOR

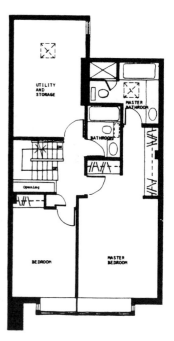

C BEDROOM LEVEL
UPPER FLOOR

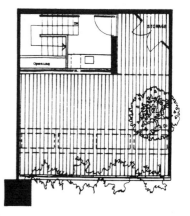

C ROOF TERRACE

2.39 Apartment building: dwelling plans.

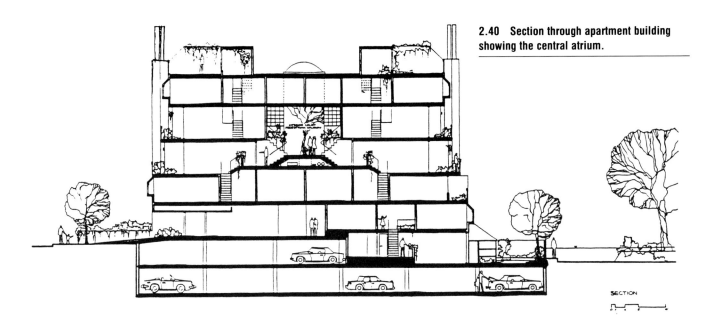

2.40   Section through apartment building showing the central atrium.

east and south and units off an atrium on the east, west and south. Most units are two-bedroom in size with end units generally being three-bedroom (Fig 2.39). In the design of the condominium apartment the architects have created the illusion that each unit is an individual house. For instance, most of the apartments are entered from a wide, high interior corridor, called Atrium Way, which has skylights for natural lighting (Figs 2.40, 2.41). There are steps up and down from Atrium Way to each of the apartments, creating a street-like atmosphere. In the upper units the kitchen and sometimes utility room windows look into Atrium Way, further enhancing the street character.

The individual units in the condominium block are on two floors with higher than normal ceilings, which is a characteristic more typical of houses in Canada than apartments. Apartments have their own fireplaces which have been designed as a feature of the external design. Further, the revealed slab on every second floor is used in the design of the elevations to emphasize the two-storey form of the apartments. All units have large terraces and on Avenue Road the balconies are enclosed with

2.41   The atrium.

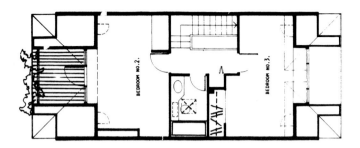

THIRD FLOOR

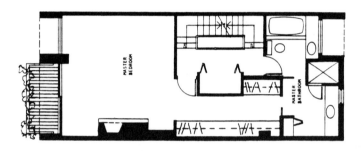

SECOND FLOOR

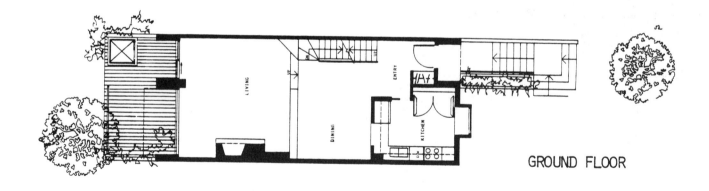

GROUND FLOOR

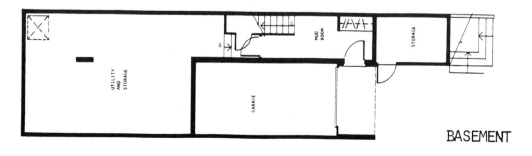

BASEMENT

2.42 Town houses: floor plans.

glass to be usable all year round as sun porches. Included in the apartment building are nine professional office suites and underground parking provision for 109 cars.

The Oaklands town houses are designed so that the living-room faces south to the private garden and the kitchen is oriented to the street (Fig 2.42). The master bedroom and bath/dressing area are on their own on the second level; there are two smaller bedrooms, one with a balcony facing south, on the second floor, with skylighted second bathroom. In the basement there is a large storage/work area with another large skylight for the back portion. The pitched roofscape of the development reflects the characteristic gables of the area and emphasizes the individuality of the houses (Fig 2.43).

Further reading
'Apartments with Inner Street', *Canadian Architect*, January 1982, vol. 27, no. 1, pp. 16–20.

'Award of Excellence', *Canadian Architect*, December 1980, vol. 25, no. 12, pp. 29–31.

2.43   Oaklands: The town houses.

Vera Co-operative Housing, Vancouver, Canada

Architect:	Henriquez Architects Urban Designers
No. of dwellings:	69 + communal building
Site area:	0.85 hectare (2.1 acres)
Density:	81 dwellings per hectare (33 dwellings per acre)
	235 (approx.) persons per hectare (95 persons per acre)

Size and no. of dwellings:		
4-person houses	105 sq m (1130 sq ft)	5
1 to 3-person flats	60–75 sq m (646–807 sq ft)	35
1 to 3-person dwellings for handicapped people	60–75 sq m (646–807 sq ft)	3
3 to 4-person town houses	75–105 sq m (807–1130 sq ft)	26

Parking/garages:	89 car parking spaces; garaging underground
Construction:	timber frame covered externally with stucco; asphalt shingle and flat membrane roofs.

2.45   The dwellings are given individual identity by the elevational treatment.

2.44   Vera co-operative housing: an aerial view.

The architects have designed a project which has the appearance of a small village with variety, yet with a definite feeling of cohesion (Fig 2.44). The scheme attempts to communicate to its occupants the concept of 'my own house' in the form of an affordable terraced housing project. The notion of an 'identifiable house' is communicated by means of a small pitched roof element added on to each unit (Fig 2.45). This simple symbol, which is derived from the most primitive image of 'house' gives the unit a feeling of being detached. Emphasized gateposts set in the walls of the rear courtyards reinforce this feeling of identity.

The dwellings are built in the form of 'stacked town houses' with partial underground parking. They are grouped on either side of a 'pedestrian street' which provides safe play space for children (Fig 2.46). Each dwelling has a front

door onto the pedestrian street and
an enclosed patio at the rear. In
order to present a sympathetic edge
to the remaining single family houses
on Ash Street, the design includes a
row of detached houses fronting the
street with driveways in between.
The dwelling plans are irregular in
form but are simple and efficient. The
three-bedroom units, for instance,
have very little wasted space. The
angled living-rooms create great
interest internally and allows sun to
penetrate into the courtyard areas in
some orientations, and face the sun
directly in others (Fig 2.47).

Further reading
'Vera co-operative housing, Marysole,
Vancouver', *Canadian Architect*, September
1988, vol. 33, no. 9, pp. 22–7.

2.46　Site layout.

PLAN UNIT TYPE 2A

PLAN UNIT TYPE 2A (HANDICAPPED)

PLAN UNIT TYPE 2B
LOWER FLOOR

PLAN UNIT TYPE 2C

PLAN UNIT TYPE 2B
UPPER FLOOR

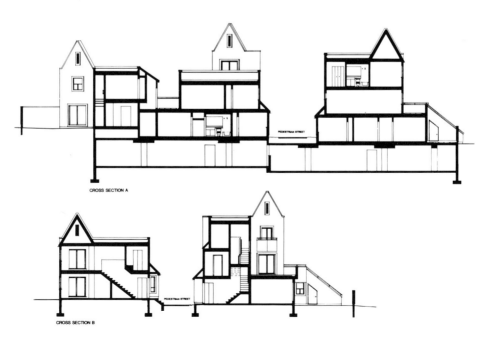

CROSS SECTION A

CROSS SECTION B

2.47 Dwelling plans and sections.

Elm Village, Camden, London (1985)

Architects:	Peter Mishcon and Associates
Clients:	United Kingdom Housing Trust Limited, Halifax Building Society, Nationwide Building Society

No. of dwellings:	162
Site area	1.74 hectares (4.3 acres)
Density:	93 dwellings per hectare (38 dwellings per acre)

Type of accommodation: mixed tenure houses and flats as follows

Type	Cost Sale	Shared Ownership (25% mortgage 75% rent)	Fair Rent	Total
1-bedroom flat	0	51	14 (including 2 designed for people confined to a wheelchair)	65
1-bedroom shared flat	0	0	4 (including 2 designed to mobility standards (i.e. for the partially disabled)	4
3-bedroom shared flat	0	0	4 (including 2 designed for use by people confined to a wheelchair)	4
2-bedroom 3-person house	50	0	4	54
3-bedroom 4-person house	0	10	0	10
3-bedroom 5-person house	0	10	1 (manager)	11
4-bedroom 6-person house	0	10	0	10
6-bedroom 8 person house designed for people confined to a wheelchair	0	4	0	4
Total	50	85	27	162

Size of dwellings:

2-bedroom 3-person house	55.6 sq m (598 sq ft)
3-bedroom 4-person house	65.3 sq m (703 sq ft)
3-bedroom 5-person house	75.94 sq m (817 sq ft)
4-bedroom 6-person house	87.6 sq m (943 sq ft)
6-bedroom 8-person house	131.53 sq m (1410 sq ft)
1-bedroom 2 person flats	45.8–48.6 sq m (439–523 sq ft)

Parking/garages:	a high level of on-street parking is provided.
Construction:	timber-framed construction and, because the scheme is built on filled ground, piles are used to reach down to the London clay below.

The site, which was formerly a railway marshalling yard, is bounded by a railway embankment to the north and the Grand Union Canal to the south-west. The scheme is a mixture of fair rent, shared ownership and cost-sale housing and was achieved by the creation of a partnership, which was unprecedented at the time (the early 1980s), of different public and private sector agencies. The fair rent housing was financed entirely by the Housing Corporation, the shared ownership by a combination of the Housing Corporation and building societies, while the cost-sale housing was financed by the building societies alone.

The density of the development required on the site was high but the architects set out to achieve this with low-rise development of not more than two storeys with gardens almost throughout (Fig 2.48). Only one block rises as high as three storeys and even here the effective height has been reduced to the pattern of London's Georgian and Victorian terraces by creating a lower ground floor or 'garden' level. This block

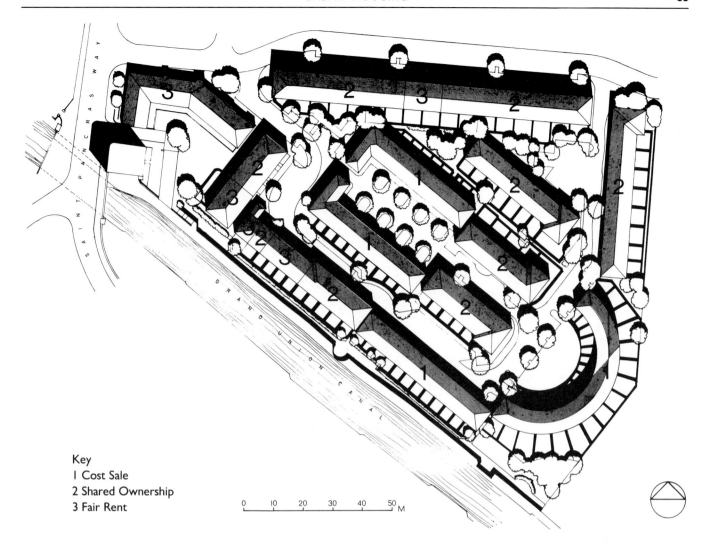

Key
1 Cost Sale
2 Shared Ownership
3 Fair Rent

0 10 20 30 40 50 M

2.48   Site layout of Elm Village.

2.49   Entrance to mews court.

consists entirely of one-bedroom flats each of which has a private entrance. The architects were keen to create a sense of identification and familiarity. This meant getting away from the uniformity which normally typifies estate housing in both the private and public sectors. Streets and pedestrian alleys are used throughout, in preference to culs-de-sac, while a crescent, a mews and a square have been incorporated to mirror some of the traditional layouts of Camden's streets (Fig 2.49). A high ratio of on-street parking is provided. Some of the effects of this are concealed by combining pedestrian and vehicular movement in a shared surface system, by introducing level changes into an otherwise flat site and by the generous use of planting.

So that homes for sale could be available to people of limited means, it was important to keep costs to a minimum. However, it was felt to be vital to the success of the venture that residents should identify not only with the area as a whole, but also with their own dwellings. To meet this end variety was introduced subtly and inexpensively by varying cladding materials, roof tiling, hard landscaping and the design of the porches.

Every house has a small rear garden and some also have a front garden (Fig 2.50). Ground-floor flats have a private garden and just under half of the upper flats have been provided with south-facing balconies. The canal frontage is opened up by a high level footpath within the village leading directly to the canal towpath. This walkway incorporates two viewing platforms which cantilever out over the two-path (Fig 2.51).

Further reading
WILLIAMS, A. and PARTNERS, 'Elm Village', *Building*, 23 November 1984, vol. CCXLVII, no. 7370, pp. 39–46.

Architects' Journal, 10 August 1983, vol. 178, no. 32, p. 18.

2.50 Dwelling plans.

2.51 A timber platform projects over the canal.

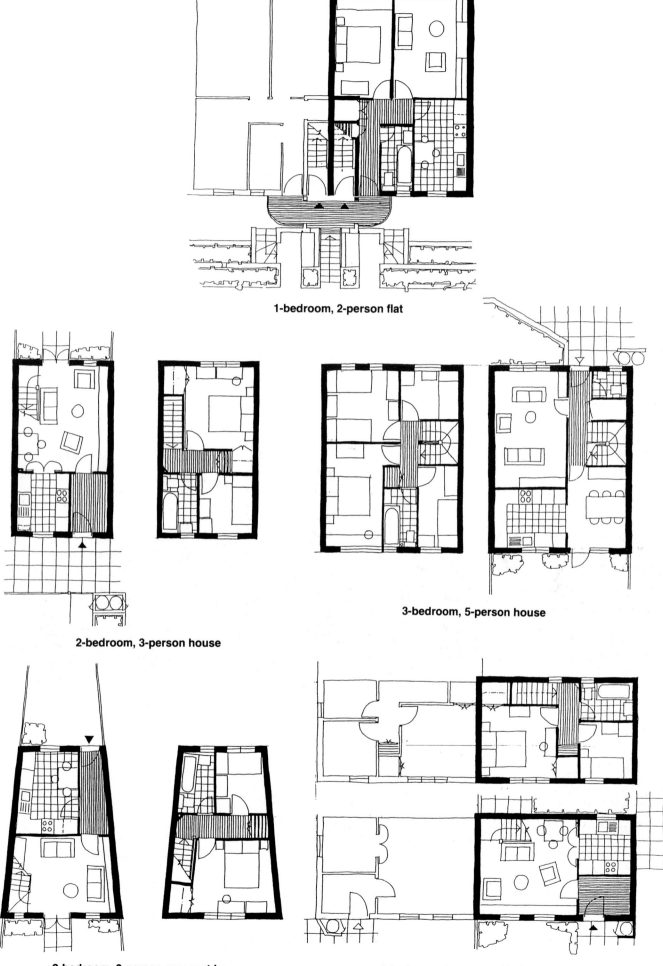

1-bedroom, 2-person flat

2-bedroom, 3-person house

3-bedroom, 5-person house

2-bedroom, 3-person crescent house

2-bedroom, 3-person wide frontage house

Kurhausplein Housing, Den Haag-Scheveningen, The Netherlands

Architects:	Architektenburo Spruit de Jong Heringa
No. of dwellings:	120
Site area (built area):	0.6 hectares (1.5 acres)
Density:	200 dwellings per hectare (80 dwellings per acre)

Typical sizes of dwellings:

1-bedroom	66.6 sq m	(717 sq ft)
2-bedroom	137.0 sq m	(1475 sq ft)
3-bedroom	167.6 sq m	(1804 sq ft)
4-bedroom	174.6 sq m	(1879 sq ft)

At the turn of the century the Kurhaus Square was a focal point of social life in Den-Haag, alive with the bustle of the carriages of the wealthy and the nobility. Its redevelopment was subject to very stringent conditions (Fig 2.52).

The 120 houses that enclose two sides of Kurhaus Square, in which the renovated *Kurhaus* forms the focal point, are built around eight 'places of ascent', i.e. with elevators and staircases which are very important to the total composition of the building complex. Great care has been taken to design the project in keeping with the style of the *Kurhaus*: the backward-sloping walls of the square with their balconies and terraces, in contrast to the other façades, emphasize more an 'inner room' than a typical urban square. The plan forms are ingenious in order to fit the shape of the external building envelope (Fig 2.53).

Further reading
'Kurhausplein Housing, Den Haag-Scheveningen, The Netherlands', *Architecture Contemporaine/Contemporary Architecture*, 1981–1982, Bibliothèque des Arts, Paris and Lausanne, pp. 37–40.

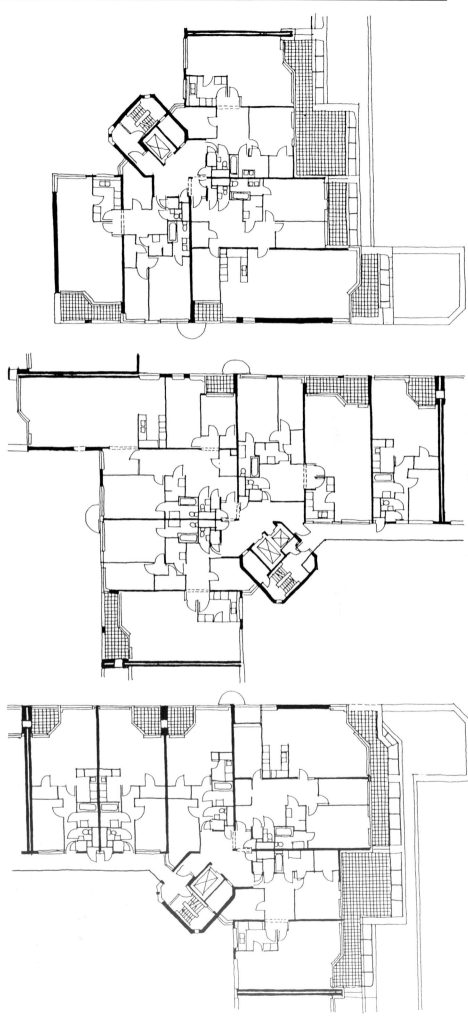

2.52   A general view of the Kurhausplaine housing.

2.53   A sample of the numerous dwelling plans.

Central Area Redevelopment at Fécamp, France

Architects:	Bastid, Bazaud and Gravayat, CRHAB
No. of dwellings:	130
Site area:	0.75 hectares (1.85 acres)
Density:	173 dwellings per hectare (70 dwellings per acre)
	546 persons per hectare (221 persons per acre)
Type of accommodation: houses with garden or a large terrace	25
apartments with a small terrace	105
Size of dwellings: houses for 1 to 6 people (there is a wide variety of sizes)	37–101 sq m (398–1087 sq ft)
apartments for 1 to 5 people (there is a wide variety of sizes)	33–94 sq m (355–1012 sq ft)
In addition there are 310 sq m (3337 sq ft) of commercial development and 100 sq m (1070 sq ft) of communal rooms	
Parking/garages:	146 parking spaces, all underground
Construction:	steel-framed construction, brick and rendered block walls.

2.55   The central square.

2.54   Central area redevelopment at Fécamp: site plan showing narrow, winding passages and central square.

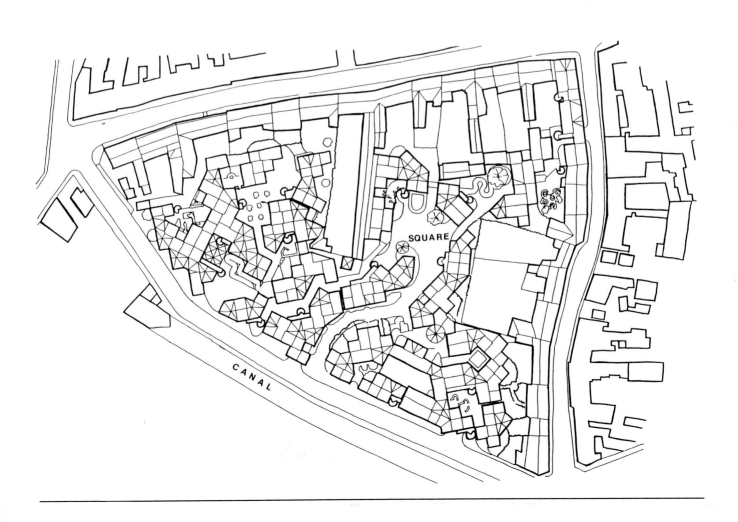

Situated in Sahlm, an ancient district of Fécamp, a seaside resort in Northern France, this project takes the place of old demolished buildings. The need for the development to fit into and reflect the character of the area was of paramount importance. The high density development of two and three storey dwellings is grouped around a series of narrow winding pedestrian passages and a central square (Figs 2.54, 2.55). The frontage overlooking the existing canal is built off the back edge of the pavement thereby retaining the street pattern of the area (Fig 2.56). Spiral staircases lead from the central square to a series of upper-level walkways and dwellings. The completely pedestrian character of the project is possible

2.56 The project viewed from the canal.

2.57 The project under construction from the same viewpoint as Fig 2.56.

2.58 Highly domestic building forms rising from the steel frame: note the podium above underground garaging.

due to the method of construction (Fig 2.57) involving the extensive use of underground car parking (Fig 2.58) which is a typical feature in French grouped housing.

The steeply pitched roofs and mixture of brick and rendered walls reflects the traditional architecture of Fécamp. The render varies in colour considerably and in places different colours are used in a highly imaginative way to create images and particular places of interest within the project. Many of the windows are decorated with small balustrades. These emphasize the Frenchness of the project which, in terms of its form, would be appropriate in any town on the English side of the Channel. Typical dwellings are also illustrated (Fig 2.59).

Further reading
'Selearchitettura – Studio Bastid, Bazaud et Gravayat, Allogginel centro di Fécamp, Seine-Maritime', *L'Architettura Cronache E Storia*, April 1982, vol. XXVIII, no. 4, pp. 250, 251.

2.59 A selection from the numerous dwelling plans.

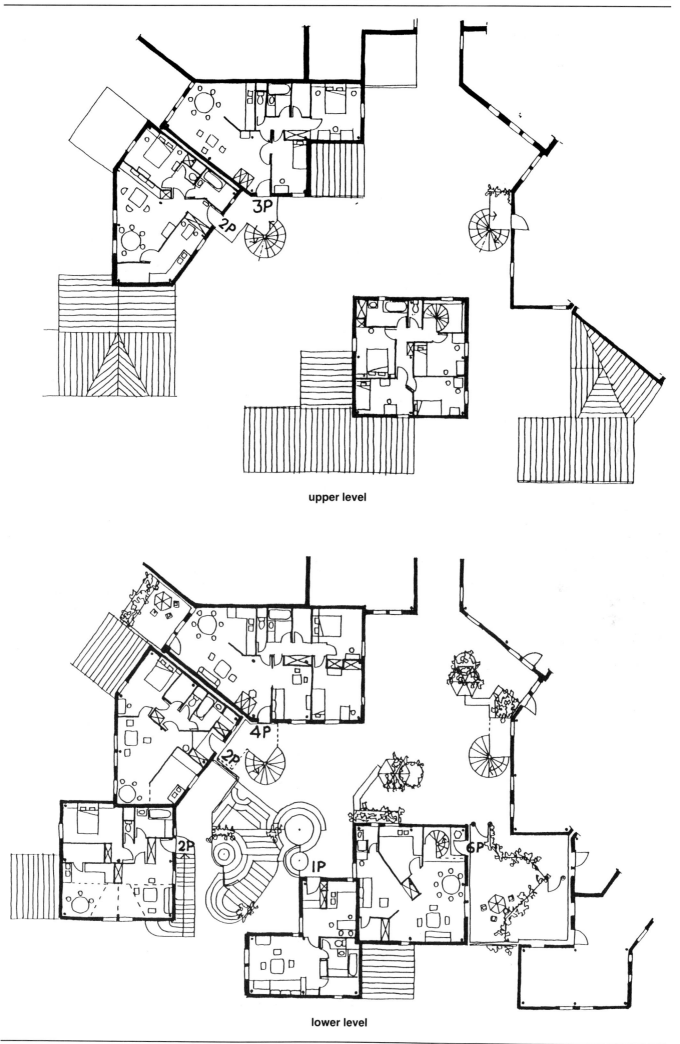

upper level

lower level

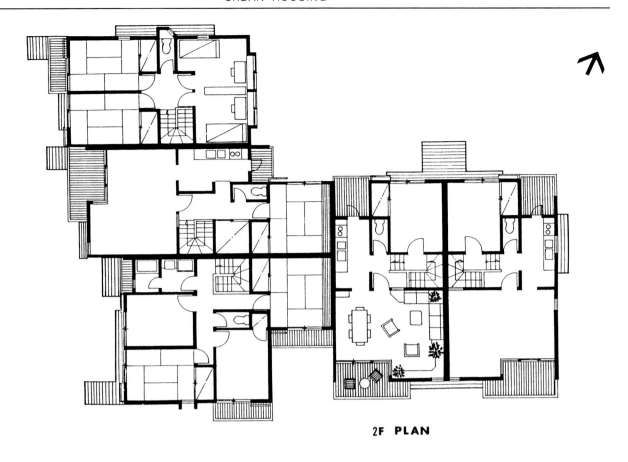

2F PLAN

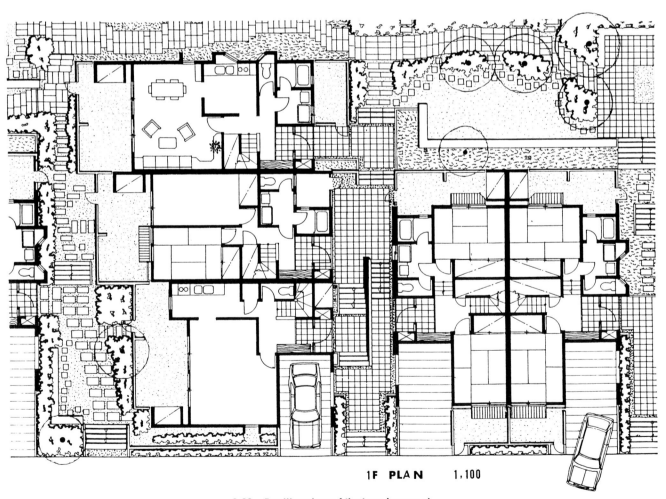

1F PLAN   1,100

**2.60   Dwelling plans of the town houses at
Higashi–Tokorozawa, Japan.**

Town Houses, Higashi-Tokorozawa, Japan

Architects:	Isshiki Architects and Partners
No. of dwellings:	39 (phase 1)
Site area:	0.49 hectares (1.2 acres)
Density:	80 dwellings per hectare (32.5 dwellings per acre)
Type of accommodation:	2 and 3-bedroom houses
Size of dwellings:	90–100 sq m (968–1076 sq ft)
Parking/Garages:	1 space per dwelling
Construction	timber framed

2.62   'Street housing'.

Phase 1 of the Saitama Prefectural Housing Supply Corporation's development at Higashi-Tokorozawa comprises 39 dwellings. Five dwellings are grouped together in one cluster under a single roof (Fig 2.60). The eight such units in the first phase of construction are grouped to enclose three communal spaces all of which connect with each other by means of narrow passages (Fig 2.61). Though they are small, these spaces provide areas where the residents can meet each other. The dwellings are reached directly from the surrounding streets, through the passageways onto which the front doors of the individual dwellings open (Fig 2.62). The living-rooms are located on the first floor to allow more daylight to enter the tightly grouped dwellings.

The project as a whole comprises 184 dwellings; the corporation's hope in building it was to produce a model for traditional housing in a present-day form which would attract public attention and acceptability.

Further reading
'Higashi-Tokorozawa Townhouses', *Japan Architect*, July 1982, no. 303, pp. 64–8.

2.61   Site layout.

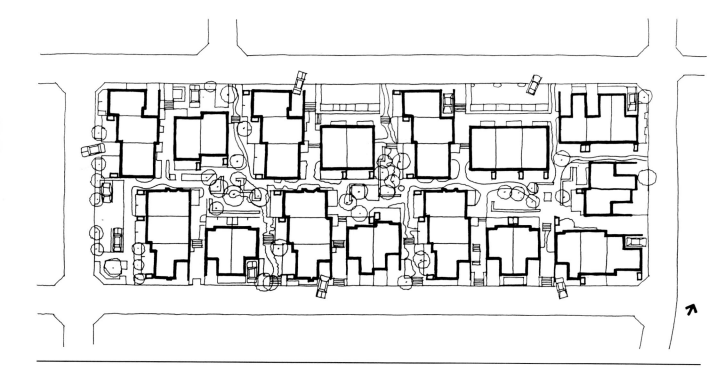

Housing near Paris: Les Arcades du Lac and Le Viaduc at St Quentin-en-Yvelines; Les Espaces D'Abraxes at Marne-La-Vallée

Architect:	Taller de Arquitectura: Ricardo Bofill

The following details apply to Les Arcades du Lac and Le Viaduc

No. of dwellings:	389 (Les Arcades du Lac)
	74 (Le Viaduc)
Density (both projects):	approximately 125 dwellings per hectare (approx.) (309 dwellings per acre)

Type of accommodation:

Les Arcades du Lac

2-bedroom dwellings	69.92 sq m (753 sq ft) 78.40 sq m (844 sq ft)
3-bedroom dwellings	85.64 sq m (922 sq ft) 99.14 sq m (1067 sq ft)
4-bedroom dwellings	99.67 sq m (1073 sq ft)

Le Viaduc 'studio' (bed-sitting type)	26.7 sq m (287 sq ft)
1-bedroom dwelling	45.13 sq m (489 sq ft)
2-bedroom dwelling	61.51 sq m (662 sq ft)
3-bedroom dwelling	88.21 sq m (949 sq ft)
4-bedroom dwelling	102.50 sq m (1103 sq ft)

The new towns around Paris contain some remarkable housing, but none so remarkable as the projects by Ricardo Bofill in St Quentin-en-Yvelines and Marne-la-Vallée, built by developers who specialize in the top category of lower-class housing. Ricardo Bofill aims to create unique and striking places in which to live – urban 'city' housing within gardens. His 'stroke of genius' was to accept the limitations of his brief and to transform what could have been very ordinary housing into decorated palaces. He has tried to revive the classical style with its columns, porticos and architraves. Everything reflects grandeur and solidity; a stage set has been created. In a television interview for the BBC programme, *Architecture at the Crossroads*, Bofill justified his approach:

In the past only the rich linked money with beauty. Today this is no longer possible. I tried to reverse this by working for the poor. I decided to make architecture for everybody. The history of architecture is not just 50 years old, it is 9000 years old. We must take this into account, not to copy history – this is the danger of post-modernism – but to find a balance

2.64 Le Viaduc. Classical housing overlooking the lake.

2.63 Site layout of Les Arcades du Lac.

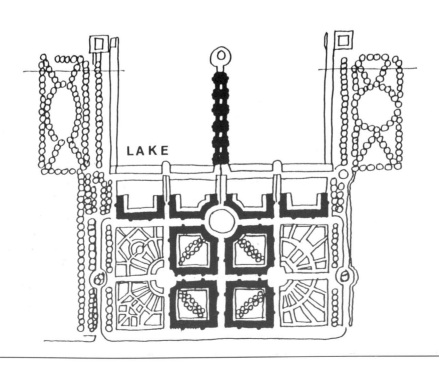

LAKE

between past and present, between classicism and new invention.

The project uses the typical French method developed for building mass housing in the 1970s, of heavy concrete panels put together by unskilled foreign labour. Here, however, the panels have an elaborate and highly decorative finish. The precision that has been achieved demonstrates that such building techniques can be successful.

In the project 'Les Arcades du Lac' at St Quentin-en-Yvelines the dwellings are arranged along cross-axial streets and around circuses, classical monuments and a large central tree-lined lake (Figs 2.63, 2.64). The hard-paved pedestrian streets (Fig 2.65) contrast with the central courts with their soft planting and avenues of tall slender trees (Fig 2.66) 'Le Viaduc' strides across the lake (Fig 2.64); its reflections in the water contribute to the grand design which re-creates the French

2.65 Housing on a monumental scale.

château in a modern housing form.
The dwellings vary in size from small
bed-sitting 'studio' flats to large four-
bedroom types. Internal planning is
somewhat dictated by the demands of
the external design but is ingenious
and varied (Fig 2.67).

'Les Arcades' contrasts significantly in scale with Bofill's other
development at Marne-la-Valle, 'Les
Espaces d' Abraxes'. This project
consists of 600 flats which are situated
in the 18-storey 'palace', the 'theatre'
– which is a great horsehoe of housing
– and an Arc de Triomphe (Fig 1.7,
2.5). It hardly looks like social housing.
It is occupied by essentially poor
people, but it nevertheless seems to
be retaining its appearance. As a place
in the new town it clearly has individual
expression: it stands out from the
endless spread of suburbia and lends
a dramatic touch to the environment.

**2.66   Les Arcades du Lac. Tree-lined
squares contrast with the hard-paved
pedestrian streets.**

Further reading
ADELMANN, M.F., 'In Ricardo Bofills Reich',
Bauwelt, 14 January 1983, vol. 74,
pp. 26–35.

CLANCY, J., 'Mistaken Monuments',
Architectural Review, June 1982, vol. CLXXI,
no. 1024, pp. 23–35.

GARCIAS, J.-C., 'Versailles for the people',
Architectural Review, November 1980,
vol. CLXVIII, no. 1005, pp. 297–300.

'Classical Concentration', *Architects' Journal*,
14 January 1981, vol. 173, no. 2,
pp. 46, 47.
'600 Logements à Marne-laVallée',
Techniques et Architecture, September 1982,
no. 343, p. 95.
'St Quentin en Yveline Housing', *A+U*,
February 1982, no. 137, pp. 49–56.

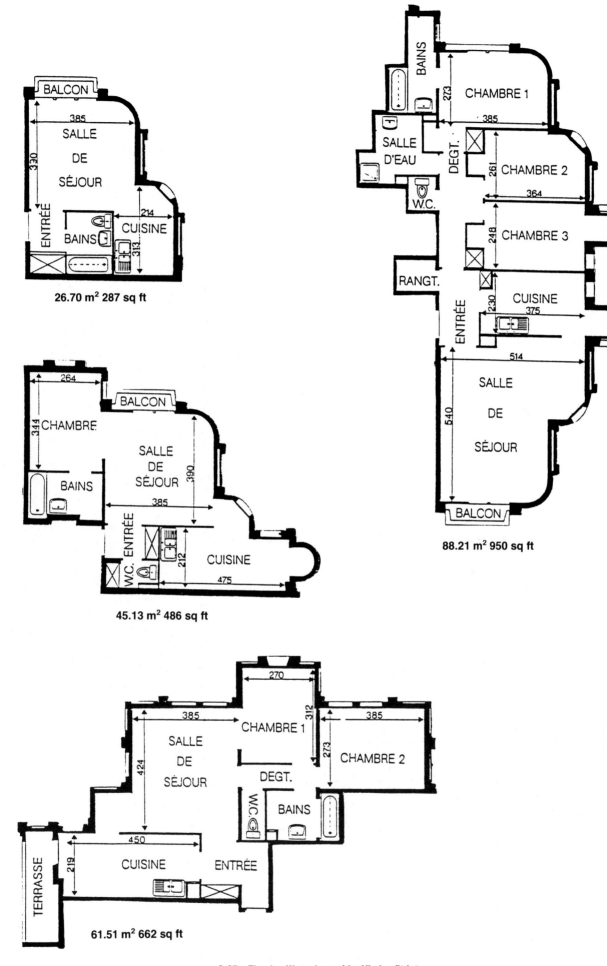

26.70 m² 287 sq ft

45.13 m² 486 sq ft

88.21 m² 950 sq ft

61.51 m² 662 sq ft

2.67 The dwelling plans of Le Viaduc fit into the sculptural shape of the architectural concept.

Les Epinettes, Evry, near Paris, France

Architect:	Alain Sarfati
No. of dwellings:	103
Site area:	0.8 hectares (1.97 acres)
Density:	128 dwellings per hectare (53 dwellings per acre)
Type of accommodation:	flats
Size of dwellings: 2 and 3-bedroom flats	75–80 sq m (807–861 sq ft)
Other accommodation:	270 sq m (2906 sq ft) commercial space
Parking/garages:	116 underground garages

In this most dynamic scheme the 103 flats are arranged on either side of a pedestrian concourse and around a central communal garden (Fig 2.68). Access to the upper dwellings overlooking the concourse is gained via series of spiral staircases capped with glass umbrellas that would grace the entrance to any Parisian Metro station (Fig 2.69). Ground-floor dwellings have small private gardens. Those opening onto the communal garden are enclosed by a variety of low walls and garden gates. The communal garden is delightfully laid out in a formal manner with pergolas and climbing plants, a covered bandstand, sculptures and lush planting of all kinds (Fig 2.70). The pedestrian concourse and the dwellings on either side of it are built above underground garaging which is

2.69   Access to the upper dwellings is via a series of spiral staircases capped with glazed umbrellas.

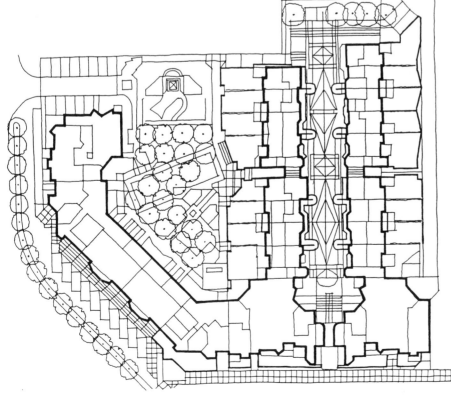

2.68   Site layout of Les Epinettes.

2.70   The communal garden.

a common arrangement for much of
the recently constructed housing in the
French new towns. The stripes painted
on the tarmac surface of the
concourse create a vivid pattern which
relates to the spiral staircases, and at
the same time are used by the
children for play (Fig 2.69).

A row of shops is located on the
ground floor of the terrace on the
further side of the communal garden.
The rendered or stucco finishes, with
the contrasting brick staircases and
blockwork balconies, the window
proportions, the eaves detail, which
casts a deep shadow across the walls
beneath, all create a harmony that
reflects, in a truly modern way, the
essential character of traditional
French architecture. It is a clear
expression of the architect's unique
approach to design.

Further reading

'Trois références valent mieux que deux',
Architecture Intérieure Crée, 1981, no. 184,
pp. 64–9.

Areas have been measured from plans
provided by the architect.

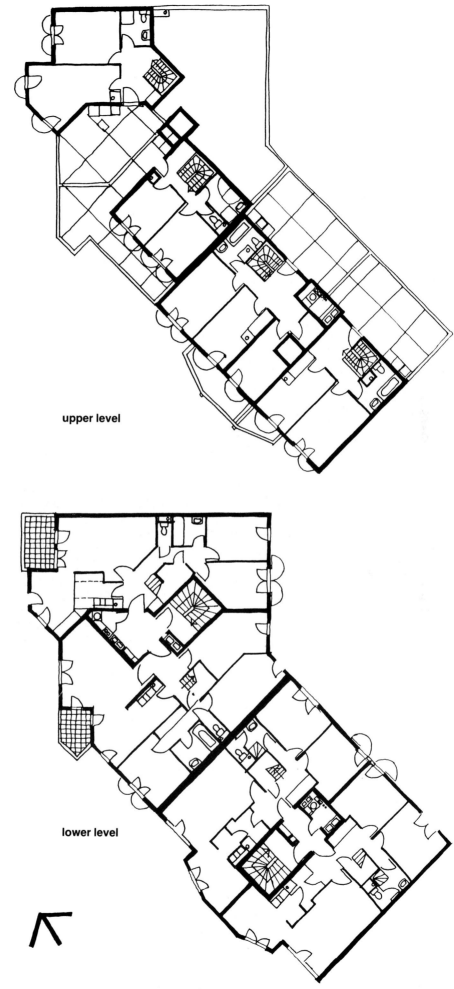

upper level

lower level

2.71 Examples of the dwelling plans.

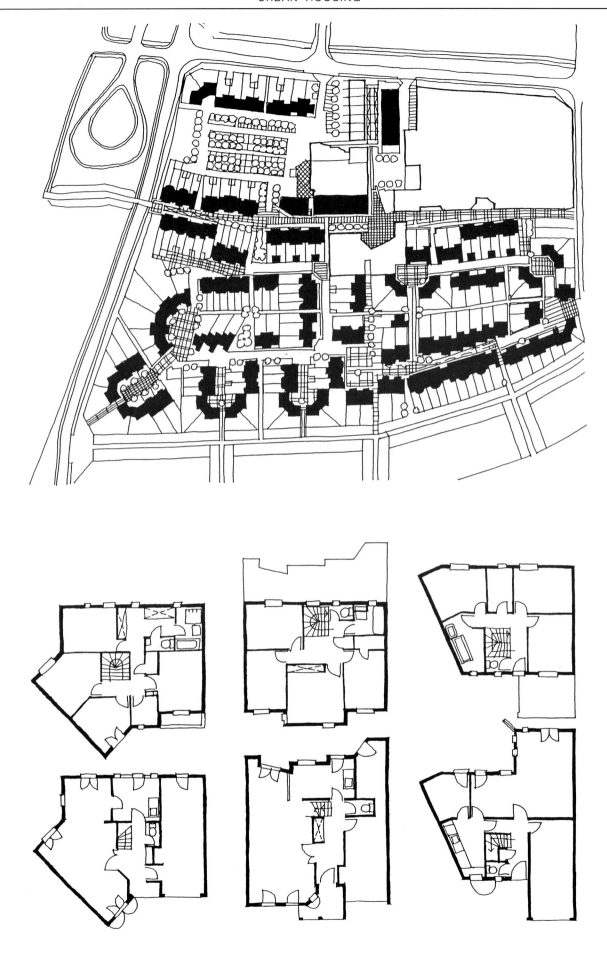

2.72 Site layout and dwelling plans of the local centre, Quartier des Eguerets (plan redrawn from *AA*, 25 February 1983, pp. 16,17).

Local Centre and Housing, Le Quartier des Eguerets, Jouy-le-Moutier, Cergy Pointoise, France

Architect:	Alain Sarfati
No. of dwellings:	202
Site area:	5.8 hectares (14.33 acres)
Density:	34 dwellings per hectare (14 dwellings per acre)
Type of accommodation:	70 apartments 132 houses

In addition there is a local shopping centre, a school and small offices.

2.74   Street housing: note the skilful handling of the integral garages.

2.73   Entrance to the shopping arcade.

Nestled on the slopes of the Côteaux de l'Hautil, in the new town of Cergy Pontoise, the Eguerets district can be seen from far away. The mosaic of roofs with their variety of colours and materials appears first. A closer look reveals Alain Sarfati's superb handling of the arrangement of the new housing and the buildings at the local centre, and particularly his skill in the design of the architectural detail. The housing is grouped around the internal road system in a manner reminiscent of a small French town or village, with the dwellings close up to the footpath or road with only a small area for planting in between them (Fig 2.72). The dwellings themselves vary in height from two to four storeys. There are about twenty different types. Many have garages carefully arranged at the front or integral to the structure. Most have private gardens at the rear.

The local centre contains a series of memorable spaces. Here the higher density of development and the built form express the function of the area by creating a true urban feel with narrow spaces, arcades and small squares. The cross-over between the road and the main footpath through the centre is particularly well handled with canopies and pergolas to provide shelter from the sun and rain and creates a positive point of arrival (Fig 2.73).

2.75 Stylish entrances and ironwork.

The essential urban character (Fig 2.74), which is achieved with a highly domestic form, is carried throughout the project, even down to the detail of the canopies and metal grills over the windows and the design of the entrance recesses and doors to the dwellings (Fig 2.75). Whilst the architecture has a hint of 'Anglo-Saxon' influence, it is in fact entirely indigenous, owing its form to the best French tradition.

Further reading

ELLIS, C. and MEADE, M., 'French Liberations', *Architects' Journal*, 25 January 1984, vol. 179, no. 4, pp. 46–54.

'Exprimer les différences', *L'Architecture d'aujourd'hui*, February 1983, no. 225, pp. 16, 17.

Apartments in the Quartier d'Habitation Elancourt Maurepas, St Quentin-en-Yvelines, France

Architect:	Henri Gaudin
No. of dwellings:	132
Area of site:	1.5 hectares (3.7 acres)
Density:	88 dwellings per hectare (36 dwellings per acre)
Type of accommodation:	Flats
Size of dwellings:	
2 bedroom flats	57 sq m (616 sq ft)
3 bedroom flats	60 sq m (710 sq ft)
Parking/garages:	Underground garaging

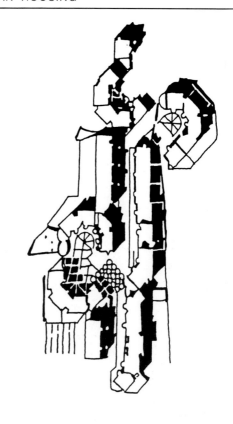

In a quiet corner of St Quentin-en-Yvelines, Henri Gaudin has built a series of apartment blocks around a pedestrian walkway (Fig 2.76). In the design of the project he has played with cubes and cylinders to create a striking architectural form (Fig 2.77). Most prominently, he has designed large circular elements clad in small white tiles which contain individual staircases. Despite its suburban location, the development has a distinct urban feel. It is amazingly sculptural and thoroughly modern in appearance. Softened by lush planting over curved metal trellis-work and by tree planting in the otherwise hard-paved pedestrian areas, it gleams white in brilliant sunshine (Fig 2.78).

Areas have been measured from plans and are approximate.

Further reading

'Des plans, des courbes et des couleurs', *L'Architecture d'Aujourd'hui*, June 1981, no. 215, pp. 58–67.

Architecture Contemporaine/Contemporary Architecture, 1982–1983, Bibliotèque des Arts, Paris and Lausanne, pp. 59–62.

'Products in Practice – wall and floor tiling', *Architects' Journal*, 4 November 1981, vol. 174, no. 44, p. 873, 903–17.

'L'a selearchitettura – Henri Gaudin: Alloggi a Maurepas', *L'Architettura Cronache E Storia*, March 1982, vol. XXVIII, no. 3, pp. 167–9.

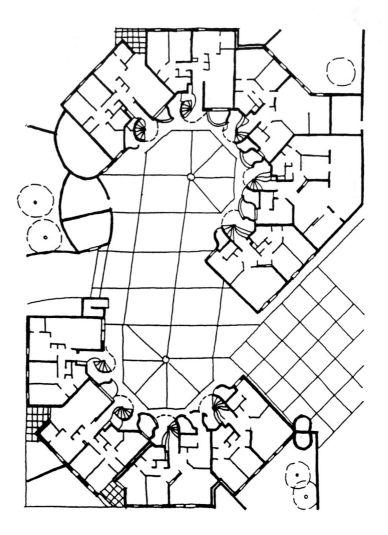

2.76 Elancourt, St Quentin-en-Yvelines; site layout.

2.77   Ceramic curves.

2.78   The project gleams white in the bright
sunshine.

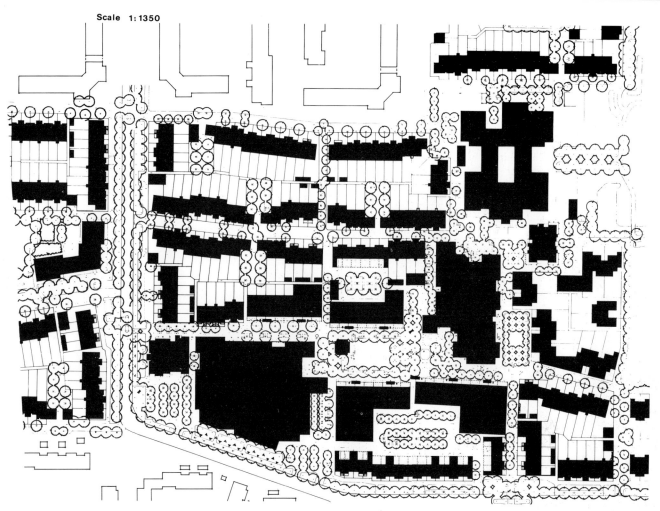

Scale 1:1350

Waterland District Centre, Spijkenisse, The Netherlands

Architect:	Reijenga Postma BV (and others)
No. of dwellings:	300 + community facilities
Site area:	8 hectares (19.5 acres)
Density:	62.5 dwellings per hectare (25.7 dwellings per acre)
Type of accommodation:	a mixture of houses and flats with some flats over shops, and other district centre uses.
Dwellings designed specifically for elderly people	40
Size of dwellings:	
4 to 5 person houses	90–110 sq m (970–1186 sq ft)
2 to 3-person flats	70–80 sq m (755–862 sq ft)
1 to 2-person dwellings for elderly people	60–70 sq m (647–755 sq ft)
3 to 4-person dwellings	80–100 sq m (862–1078 sq ft)
Parking/garages:	450 car parking spaces

The task of designing multi-function district centres with housing, shops and other community facilities is a common problem for many architects. At Waterland the architects designed a district centre for 10,000 people which comprises shops, a library, social/cultural facilities, a swimming pool and sports hall, a meeting and entertainment room, an elementary school, a bar-bistro, and small scale office and workshop accommodation, together with four doctors' houses and consulting rooms, and a Chinese restaurant.

The brief was to achieve optimum integration of the various facilities and to provide the people of the district with a place of enough character and atmosphere for them to be able to meet there in comfort. Prior to the appointment of the architects, separate sites had been earmarked for the different functions of the centre: the non-housing facilities were to be located in a single building and the housing in high rise development around. This was not considered suitable and the brief was changed to provide for an integration of facilities (Fig 2.77) designed in accordance with the following principles.

2.79   Waterland District Centre, Spijkenisse, The Netherlands: site layout showing hierarchy and variety of spaces.

The development of an 'urban tissue' for the entire centre, consisting of buildings and open spaces, the latter being clearly recognisable in the shape of streets, squares, alleys, gateways, courtyards, etc. The chief function within the centre is living: the scale and size of buildings and open spaces should be based in the first place on residential function; the other facilities will be fitted into this residential scale. Pedestrians and cyclists will be the main traffic in the Waterland Centre. In case car traffic is necessary, it must be adapted to the pedestrian's behaviour as far as possible.

The resultant design does successfully achieve these aims with its interweaving of streets, paths and alleys, and its open spaces of a more special purpose, such as a piazza, a square and an *agora*. The piazza is formed by shops, the sports hall and houses, with the community centre and its café as a focal point (Fig 2.80). The *agora* is formed by the school and community centre buildings. Typical dwelling plans are illustrated (Fig 2.81).

Details of the brief are from a description provided by the architects.

Further reading
'Wijkcentrum Waterland te Spijkenisse', *Bouw*, 2 February 1980, no. 3, pp. 53–7.

2.80 A high level of integration between housing and commercial uses has created urban spaces that are full of interest.

2nd floor   **3rd floor**

1-bedroom maisonette

ground floor   **1st floor**

2-bedroom maisonette

2.81 Typical dwelling plans.

'Sol òg Vind', Aarhus, Denmark

Architect:	Arkitektgruppen Regnbuen
No. of dwellings:	25
Site area:	1.27 hectares (3.15 acres)
Density:	19.7 dwellings per hectare (8 dwellings per acre).
Type of accommodation:	3-bedroom houses with living-room on the first floor and bedrooms on both floors (Fig 2.85)
Size of dwellings:	75.5 sq m (813 sq ft) to 94.0 sq m (1012 sq ft)
Size of community centre:	400 sq m (4,036 sq ft)

Energy conservation was the principle influence on the design of this project 'Sol og vind' ('Sun and wind'). The dwellings and the community centre have been grouped together in rows, aligned east-west (Figs 2.82, 2.83). This arrangement permits full advantage to be taken of passive solar heat coming through south-facing windows, and active solar heat

2.83 Large, south-facing conservatories create the maximum opportunity for passive solar gain.

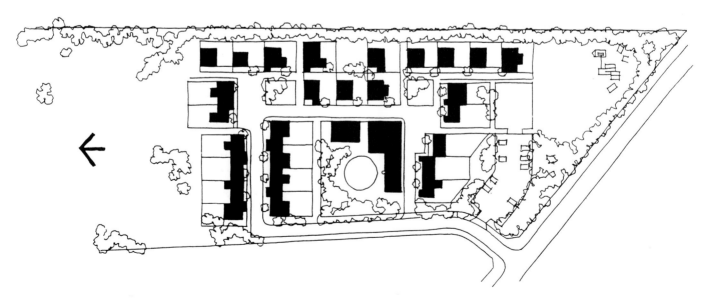

2.82 Site layout of 'Sol og Vind', Aarhus.

2.84 The walls are solid and have small windows to reduce heat loss.

collected by large panels mounted on the roof of each building (Fig 2.83). The windows in the other elevations are small to prevent heat loss (Fig 2.84).

The development was one of the first Danish examples to illustrate how energy considerations influence both the layout of a housing scheme and the design of the external walls, especially the size of the windows. In its description of the scheme, the *Danish Journal* compares energy conservation with density of development as follows:

> The dense/low rise dwelling with its smaller outer surfaces, needs less energy than a detached unit. Energy considerations alone would appear to be sufficient reason for building single-family dwellings in tighter

clusters. (Hansen and Larsen 1981:21)

The project clearly demonstrates that a quality environment can be provided alongside the most stringent energy conservation requirements.

Further reading

HANSEN, P. and LARSEN, F.A. (eds.), 'How the Danes live', a special issue of the *Danish Journal*, Royal Danish Ministry of Foreign Affairs, Copenhagen.

ground floor　　　　**family houses**　　　　**first floor**

2.85　Plans of family houses and community centre.

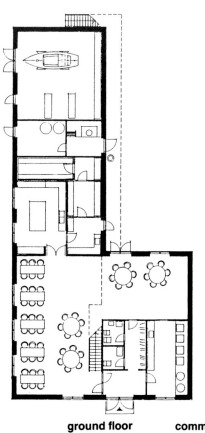

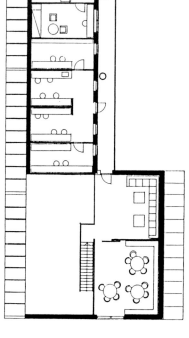

ground floor　　　　**community building**　　　　**first floor**

Old Hall 1: Housing for rent at Warrington New Town, Cheshire, England

Architect	Warrington and Runcorn Development Corporation; Hugh Cannings, Chief Architect and Planner

No. of dwellings:	115
Site area:	2.4 hectares approx. (5.9 acres)
Density:	48.3 dwellings per hectare approx. (19.5 dwellings per acre) 185 persons per hectare (74.9 persons per acre)

Type of accommodation:

1-bedroom 1-person flats	9
2-bedroom 3-person flats	39
2-bedroom 4-person houses	21
3-bedroom 5-person houses	46

Size of dwellings:

2-bedroom flats	47.5 sq m (511 sq ft)
2-bedroom flats	62–62.5 sq m (667–673 sq ft)
2-bedroom houses	81 sq m (872 sq ft)
3-bedroom houses	93 sq m (1001 sq ft)

Parking/garages:	1.25 parking spaces/garages per dwelling
Construction:	Traditional brick cavity-wall and tiled roof construction.

The project was designed for rent, but the facility of the dwellings being sold to the occupants was an important aspect of the brief. The objectives of the project are listed below.

1 To provide a residential ambience which exhibited the best characteristics of private housing for sale and eliminated the worst features of municipal housing.
2 To devise a familiar vocabulary of housing forms that would be attractive both outside and inside to the occupiers/potential owners.
3 To create distinct settings for groups of dwellings.
4 To exploit the proximity of the adjoining Sankey Valley Linear Park for both access and views.
5 To provide a distinct and appealing character on approaching the site.
6 To provide convenient, identifiable car parking spaces.

To achieve these objectives, the dwellings were grouped to provide views into landscaped extensions of the park (Fig 2.87). The provision of a low eaves line at the front to enhance the 'court' groupings (Fig 2.86), gives a pleasant, airy quality to the spaces between the dwellings and privacy to

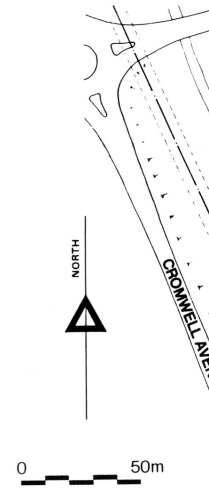

2.86 'Court' groupings.

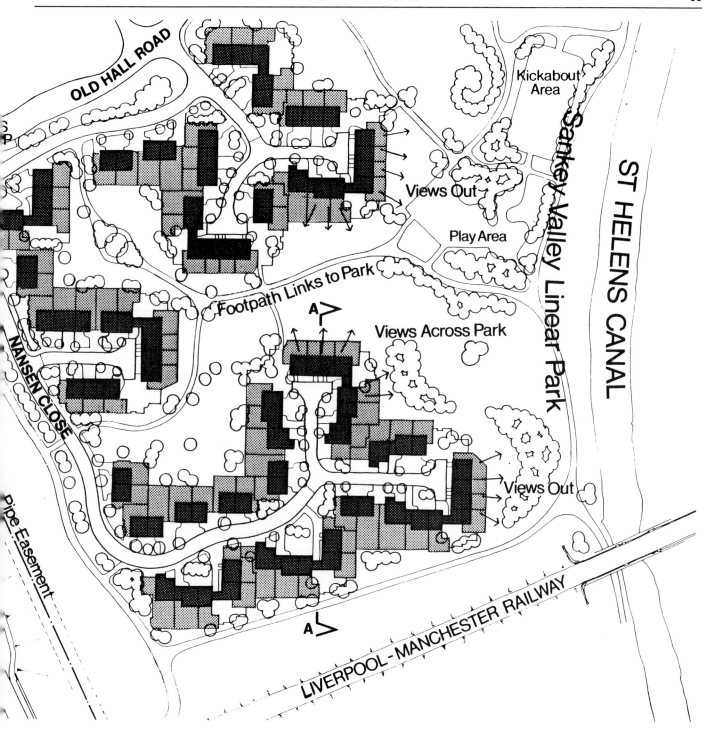

2.87   Old Hall 1: site layout.

first-floor rooms and a distinctive front and back.

There are a variety of dwellings in each group with 'L' shaped houses and flats to utilize spaces in external corners. There is a predominance of 'semi-detachedness', and space for future garages to be constructed without this being at all obvious. Some dwellings are in terraces but the maximum length of a terrace is four units, with integral parking for one of the mid-dwellings. All flats have a front door at ground-floor level and a balcony at first-floor level. Dwellings have front gardens with potential for personalized enclosures wherever possible. Car parking is on plot or in adjacent parking spaces. In addition there are spaces for visitor parking and toddlers' play provision in each housing group.

Areas of dwellings have been measured from the plans provided.

Further reading

DOE, NHBC, RIBA: *Housing Design Awards 1987*, a *Building* publication, p. 57.

Old Hall 2: Housing for rent at Warrington New Town, Cheshire, England

Architects:	Warrington and Runcorn Development Corporation; Hugh Cannings, Chief Architect and Planner

No. of dwellings:	295
Area of site:	8 hectares (19.7 acres)
Density:	36.9 dwellings per hectare (15 dwellings per acre) 110 persons per hectare (44.7 persons per acre)

Type of accommodation:

1-bedroom 2-person houses	30
2-bedroom 3-person houses	49
2-bedroom 4-person houses	40
3-bedroom 5-person houses	66
1-bedroom 1-person flats	67
2-bedroom 3-person flats	38

Size of dwellings illustrated in Fig 2.88.

1-bedroom 1-person flat	31.5 sq m (339 sq ft) and 42 sq m (452 sq ft)
1-bedroom 2-person flat	49.5 sq m (533 sq ft)
1-bedroom 2-person bungalow	49 sq m (527 sq ft)
3-bedroom 3-person house	93.8 sq m (1010 sq ft)

Parking/garages:	1.25 parking spaces/garages per dwelling

Construction:	traditional brick, timber and roof tiles.

The design objectives of this project of 295 flats and houses for rent were as follows.

1 To provide in a relatively large scheme and on a flat, featureless site, a clarity and sense of identity in the layout and built form.

2 To respond to external environmental constraints presented by the surrounding road pattern and the large-scale industrial buildings close to the western boundary.

3 To both respond and contribute

Structure Plan

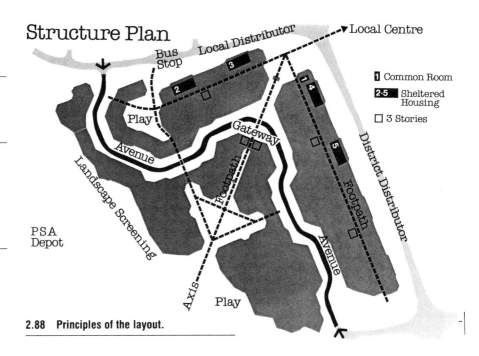

2.88   Principles of the layout.

2.89   The central spine road meanders through the development.

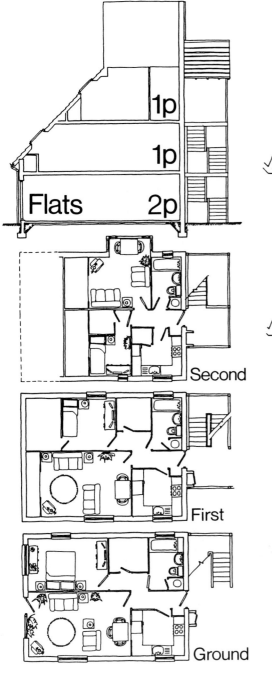

2.90 Dwelling plans.

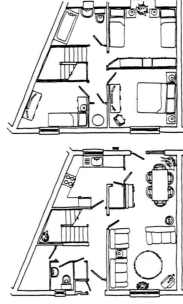

5p house

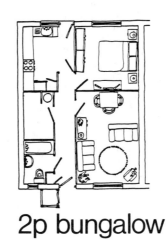

2p bungalow

0 _____ 5m

to the location of the local centre.

4 To integrate within the layout a group of sheltered dwellings.

5 To develop a distinctive style and grouping of buildings which would display variety.

6 To incorporate individual, convenient and identifiable car parking spaces.

The design of the project responds to these criteria in a most imaginative way. A 'spinal' access road designed as a familar tree-lined avenue with frontage housing and a flowing alignment to limit traffic speeds, passes through a variety of different spaces within the development (Fig 2.88). From this road, access is gained to contrasting pedestrian/vehicular courts of mixed housing developments. A simple direct footpath system focuses on a 'gateway' at the north-east corner of the site opposite the local centre. The layout concept is complemented and reinforced by a generous landscape framework. The building form complements and gives visual emphasis to the pedestrian and vehicular access arrangements (Fig 2.89). Careful orientation of the dwellings minimizes visual and noise problems from the perimeter roads on two sides of the development. The sheltered housing with a day-room for elderly people is well integrated by being located at the gateway. The character of the project is enhanced by the use of the Cheshire tradition of separating the wall and the roof elements visually, which assists considerably in the creation of a familiar and friendly atmosphere. A number of dwelling plans are illustrated (Fig 2.90).

Areas have been measured from plans provided by WDRC.

Further reading

DOE, NHBC, RIBA: *Housing Design Awards 1985*, Sabrecrown Publishing, pp. 30, 31.

2.91 'House of Symbols', Zurich: the south elevation is distinguished by perforated cupolas.

'House of Symbols', Zurich, Switzerland

Architects:	Prof. Dr Sc. Tech. Justus Dahinden, SIA, Hon FAIA. Walter Toschi
Sculptor:	Bruno Weber

No. of dwellings:	8
Site area:	0.19 hectare (0.47 acre)
Density:	42 dwellings per hectare (17 dwellings per acre)

Type of accommodation:

flats	8

There is also an architects office on the ground floor

Size of dwellings:

2–4 person dwellings	850 sq m (9149 sq ft) (area of total dwelling space);
office	250 sq m (2691 sq ft)
Parking/garages:	2 parking spaces; 10 garages (within building structure)

2.92 Central fireplace located within the circular bays at the ends of the dwelling block.

'The House of Symbols' (Figs 2.91 to 2.93) is situated on a hill in the City of Zurich. It provides living and separate office space on the ground floor (Fig 2.93). The freestanding column which dominates the northern entry-court, containing the chimney, is raised by a sculpture of three taurus-heads as symbolic guards of the house entrances. The edges of the building's south façade are distinguished by large circular oriels crowned by perforated cupolas (Fig 2.91). They surround the living areas containing central fireplaces. The design (Fig 2.92) is unique: it

attempts to express a new kind of poetry in architecture. Traditional elements have been transformed without reference to post-modernism: the Taurus head symbolizes vigour and earthiness (Figs 2.94 and 2.95). This impression is complemented by serene decorations on the pinnacle symbolizing the duality of man and woman: an old German symbol of fertility. The two golden cupolas give the house a festive touch symbolizing what Professor Dahinden describes as 'the alliance with the sun and the cosmos'.

Further reading
'Maison–Zum Erker–Zurich Suisse', *Architecture Contemporaine/Contemporary Architecture*, 1983–1984, Bibliothéque des Arts, Paris and Lausanne, pp. 59–63.

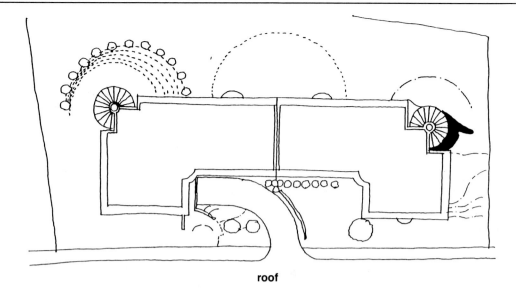

roof

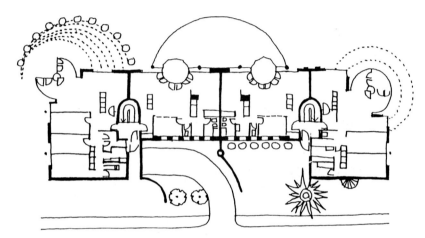

second floor

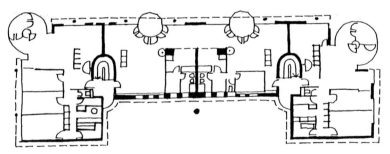

first floor

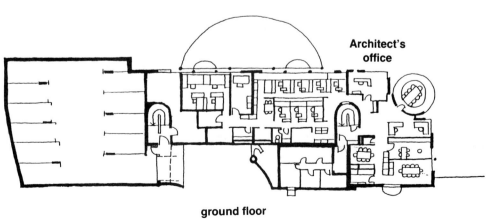

Architect's
office

ground floor

2.93 Floor plans.

2.94   The north elevation.

**2.95   The Taurus head symbolizes vigour
and earthiness.**

Cluster Housing, Seminole Beach, Florida, USA

Architects:	William Morgan Architects
No. of dwellings:	15
Site area:	0.66 hectares (1.6 acres)
Density:	23 units per hectare (9.4 units per acre) (Net density – land taken up with housing – 49.4 dwellings per hectare, 20 dwellings per acre)
Type of accommodation:	houses 15
Size of dwellings:	137.3 sq m–142 sq m (1479–1532 sq ft)
Parking/garages:	15 car ports
Construction:	timber-framed construction with diagonal cedar external cladding, cedar decks and machine-cut cedar shingles; the interiors consist of white painted gypsum wall board, carpeted floors and acoustical sprayed ceilings.

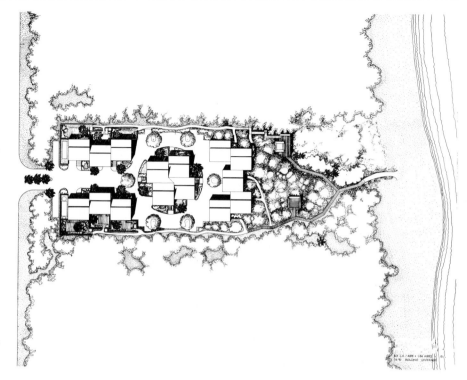

2.96   Cluster housing at Seminole Beach, Florida: site layout.

The 150 ft (46 m) ocean-front site consists of a 30 ft (9.15 m) high primary dune covered with native oak, laurel and magnolia trees. The owners' requirement of a density of 9.4 units per acre (23 units per hectare) was achieved by placing 15 units around a circular drive on the west end of the site, thus preserving the primary dune and its existing vegetation (Fig. 2.96). Two large cedar-decked viewing

platforms with built-in seating are situated on the highest sand dune; these provide an uninterrupted view of the sea. Cedar walkways lead from the houses through the densely wooded site to the ocean front. The houses are built into four clusters of three, four and five units 2.97. Within each cluster, the three-level units are sited so that the outdoor living areas of

2.97   Timber housing in the best American tradition.

adjoining units are isolated from each other, so that windows face forwards to the beach or the outdoor living area, never another houses (Fig 2.98). Thus, even though the project was built to an unusually high density for US housing, the owners have almost as much privacy as they would have in single-family houses. All houses have two-storey-high living-rooms (Fig 2.99) with north-facing clerestory windows and have either three or four bedrooms. All have outdoor living decks with cedar garden walls. All units have car ports with outdoor storage.

Further reading
'Three mini-site winners – in Atlantic Beach, Fla, 1.6 acres, with 15 townhouses', *Housing* (New York), December 1980, p. 57.

2.99   Section through a typical dwelling showing mezzanine and double height living-room.

2.98   Dwelling plans.

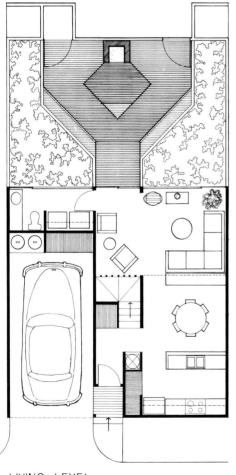

LIVING LEVEL

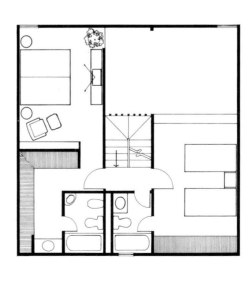

BEDROOM LEVEL

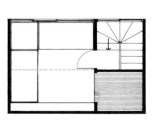

LOFT LEVEL

2.100 Four houses at Bekkestua, Norway – a delightful cluster of roofs in a winter setting.

Courtyard Housing at Bekkestua, Norway

Architect:	Per-Johan Eriksen and Bengt Espen Knutsen
Site area:	0.27 hectares (0.66 acres)
No. of dwellings:	4
Density:	14 dwellings per hectare (6 dwellings per acre)
Type of accommodation:	3-bedroom bungalows
Size of dwellings:	215 sq m (2318 sq ft)
Parking/garages:	8 (4 double) garages

This small scheme of four dwellings is a superb example of traditional Norwegian architecture at its best (Fig 2.100). Constructed in timber the 'L'-shaped single-storey houses are

arranged with their garages to provide a continuous built form on the perimeter of the site (Figs 2.101, 2.102). Within the development, the individual patios open on to a central communal area which is superbly landscaped with rocks, trees and plants (Fig 2.103). The space under the roof is free of structural supports and could be used as a small apartment or office.

2.101 A continuous built form has been achieved although the dwellings are detached.

Further reading
'Boliggruppe Nadderual', *Byggekunst*, August 1981, pp. 402–5.

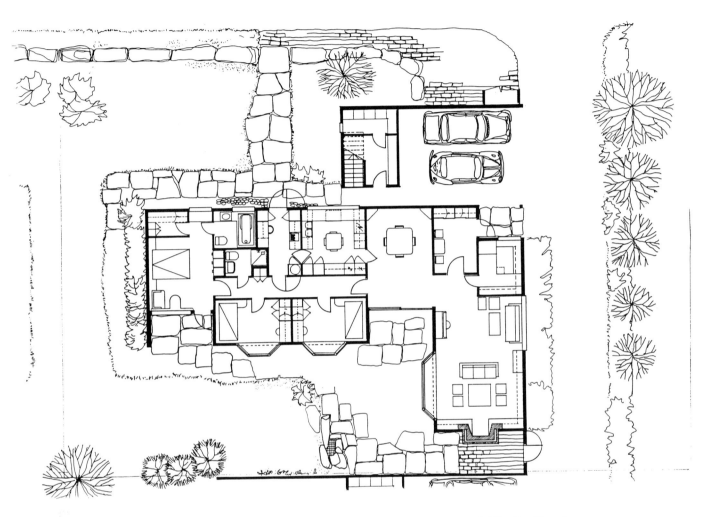

2.102   Dwelling plan.

2.103   The central communal garden.

Courtyard Housing at Belapur, Bombay, India

Architect:	Charles Correa
No. of dwellings:	557
Site area:	6.28 hectares (15.5 acres)
Density:	89 dwellings per hectare (36 dwellings per acre)
	445 persons per hectare (180 persons per acre)
Type of accommodation:	
Houses	(407 are single-storey and suitable for elderly people)
Size of dwellings:	
4/5 person	26.19 sq m–75.37 sq m (279 sq ft–811 sq ft)
Construction:	load bearing brick wall construction with Mangalore tile roofing on timber scantlings.

2.104   The housing at Belapur is arranged as a series of informal, inter-locking courts.

Charles Correa's housing at Belapur, Bombay, uses and reinterprets traditional Indian courtyard housing (Fig 2.104). Correa believes that houses should be capable of being extended, i.e. built using an incremental method which is the tradition in India; as R. Saini points out:

> To build reasonable living environments for the maximum number of people governments should not concentrate on building houses but should leave this to the resources of the people themselves.

In proposing this solution Correa is of course fully aware that self-help housing has been most successful in rural areas, where people have access to building materials and sufficient spare time on their hands to construct their own shelter.

It is much more difficult to accomplish this task in urban areas, and here lies the challenge of architects to use their expertise and innovative abilities to generate low-cost building activity. (in Morgain and Naylor 1987:187)

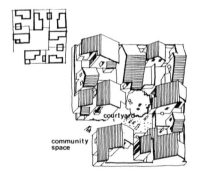

b)   Three clusters combine to form a larger module of 21 houses, surrounding an open space (12m × 12m) (39ft 4in. × 39ft 4in.).

a)   The dwellings are clustered around small community spaces. At the smallest scale, seven units are grouped around an intimate courtyard (approx. 8m × 8m) (approx. 26ft 3in. × 26ft 3in.).

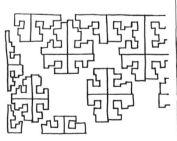

c)   Three such modules interlock to define the next scale of community space (approx. 20m × 20m) (65ft 7in. × 65ft 7in.).

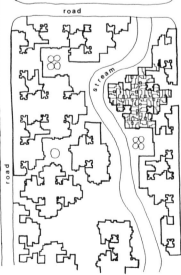

d)   This spatial hierarchy continues up to the largest neighbourhood spaces where facilities such as primary schools are located. Down the centre runs a small stream for drainage during monsoons.

2.105   Housing layout principles.

At Belapur the dwellings have pitched roofs, yards and raised terraces. The houses are arranged in clusters that aim to create a sense of place and community: seven houses are grouped around a small court which is about 8 sq m (80 sq ft) in size. Three of these clusters combine to form a larger 21-house unit. Three of the larger clusters interlock to form the next size of community space (Fig 2.105). The accommodation is formed of 16 types of structurally independent one and two-storey houses on individual plots of 75 sq m (807 sq ft) and 45 sq m (484 sq ft). The structural independence has been achieved by building the principal load bearing walls for each dwelling separately from the neighbouring dwelling, whilst the whole terrace is covered with a continuous roof form (Fig 2.106).

In an attempt to give the various courts a greater degree of individual character, traditional earth colours have been introduced to the rendering: this gives each court its own colour theme and identity. The dwellings are constructed entirely by local labour.

The incomes of the richest occupants are five times those of the poorest — a quite astonishing ratio when compared to the socio-economic mono-cultures of western housing estates. It is still effectively a middle-class housing scheme, but nevertheless one that address itself successfully to the problems of housing design in one of the poorest countries in the world.

Further reading

CRUICKSHANK, D., 'Variations and traditions', *Architectural Review*, August 1987, vol. CLXXXII, no. 1086, pp. 51–8.

DAVEY, P., 'Correa Courts', *Architectural Review*, October 1985, vol. CLXXVIII, no. 1064, pp. 32–5.

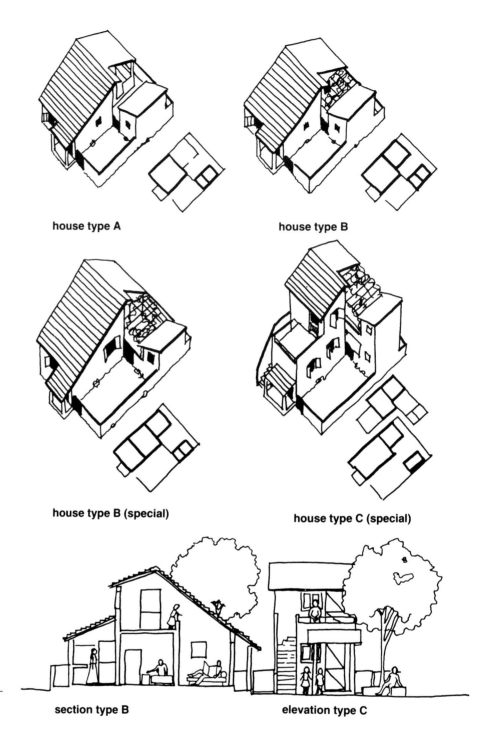

house type A

house type B

house type B (special)

house type C (special)

section type B

elevation type C

2.106   Typology of house design.

Private Housing at Dalkey, near Dublin, Eire

Architects:	Raymond MacDonnell
No. of dwellings:	7 (excluding existing housing)
Site area:	0.68 hectares (1.7 acres)
Density:	10.3 dwellings per hectare (4.1 dwellings per acre)
Type of accommodation:	3 houses and 4 bungalows
Size of dwellings:	houses 158 sq m (1700 sq ft) bungalows 153.3 sq m (1650 sq ft)
Parking/garages:	1 car parking space and 1 garage per dwelling
Construction:	conventional cavity walling, outer leaf in concrete brick finished externally with white acrylic paint; roof covering brown inter locking concrete tiles; pine windows with hardwood cills; taught chains are generally used in lieu of conventional rainwater pipes where there are large overhangs in the bungalows.

2.107 Private housing at Dalke: site layout, dwelling plan and section.

The design of the layout was primarily governed by the natural rock outcrops on the site and the fact that there were large fissures and abrupt changes of level in the rock formation. The seven dwellings are grouped around a short cul-de-sac (Fig 2.107). An existing two-storey house in the south-east corner of the site has been incorporated into the grouping of the dwellings. The three houses are situated at the south of the site, on the flatter land, whilst the four bungalows occupy the northern part of the site. The bungalows all have similar plans, but they are varied where necessary, to avoid digging into the natural rock (Figure 2.108). The changes in level

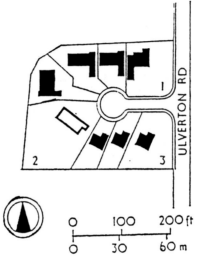

a) site layout: 1 house type A
2 existing house
3 house type B

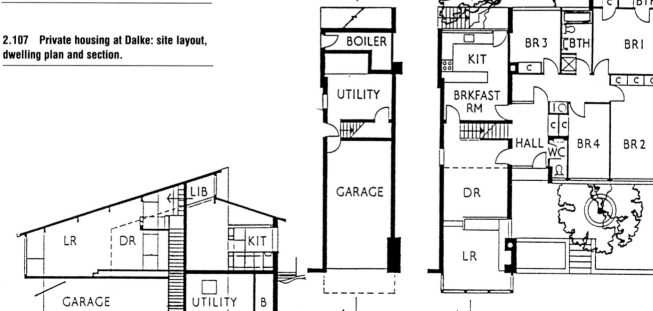

b) section AA

c) lower ground and ground floor plans of house type A

have allowed garages to be built beneath three of the bungalows (Fig 2.106) and double height spaces to be created internally in others (Fig 2.109). The existing trees on the site have been carefully preserved and, together with the use of large pieces of rock, they help to create the natural wooded environment.

Further reading
'Private housing, at Dalkey', *Architects Journal*, 20 and 27 December 1972, vol. 156, no. 51, pp. 1415–20.

2.108 The existing trees and natural rock outcrop on the site have been carefully preserved in the design.

2.109 Double height living-room and gallery.

3 INFILL DEVELOPMENT

SINCE the mid 1970s, there has been a significant switch from the demolition and redevelopment of old residential areas to the refurbishment of older properties and the construction of new, sensitively designed housing on the small infill sites where clearance has taken place. New 'street' housing and town houses now abound in cities and towns from San Francisco to Sydney, Amsterdam and London to New York, as people move back to the urban life-style that living in town can offer. The design principles that make these schemes successful are set out below.

1 The development relates to the street pattern and the lines and heights of the existing buildings. The buildings themselves are usually close to the back edge of the pavement. Just as importantly, any spaces within the development resemble those which are familiar to the locality and to the people who already live there.

2 The new architecture reflects – without necessarily copying – the existing character of the area.

3 The density of development is similar to the building form of the location in which the housing is built.

The quality of the schemes in Canada, the United States and Britain which follow illustrates this renaissance. The Canadian scheme contains terraced town houses built up to the back edge of the streets (Figs 3.1 to 3.4). The form of the development is highly urban but there is a high degree of individuality given to each of the narrow-fronted houses in the terrace (Fig 3.2).

The American projects all have a fresh approach in the way that tradition has been interpreted without undue reference to the past. They all contrast to the high-rise development that would usually present itself as the only economic option for sites in such central locations. Greenway Gables in Minneapolis recreates a series of streets and squares (Fig 3.5) within a relatively small infill site. The form of the layout and the scale of the development are highly urban whilst the overall appearance is that of a small New England town (Fig 3.6). The extensive use of gables not only creates individualism, but helps to establish the correct ratio of space between the buildings and their height which is important to the creation of urban scale.

The projects in San Francisco by Daniel Solomon and Associates (Figs 3.8 to 3.13) are important examples in demonstrating how to make the best use of very small sites. All establish a sensitive balance between the common and private requirements of the residents. All have small courtyards within the project to provide quiet outdoor space for common use, yet the dwellings are designed to have an individual identity, achieved by the use of features such as projecting oriel windows and a variety of different means of access from the street to front doors. This theme is echoed in the projects by Michael Folonis in California (Figs 3.14 to 3.15) and Alfredo de Vido in New York (Figs 3.16 to 3.18). Macondray Terrace in San Francisco by Hood Miller Associates not only tackles the problem of relating to an existing street frontage and creating an individual identity, but also copes with a steeply sloping site (Figs 3.19 to 3.23).

The British examples (Figs 3.24 to 3.27 and 3.21 to 3.32) illustrate solutions to the design of two typical kinds of infill site. At Caversham Road, London, architects Colquhoun, Miller and Partners have joined new housing on to the ends of two existing parallel rows of Victorian terraced houses. The result is a fresh architectural solution that is harmonious in scale and appearance with its surroundings, (Figs 3.24 to 3.27). At Bowland Yard, Belgravia, London, Donald Insall and Associates show the way to develop a small piece of back land such as is frequently found behind existing buildings in urban areas. The site required the development of special, single-aspect dwelling types which could be located close to the boundaries of the site, thereby maximizing the area of open space at the front of the dwellings (Figs 3.31 and 3.32). It is a skilful piece of design of an urban quality reminiscent of a Victorian mews. The example from the Netherlands (Figs 3.28 to 3.30) illustrates the quality of the achievement of the 'New Amsterdam School' of Architects in the area of urban regeneration.

Frankel Lambert Town Houses, Toronto, Ontario, Canada

Architects:	Ernest Annau Associates
No. of dwellings:	66
Site area:	0.6 hectares (1.5 acres)
Density:	110 dwellings per hectare (44.5 dwellings per acre)
Type of accommodation:	2-storey narrow frontage houses with additional basement

Size of dwellings:	
type A	98.4 sq m (1059 sq ft)
type B	96.8 sq m (1204 sq ft)
type C	92.6 sq m (998 sq ft)
type D	144.2 sq m (1552 sq ft)

Parking/garages:	1 space per dwelling
Construction:	4.1 m cross wall with timber infill panels; shingle roof.

3.1   Frankel Lambert town houses – the site layout relates to the existing street pattern.

The project consists of 46 very narrow-fronted town houses and ten duplex units on a new block within a large city-administered infill project in downtown Toronto. The design reflects in a modern way the traditional patterns of street, block, and lot ownership, while anticipating the sense of neighbourhood to be achieved in the completed project (Fig 3.1). Two-storey townhouses with three different internal layouts (Fig 3.3) and external treatments are located along Wychcrest Avenue and Melita

3.3   Considerable variety of elevational treatment has been produced from identical, narrow-fronted dwellings.

Crescent, providing choice of unit and variety of streetscape (Fig 3.2). Further choice is provided by the three-storey duplex units along Melita Crescent, each with separate unit entries from the street. The use of external stairs from the street to the entrance of the upper dwellings is a traditional feature of housing in Canada and the USA (Fig 3.2).

Wychcrest Avenue   **cars in**

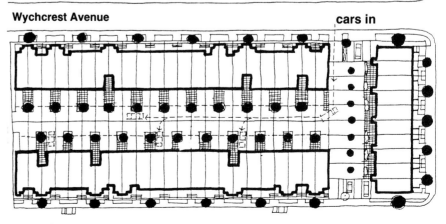

Melito Crescent

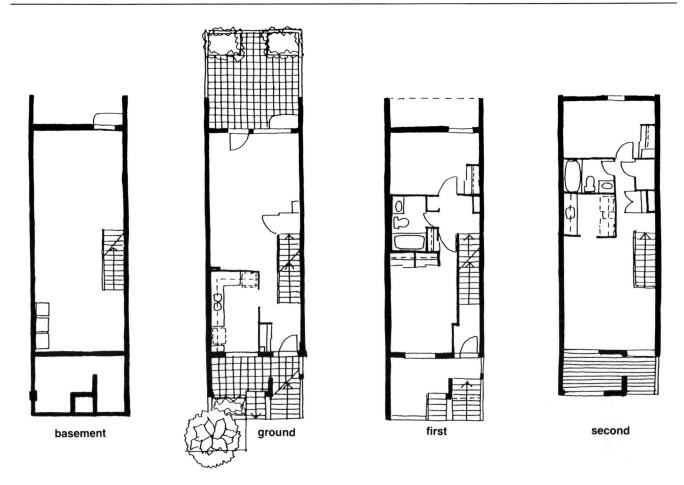

basement ground first second

**2-storey, 2-bedroom duplex town house with self-contained
1-bedroom apartment on the 3rd level**

**3.3 A selection from the numerous
town house plans.**

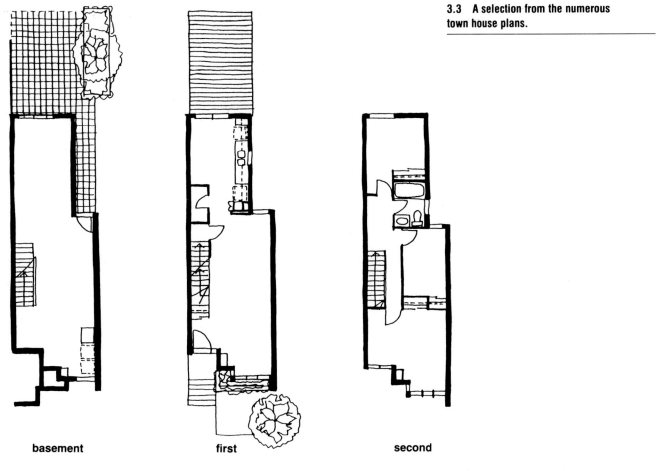

basement first second

2-storey, 2-bedroom duplex town house

3.4   Staircases to first-floor entrances.

Further reading
'Townhouses with Internal Street', *Canadian Architect*, March 1983, vol. 28, no. 3, pp. 20–3.
'Award of Excellence', *Canadian Architect*, December 1980, vol. 25, no. 12, pp. 32–4.

Greenway Gables, Minneapolis, Minnesota, USA

Architects:	Frederick Benz/Milo Thompson/Robert Rietow Inc, Architecture and Urban Design
No. of dwellings:	43
Site area:	1.0 hectares (2.6 acres)
Density:	43 dwellings per hectare (16 dwellings per acre)
Type of accommodation:	43 town houses
Size of dwellings:	
2-bedroom	200 sq m (2152 sq ft)
3-bedroom	232 sq m (2499 sq ft) to 300 sq m (3226 sq ft)
Parking/garages:	22 visitor spaces 43 double garages
Construction:	concrete footings; concrete block foundations; timber frame with redwood board cladding stained grey on exterior; asphalt roof shingles.

This scheme is a positive attempt to create, in a downtown area of Minneapolis, an urban form of housing using single family dwellings. The layout concept uses a traditional pattern of town streets and squares (Fig 3.5). Access to the entrances of the dwellings is from private culs-de-sac leading into the site from Yale Place. Every dwelling has an enclosed rear garden which leads onto spaces which are communal only to the dwellings. These spaces lead through keyed gates to a pedestrian greenway which passes through the area. To provide adequate security to the project as a whole, the frontage to the greenway is completely walled. The architectural character is traditional, with gables, bay windows, tall chimneys and timber boarding (Fig 3.6), yet the feeling created is very much of the present day. Each dwelling has its own identity which contributes to the diverse but integral

YALE PLACE

LORING GREENWAY

WILLOW STREET

0 16 32

N

3.5 The Greenway Gables housing, Minneapolis, is grouped around traditional streets and squares.

3.6 Two-storey houses looking onto small communal gardens.

character of the design. All dwellings have a double garage and basement at street level, with the major living spaces on the two floors above (Fig 3.7). Lifts are provided in dwellings when requested by the owners.

Further reading
'Three mini-site winners – in Minneapolis, 2.6 acres, with 43 townhouses', *Housing* (New York), December 1980, pp. 54, 55.

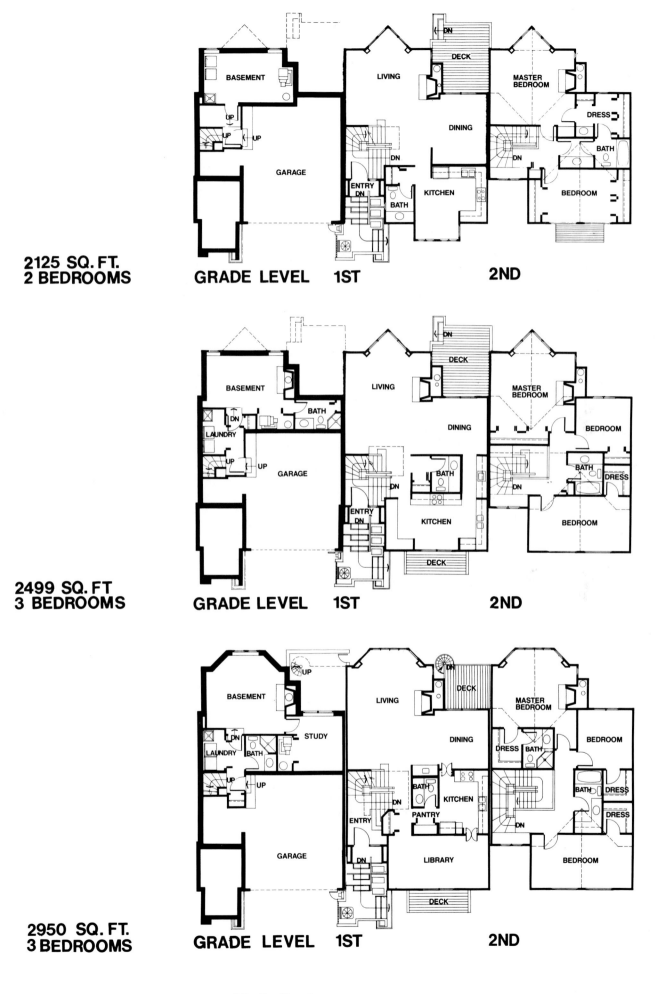

2125 SQ. FT.
2 BEDROOMS

GRADE LEVEL   1ST   2ND

2499 SQ. FT
3 BEDROOMS

GRADE LEVEL   1ST   2ND

2950 SQ. FT.
3 BEDROOMS

GRADE LEVEL   1ST   2ND

3.7 Dwelling plans.

Castro Common, San Francisco, California, USA

Architects:	Daniel Solomon and Associates
No. of dwellings:	12 (all flats)
Site area:	0.18 hectares (0.44 acres)
Density:	66 dwellings per hectare (27 dwellings per acre)
Size of dwellings:	88 sq m (950 sq ft)
Construction	timber frame; clapboarding.

3.8   The development at Castro Common, San Francisco, fits snugly into the irregular shape of the small site.

Castro Common is an infill housing scheme on a downtown site conceived principally for single people who are the predominant population in the surrounding neighbourhood. The distinguishing features of the design are its urban design qualities, i.e. the way it fits into a small, irregularly shaped infill site (Fig 3.8), and its unit planning, which responds to living patterns somewhat different from those in conventional housing. The scheme stands out, white and modern (Fig 3.9): it is visible but separate from its surroundings, standing high above a city plaza. Beyond its secured theatrical façade, the project opens into a small courtyard (Fig 3.10).

The larger units are designed for purchase by two single people and have two master bedrooms and bathrooms, all with equal amenity and privacy (Fig 3.11). This pattern permits two people, who have moderate

3.9   Screening across the entrance to the site increases the privacy within.

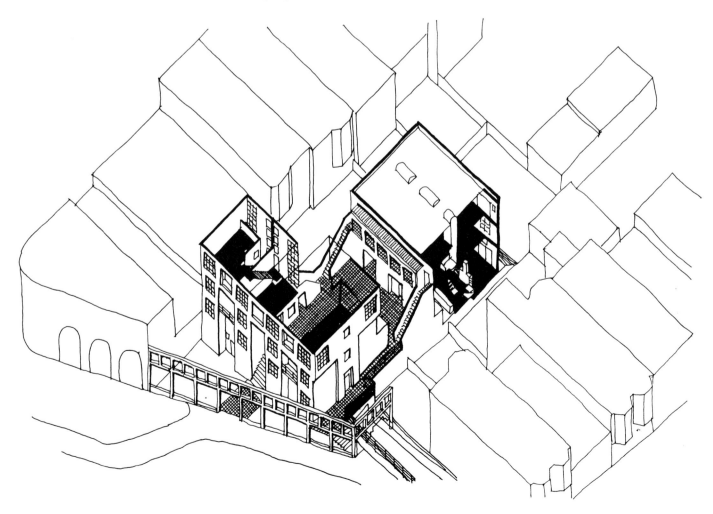

incomes and are both independent, to purchase new inner-city housing. There are 12 units, each averaging 88 sq m (950 sq ft) in size. Most units have two-storey spaces, fireplaces and private open space.

Further reading
'Courtyard Complex', *Architecture* (the AIA Journal) October 1983, vol. 72, no. 10, pp. 56, 57.

3.10 Internal courtyard.

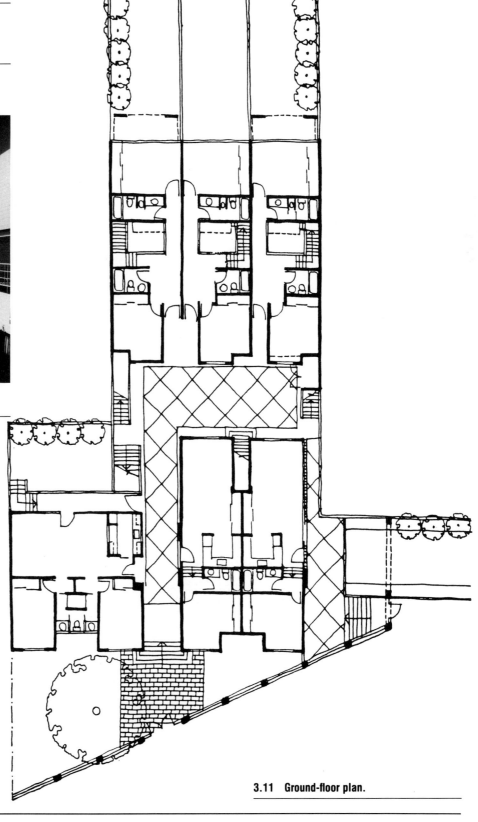

3.11 Ground-floor plan.

Washington House, 6620 Geary Boulevard, San Francisco, California, USA

Architects:	Daniel Solomon and Associates
No. of dwellings:	13
Site area:	0.09 hectares (0.22 acres)
Density:	144 dwellings per hectare (59 dwellings per acre)

Type size and no. of accommodation:

			Car parking
Ground floor First floor	4/2-bedroom flats	107.8 sq m (1160 sq ft)	1
Second floor	2/2-bedroom flats	98.3 sq m (1058 sq ft)	1
	2/3-bedroom flats	127.3 sq m (1370 sq ft)	1
Third floor	1/1-bedroom flat	96.0 sq m (1034 sq ft)	1
	2/2-bedroom flats	113.9 sq m (1226 sq ft)	1
	2/bed-sitting flats	33.4 sq m (360 sq ft)	1

Parking/garages:	13 parking spaces
Heating:	gas central heating in 3 dwellings; solar heating in 10 dwellings
Construction:	timber frame: stucco finish.

Washington House comprises 13 units of infill housing in San Francisco. Whilst being an apartment block, the scheme takes the form of the traditional row-house found in the city (Fig 3.12). The site is 100 ft by 100 ft (30.5 m by 30.5 m) but the building is organized on a 25ft (7.6m) grid which is the historical unit of land division in San Francisco. Party-walls between units relate to this dimension. The lower two units of each outer bay (four units in total) are walk-ups with their own street entrances. The remaining nine units are served by a central two-storey lift lobby (Fig 3.13). The multiple entrances also recall the scale of smaller buildings, concealing the parking behind them and providing an animated street frontage.

The interior is ingeniously planned to ensure that all rooms have natural daylight: bathrooms and some kitchens are lit from small light wells.

Ten of the 13 units are heated by a passive solar system. Glazed versions of traditional San Francisco bay windows serve as heat collecting solaria facing south. Heat is directed from these solaria to the north end of the units. The solaria also serve as indoor garden rooms and as acoustic buffers between the bedrooms and the noise of the street.

**3.12   Washington House, San Francisco –
street housing at its best.**

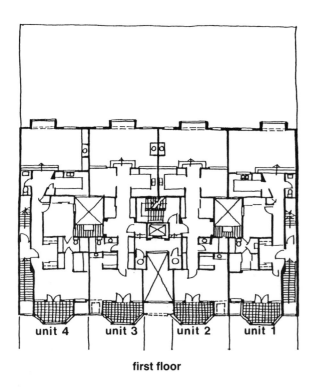

first floor

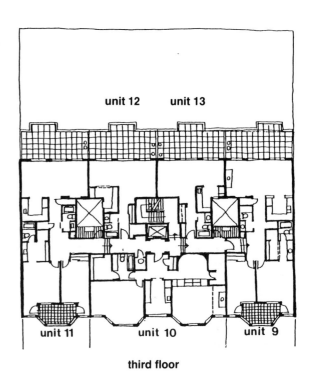

third floor

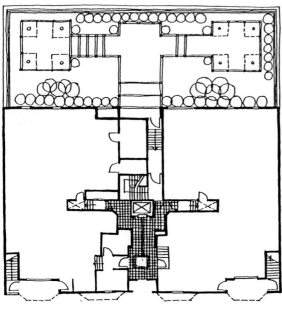

ground floor

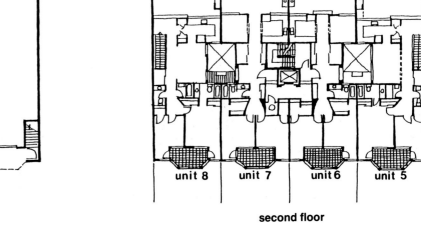

second floor

3.13 Dwelling plans.

Barrington Avenue Street Housing, West Los Angeles, California, and 831 Pacific Street, Santa Monica, California, USA

Architect:	Michael W. Folonis, AIA and Associates
No. of dwellings:	5
Site area:	0.6 hectares (0.14 acres)
Density:	88 dwellings per hectare (36 dwellings per acre)
Construction:	timber-framed construction with stucco exterior and drywall interior; concrete slab above the garage level and at first floor level.

The project is located on a major residential street in West Los Angeles, in a neighbourhood consisting of single and multiple family dwellings. The site is bounded by two streets and a single-family residence. Within strict economic constraints, the client wished to maximize the interior space while allowing ample private exterior balconies. The project was designed to achieve a strong identity and each unit was to have a separate entrance close to the garage. Entry stairs, parking gates and planters combine to individualize and separate each unit. The rounded elements serve to identify the entrances and vertical circulation and separate the exterior balconies (Fig 3.14). The second level

3.14   At 831 Pacific Street planes and voids create a distinctive architectural appearance which is highly appropriate for the Californian climate.

contains two bedrooms. Seclusion from street traffic is achieved by recessed wall planters between the windows and the street. The third level contains the kitchen and living area. The mezzanine level above covers only one-third of the living area, which is consequently opened up to become a double height space.

Michael Folonis has designed other projects of a similar quality. At 831 Pacific Street, Santa Monica, designed in 1980, the theme of Barrington Avenue is further exploited to create a highly imaginative development which owes its form to the total acceptance of twentieth-century architecture to provide a unique habitat (Fig 3.15). The building's three levels rise above a concrete block and concrete underground garage containing two parking spaces per unit as well as storage space, water-heater and individual entry stairs. The first living level consists of two bedrooms, two bathrooms, an entry area and a laundry area. The second level consists of living, dining, kitchen, bath and exterior dining area. The third level (mezzanine) overlooks the living area and has an exterior deck and staircase leading to a roof sundeck. The mezzanine decks are separated by diagonal fin-walls which have semi-circular openings for emergency stair access. These walls also reinforce the articulation of the units above the second level.

Further reading

FRAMPTON, K., 'The Utopian Legacy', *Architectural Review*, December 1987, vol. CLXXXII, no. 1090, pp. 30, 31.

3.15 Barrington Avenue, San Francisco – the elevations how a skilful modelling of receding floor levels and circular staircase elements.

222 Columbia Heights, New York City, USA

Architects:	Alfredo de Vido Associates
No. of dwellings:	4
Site area:	0.3 hectares (0.74 acres)
Density:	13.3 dwellings per hectare (5.4 dwellings per acre)
Type of accommodation:	apartments
Size of dwellings:	130 sq m (1399 sq ft) and 450 sq m (4844 sq ft)
Construction:	masonry bearing walls with steel joists supporting the floors.

Brooklyn Heights is a landmark preservation district within New York City. It is notable for its four-storey brownstone houses, many of which were completed in the late nineteenth century in Renaissance Revival style. The original brief called for a two/three-storey house to be built on a vacant piece of land terminating a row of handsome brownstone houses. Initial discussion with the Landmarks Commission caused a revision of this brief which increased the height of the building to equal that of adjacent structures. The addition of a rental apartment and second condominium enabled the new construction to reflect the scale of the neighbourhood (Fig 3.16).

Externally, the elevations are modern, but totally in keeping with the surrounding buildings. The use of brown brick, stoop and bay windows and high profile 'Torck'-profile sills, string courses and cornices all enliven the façades. The interiors contain light-filled double height spaces which create an open plan (Fig 3.17) from which are gained extraordinary views of the Manhattan commercial district (Fig 3.18).

3.16   222 Columbia Heights provides a present-day solution to building onto the end of a Victorian Terrace.

Further reading
'Learning to live with landmarks', *Architectural Record* July 1982, pp. 82–5.

3.17   Superb views of the Manhatten skyline.

3.18   Dwelling plans.

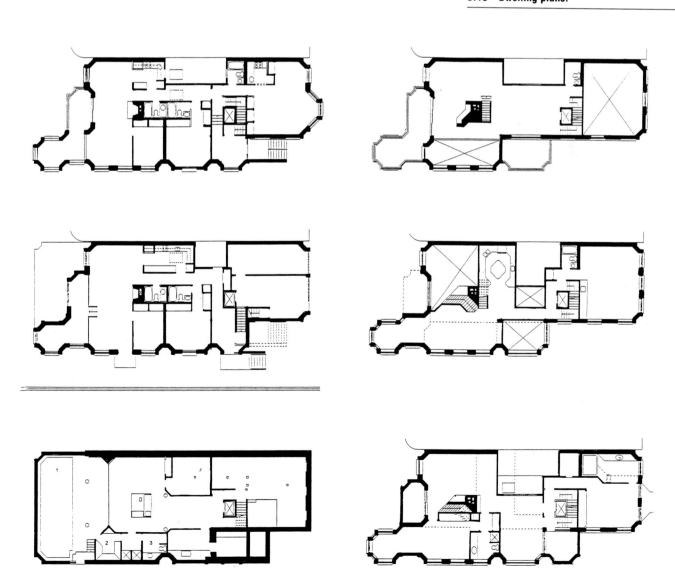

Macondray Terrace Condominiums, 945 Union Street/44 Macondray Lane, Russian Hill, San Francisco, California, USA

Architects:	Hood, Miller Associates
No. of dwellings:	13
Site area:	0.7 hectares (0.16 acre)
Density:	195 units per hectare (79 units per acre)
	400 persons per hectare (160 persons per acre)
Type of accommodation:	
flats	13 condominiums with 10 different floor plans, 1–3 bedrooms
Size of dwellings:	
2–6 person dwellings	83.6 sq m (900 sq ft) to 195.09 sq m (2100 sq ft)
Parking/garages:	16 car parking spaces; garage built into the structure on two levels
Construction:	western platform timber frame; timber cladding externally with rustication similar to traditional San Francisco architecture; double-glazed windows.
garage levels	the side and back walls are constructed in heavily reinforced concrete with tie backs into the hill; the front wall is of split-faced concrete block; concrete slab floors.
storage levels	reinforced concrete block with concrete slab floors.

3.19 The 13-unit condominium complex is split into two levels and linked by a glass-enclosed elevator.

The site is close to the centre of San Francisco on the very steep northern slope of Russian Hill. On the uphill side it is bordered by a pleasant pedestrian street, Macondray Lane, whilst on the lower side it is bounded by a busy thoroughfare, Union Street (Fig 3.20).

Vehicular access is from Union Street and cars park on two levels, one of which is situated on the uphill side and the other on the downhill, thereby avoiding the need for internal ramps. To preserve the existing pattern of mid-block open space, the project is split into two buildings connected by an inclined glass-

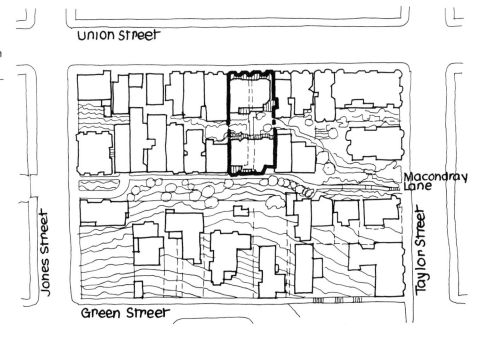

3.20 Site plan of the Macondray Terrace condominiums.

enclosed elevator which links parking, living levels and the Union Street and Macondray Lane entrances (Fig 3.19). The project has distinct unity and yet responds in different ways to its public façades. The Union Street façade is formal and symmetrical, reflecting the strong pattern of Victorian façades throughout the block (Fig 3.23). There is a two-storey atrium which opens the interior to the informal and rustic landscape. A pedestrian walkway and the inclined elevator make it possible for anyone living in either building to reach his or her condominium and to admit visitors by either entrance. Except for repeating floor plans on the first two floors, all the units are different

3.22 The development enjoys sweeping views across San Francisco Bay.

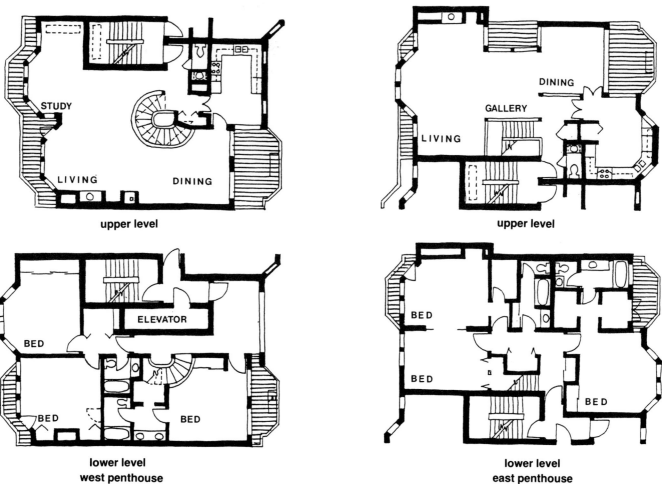

upper level

upper level

lower level
west penthouse

lower level
east penthouse

3.21 Dwellings plans.

ranging in size from one to three bedrooms (Fig 3.21). The living-rooms have fireplaces and spectacular views over San Francisco Bay (Fig 3.22). The units are extremely energy efficient due to double glazing, heavy insulation and minimum exterior walls exposed to the elements. The physically handicapped have access to 11 of the 13 units by the elevator.

Further reading
'AIA Honor Awards 1982', *Architecture* (the AIA Journal), mid-May 1982, vol. 71, no. 6, pp. 225–35.

'Macondray Terrace, San Francisco – 1982 Honor Award', *Architecture California*, July/ August 1982, vol. 4, no. 4, pp. 22, 23.

3.23 Union Street façade.

Caversham Road/Gaisford Street, London

Architects:	Colquhoun, Miller and Partners
No. of dwellings:	7
Site Area:	0.15 hectares (0.37 acres)
Density:	47 dwellings per hectare (19 dwellings per acre)
	267 persons per hectare (108 person per acre)
Type of accommodation:	2-storey maisonettes
Size of dwellings:	
6-person maisonette	102 sq m (1098 sq ft)
5-person maisonette	88 sq m (947 sq ft)
Parking/garages:	on-street parking
Construction:	load bearing concrete blockwork walls; reinforced concrete intermediate floors between maisonettes and timber intermediate floors within the maisonettes; roofs are of timber rafters on steel trusses and specialist timber trusses; external walls are finished with white render; windows have dark brown aluminium slides and casements; staircases and balconies are finished with black quarry tiles.

Architects Colquhoun, Miller and Partners have clearly demonstrated with this small project for the London Borough of Camden that it is not necessary to copy the architectural styles of the past to achieve sensitive infill development (Fig 3.24).

The site comprises two small areas of land on parallel streets of four-storey housing, built virtually up to the back edge of the pavement. The gap in Gaisford Street was filled with a block of five new maisonettes, all with direct access from street level. The steps leading to the upper-floor dwellings resemble the stairs up to the front doors of the adjoining terraced housing (Fig 3.25). In Caversham Road, the previous semi-detached block was replaced by two maisonettes with access from street

3.24 A view of the infill housing from Gaisford Road.

level. A hipped gable roof was
provided to match the adjoining house.
A pedestrian walkway through the site
links both sides of the scheme with a
common playspace and a future
tenants' hall (Fig 3.26). The route is
gated to prevent use by non-residents.
The dwelling plan fronting Gaisford
Street is illustrated (Fig 3.27).

Further reading

SUDJIC, D., 'Fitting Trilente', *Building Design*,
10 August 1979, no. 458, pp. 12, 13.

'Preview 78', *The Architectural Review*,
January 1978, vol. CLXII, no. 971, p. 9.

'Colquhoun and Miller, Caversham Road/
Gaisford Street Housing', *Architectural
Design*, March/April 1981, no. 51, pp. 10, 11.

'Miethäuser in London', *Baumeister*,
November, 1982, pp. 1078–80.

'Public Housing: Caversham Road and
Gaisford Street', *A+U*, April 1982, no. 139,
pp. 92–4.

'Caversham Road y Gaisford Street',
Arquitectura, February 1983, vol. LXIV,
no. 240, pp. 53–7.

**3.25 Staircase entrance to upper-floor
maisonettes.**

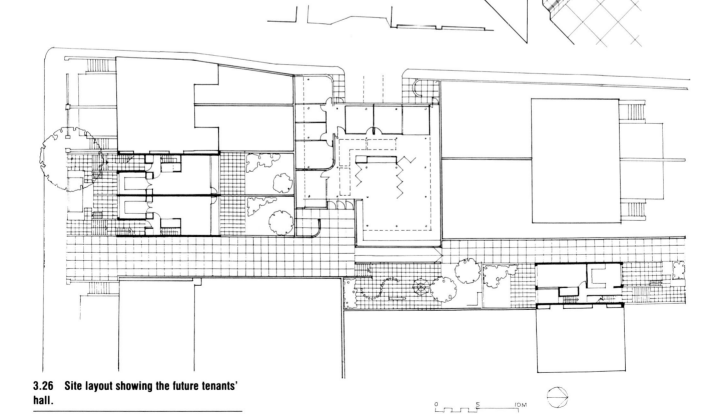

**3.26 Site layout showing the future tenants'
hall.**

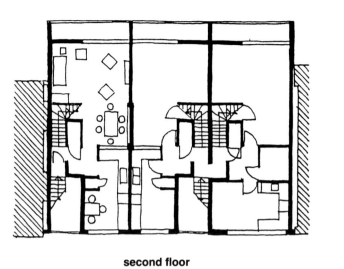
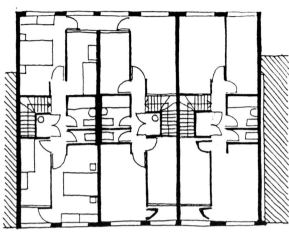

second floor

Third floor

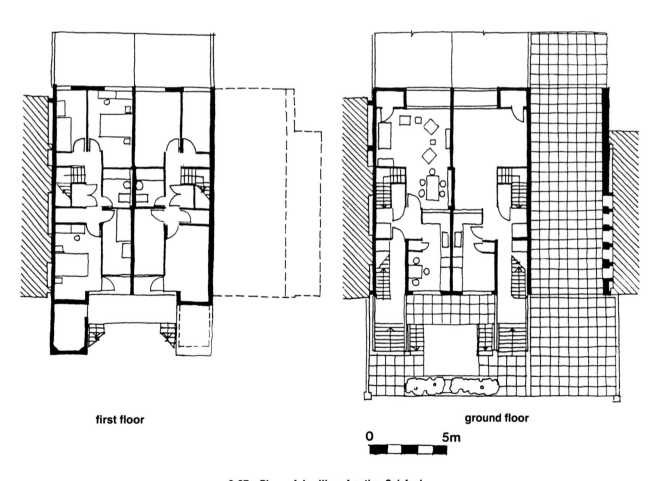

first floor

ground floor

0   5m

3.27 Plans of dwellings fronting Gaisford Road.

Oude-Schans, 31–33 Uilenburg, Amsterdam, The Netherlands

Architect:	Paul de Ley
No. of dwellings:	12
Site area:	0.4 hectares (1.0 acre)
Density:	30 dwellings per hectare
Type of accommodation:	4/2-roomed dwellings
	4/3-roomed dwellings (maisonettes)
	4/4-roomed dwellings (maisonettes)
Size of dwellings:	
1-bedroom flats	39.3 sq m (423 sq ft)
2/3-bedroom maisonettes	78.6 sq m (846 sq ft)
2-bedroom maisonettes	73.8 sq m (794 sq ft)
Construction:	brick walls; reinforced concrete floors; painted wooden window frames; painted steel railings.

3.28   Sensitive canal-side infill development on the Oude-Schans, Amsterdam.

This infill scheme on the Oude-Schans echoes the symmetrical and gable form of the traditional buildings which front the canals in Amsterdam, but added are bay windows and conservatories at the tops of staircases which lead onto roof terraces (Fig 3.28).

Rather than attempting rigidly to copy the style of its neighbours, the fenestration is a genuine continuation of the internal planning: living-rooms have tall windows and bedrooms less tall ones on alternate floors. The result is an extremely successful solution to the problem of infill development (Figs 3.29, 3.30).

Further reading

BUCHANAN, P., 'The New Amsterdam School – Paul de Ley', *Architectural Review*, January 1988, vol. CLXXVII, no. 1055, pp. 36–8.

'Bebauung einer Baulücke an der Oude Schans', *Deutshe Bauzeitung*, April 1980, pp. 22, 23.

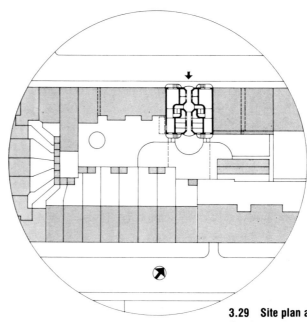

3.29   Site plan and ground-floor plan of the development.

Bowland Yard, Belgravia, London

Architect:	Donald W. Insall and Associates Ltd
No. of dwellings:	8
Site area:	0.05 hectares (0.12 acres)
Density:	173 dwellings per hectare (72 dwellings per acre)

Type of accommodation:

1-bedroom flats	2
2-bedroom maisonettes	1
3-bedroom maisonettes	1
3-bedroom houses	4

Size of dwellings:

1-bedroom flats	48 sq m and 59 sq m (517 sq ft and 635 sq ft)
2-bedroom maisonette	56 sq m (603 sq ft)
3-bedroom maisonette	131 sq m (1410 sq ft)
3-bedroom houses	153 sq m (1647 sq ft)

The area of the dwellings has been measured from the plans.

3.31   The view along Bowland Yard from an upper floor.

3.30   A typical floor plan.

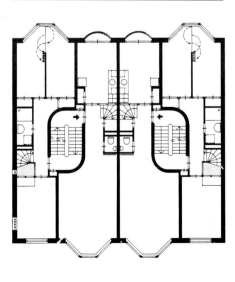

London is renowned for its mews housing, constructed in the nineteenth century, at the rear of the great terraces to accommodate the servants, coaches, etc. These have now become much sought after city residences. The opportunity to design new housing in such locations is extremely rare and poses a great challenge when it arises. At Bowlands Yard, Belgravia, Donald Insall designed this project to create an enclosure in the spirit and tradition of the neighbourhood. (Fig 3.31). The houses replace an industrial building which was considered a fire hazard to the small residential area. All the building materials had to be brought through the existing, narrow entry. The dwellings are skilfully grouped in an 'L' on two sides of the yard with the principal rooms facing into the yard (Fig 3.32). The use of bay windows at higher level provides views along the length of the yard. To enable the development to be built right up to the boundaries of the site, single aspect dwelling forms have been used together with small courts at the rear of each dwelling. The pedestrian circulation links with adjoining mews. In 1989 the project was awarded the Europa Nostra Diploma of Merit for the sensitive residential development of a typical London mews.

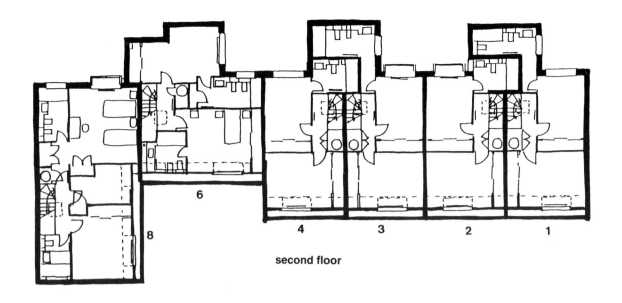

second floor

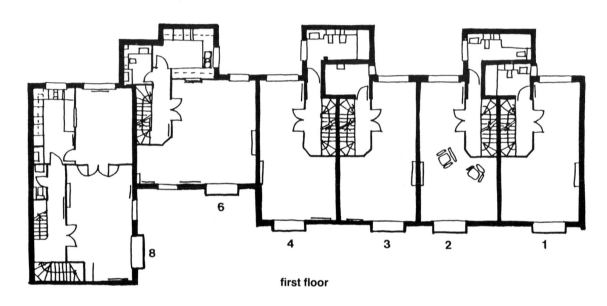

first floor

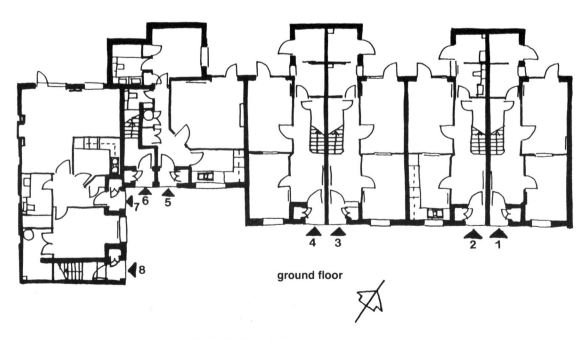

ground floor

3.32 Dwelling plans.

4 HOUSING ON HILLSIDE SITES

SLOPING sites or sites on the ridge of a hill can offer some of the greatest opportunities to the imaginative architect in terms of site planning and architectural design. Changes in level offer many options for building-to-building relationships, parking and garaging of cars and the design of open spaces. Today, houses with a view are frequently prized, yet such sites are all too often developed with housing more suited to flat land.

The design solutions for sloping sites vary, from the construction of simple terraced housing along the contours of sites with moderate gradients (Fig 4.1) to the design on steeply sloping sites of split-level housing with living-rooms on the first floor, affording extensive views over the roof-tops of dwellings below. Some sites are so steeply sloping that they call for very special design solutions (Figs 4.14 to 4.21).

The construction of housing on sloping sites can be more costly than building on a flat site, as a substantial extra investment is required for the construction of retaining walls, roads, which may have to zigzag diagonally across the site (Fig 4.2), foundations, drainage and possibly earth moving. However, such costs may be offset by a higher density of development, arising from the construction of the housing in terraced

4.1 Hillside villas, Kooralbyn, Queensland, Australia.
Architects: Harry Seidler and Associates Pty Ltd.

form and the potential for grouping dwellings closer together than the distances required on flat sites to ensure reasonable privacy. On sloping sites, privacy, in the direction of the view, can be obtained from the use of single-aspect, wide-frontage housing looking out over the roof-tops of the dwellings below. Furthermore, the benefits of a good view can considerably reduce the desire for detachment and thereby enable genuinely urban housing forms to be constructed in urban locations.

Sites on the brow of a hill can usually be seen from a distance and the housing is easily identifiable; it therefore needs to be designed with this in mind. Housing, built in long continuous forms, is particularly suitable because of its scale and its potential to dramatize the silhouette of the hill. However, forms without some variety of roof line can be monotonous and often require relief as in Figs 4.23 and 4.25. It is more difficult to succeed with small houses as a tooth-and-gap silhouette will result, unless the grouping creates a clustering of roofs

and gables. If all the houses are detached or semi-detached and are to be built in long rows, it is safer to confine them to the lower slopes, leaving the crown of the hill as natural landscape.

The projects which follow illustrate these principles. Exwick Farm (Figs 4.2 to 4.5) is a typically well-designed British project on a site with a steep gradient. Oksvaal III (chapter 6 and Figs 6.35 to 6.37) shows a Norwegian approach to developing a site which was not only steeply sloping, but also had outcrops to be incorporated into the design. The 'duplex' housing at the foot of Mount Fiji (Figs 4.6 to 4.9) and Cranmore Woods Condominiums in New Hampshire, USA (Figs 4.10 to 4.13), illustrate split-level house forms on steeply sloping sites, whilst the Rokko Housing in Japan (Figs 4.15 to 4.18) and Albany Oaks in California (Figs 4.19 to 4.22) demonstrate special design solutions to very steeply sloping sites. The remaining projects (Figs 4.23 to 4.40) are all hill-top projects. Macondray Condominiums in San Francisco,

which is described in chapter 3 (Figs 3.19 to 3.23), also illustrates a special design solution to a very steeply sloping site: it is a superb example of the potential for high density hillside housing in an urban infill location.

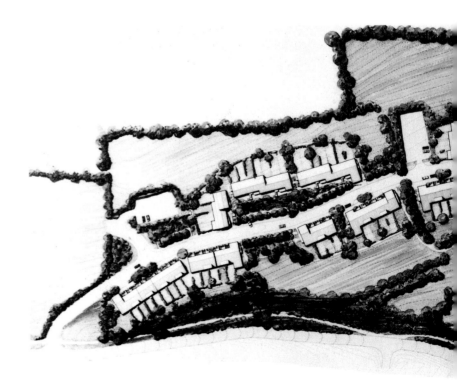

Exwick Farm, Exeter, England

Architects:	Smith, Hutton, Nichols
No. of dwellings:	188
Site area:	3.9 hectares (9.6 acres)
Density:	47.96 dwellings per hectare (118.5 dwellings per acre)
	156 persons per hectare (385.5 persons per acre)

Type of accommodation:	
	houses 31
	flats 113
	44 of these dwellings were specifically designed for elderly people

Size of dwellings: all to Parker Morris standards:	
5-person houses	90.5 sq m (974 sq ft)
6-person houses	105.3 sq m (1133 sq ft)
2–5-person flats	48.6 sq m–89.1 sq m (523 sq ft–959 sq ft)
1, 2 and 3-person dwellings for elderly people	33.4 sq m–57.0 sq m (360 sq ft–614 sq ft)

Parking/garaging:	155 car parking spaces
Construction:	traditional cross wall construction; deep strip and pile foundations with undersoil drainage; brick cavity walls; concrete party floors and timber intermediate floors and roof; concrete interlocking roof tiles; stained timber windows.

The south-facing slope of the site is very steep with a general gradient of 1 in 4 and one area of 1 in 2.5. House types have been devised to exploit these gradients and to take full benefit of the extensive views to the south-east towards Exeter Cathedral and to the south west over open countryside. Road design along the contours was critical, both to conform to acceptable gradients and to minimize cut and fill (Figs 4.2). Parking bays have been formed directly by the roads, except for a separate parking court for the elderly persons' dwellings.

The general disposition of housing is set out below.

1　Above the roads there are single level flats, and above these are two-storey houses which have direct access to their own gardens (Fig 4.3).

2　Situated below the roads there are single-level flats, and below them are two-storey houses which have direct access to their own gardens (Fig 4.3).

3　At the ends of terraces the building form has been deepened to provide a variety of extra accommodation which takes advantage of light and access through the gable wall.

4　Two-storey stepped terrace-houses are located at right angles to the contours which serve to define 'public places' (Fig 4.4).

4.2　Site layout of Exwick Farm.
Architect: S. Benedetti.

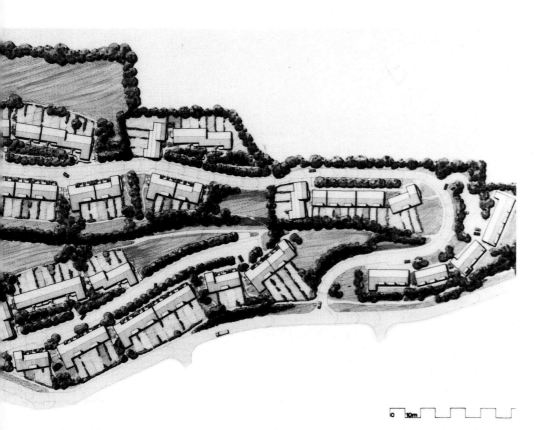

4.3   A view showing the relationship of the housing to the spine road through the development.

4.4   Section through Exwick Farm – note how the location of dwellings down the slope help to close off the vistas along the spine road.

5   Narrow frontage three-storey houses have been used to adjust the terraces to the contours or simply to provide for larger accommodation.

6   In the area of the site nearest Exwick Village, a group of four terraces has been designed for elderly people (category 1 housing), together with a meeting hall and superintendent's house.

The layout of the housing on the site has been designed to fit closely to the original field pattern, forming a series of unique and well defined 'places' which respond to the various conditions and characteristics of the site. By avoiding an even spread of dwellings, large, open landscape areas have been preserved which exploit the special qualities of the hillside, and respect the very important distant views from the city centre.

A selection of dwelling plans are illustrated (Fig 4.5).

Further reading

DOE, NHBC, RIBA, 'Exwick Farm (phase 1 of stage 1)', *Housing Design Awards 1983*, Housing Design Awards Steening Committee, p. 46.

'Wohnquartier in Exeter', *Baumeister*, March 1983, pp. 240–3.

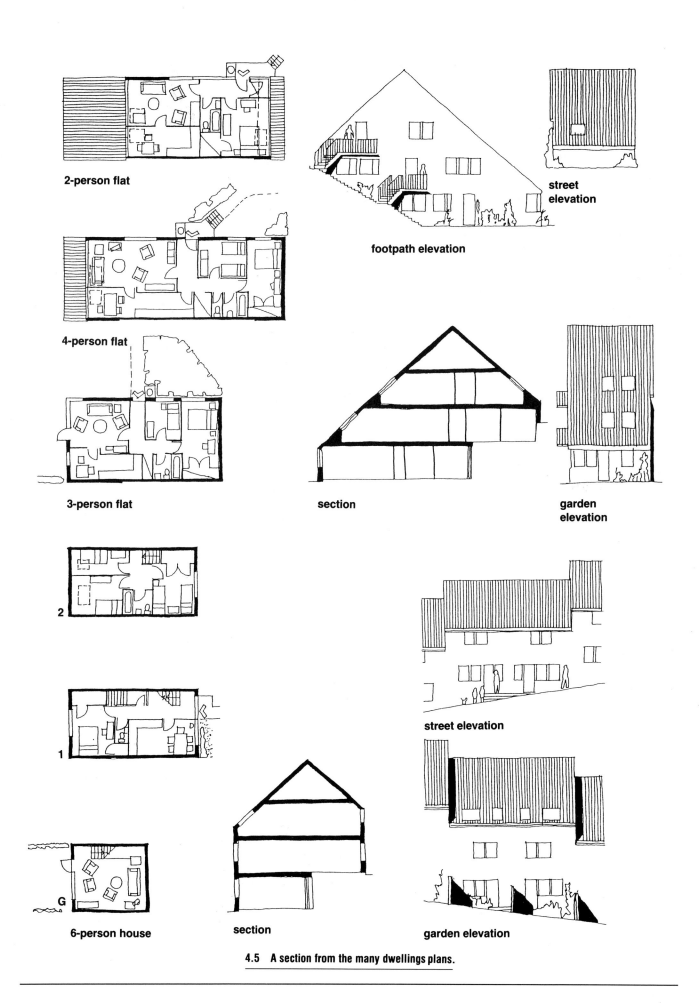

2-person flat

footpath elevation

street elevation

4-person flat

3-person flat

section

garden elevation

2

1

6-person house

section

street elevation

G

garden elevation

4.5 A section from the many dwellings plans.

Duplex Housing at the Foot of Mount Fuji, Japan

Architect:	Tsukasa Yamashita
No. of dwellings:	10
Site area:	0.6 hectares (1.5 acres)
Density:	16 dwellings per hectare (6.5 dwellings per acre)
Size of dwellings:	100 sq m (107 sq ft)
Parking/garages:	20 car parking spaces
Construction:	reinforced concrete.

These dwellings take full advantage of the steeply sloping north-west-facing site (Fig 4.6). The internal spaces cascade at several levels down the slopes; the curved balconies create a distinctive architectural form (Figs 4.7, 4.8). The entrances to the houses are on the upper level, along with the bathroom, toilet and master bedroom (Fig 4.7). A staircase leads down into the high-ceilinged living/dining-room which has a balcony projecting at mezzanine level (Fig 4.9). The acrylic dome skylights in the living/dining-room ceilings admit bright sunlight during the day into the centre of the dwelling. The rhythmical design of the north sides results from the repeated curving lines of the dining-room windows and the projecting semi-circular balcony terraces.

Further reading
'Duplex houses at the foot of Mount Fiji', *Japan Architect*, August 1982, no. 304, pp. 58–62.

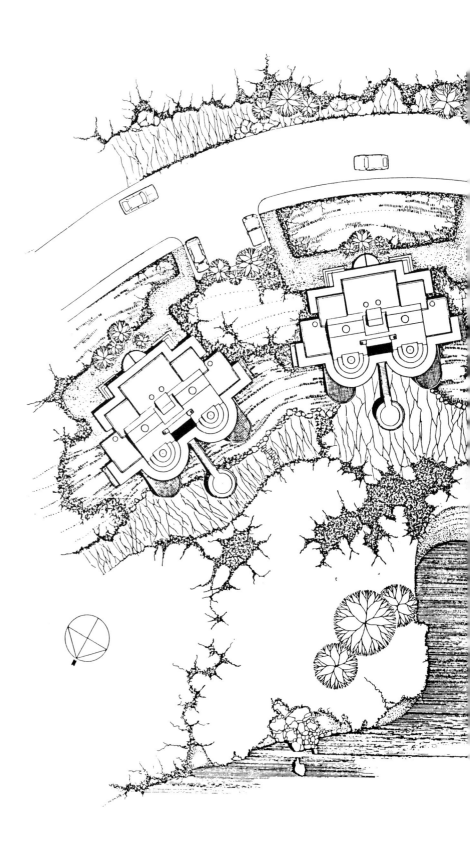

4.6   Site layout of the duplex houses at the foot of Mount Fuji, Japan.

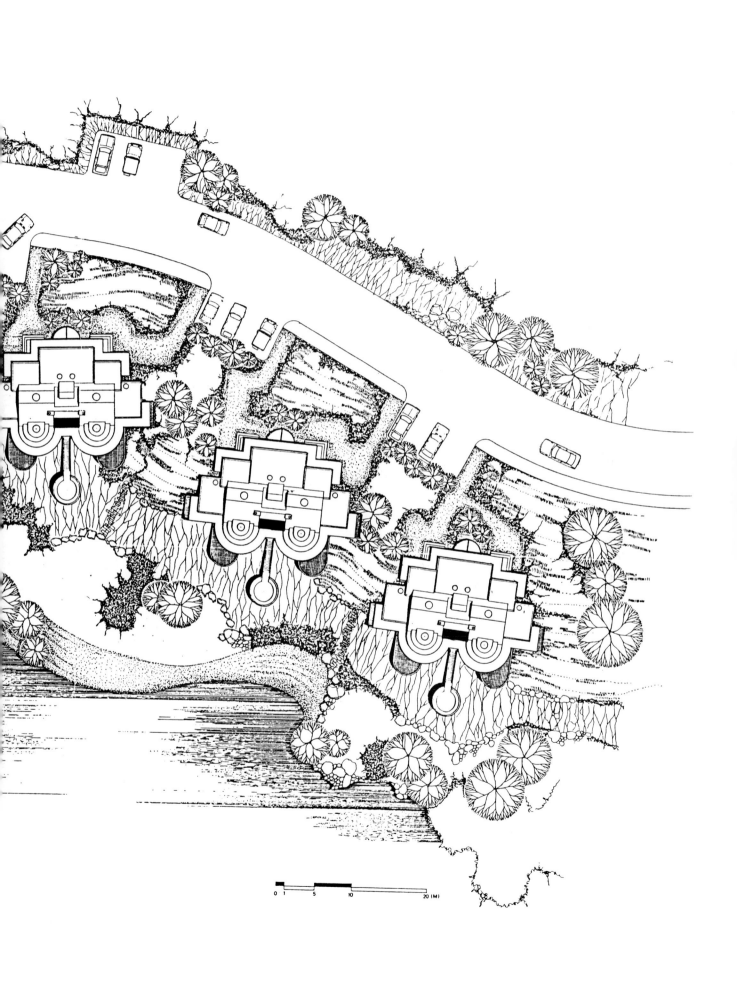

0 1 5 10 20 (M)

4.7   Section through the site.

**4.8   The houses with Mount Fuji in the
background.**

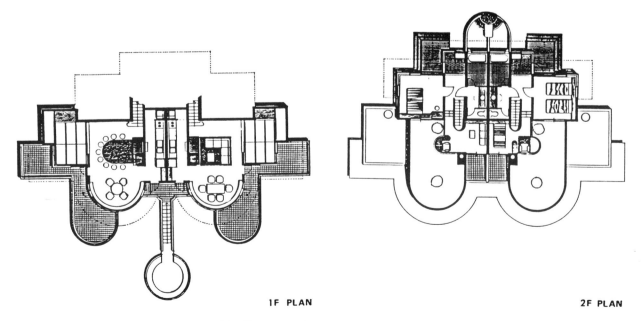

1F PLAN   2F PLAN

4.9   Floor plans of the dwellings.

Cranmore Woods Condominiums, North Cornway, New Hampshire, USA

Architects:	Banwell, White, Arnold and Hemberger
No. of dwellings:	15
Site area:	3.03 hectares (7.5 acres)
Density:	4.95 persons per hectare (2 dwellings per acre)
Type of accommodation:	houses
Size of dwellings:	293.5 sq m (3160 sq ft)
Parking/garages:	30 car parking spaces
Heating:	passive solar and electric 'baseboard' heating; wood stove in lower level
Construction:	poured concrete foundation walls; timber-framed construction with shiplap pine boarding externally; masonry party walls; double glazed windows; sliding doors and skylights; 1-inch tempered insulating glass in aluminium frame at solarium roof, combined with motorized thermal shade for passive solar heating.

The 15 condominiums nestle harmoniously onto a woodland site with gentle slopes towards the south west. The site presented a good opportunity to develop a passive solar scheme, whilst simultaneously opening to westerly views of the White Mountains (Fig 4.10).

Site planning resulted in an approach to each dwelling from the north with the units organized around a crossing of the east-west and north-south axes (Fig 4.11). The north entry leads directly south through the unit into the dining-room/solarium and beyond to the adjoining balcony. The unit plan is arranged on three floors: living spaces are located on the main entry level; sleeping areas on the upper level; recreation room, utilities, storage and, at the owner's option, additional bedrooms or play spaces on the lower level (Fig 4.12). The unit plans are repetitive to comply with building economy and market

4.10   The houses nestle amongst the trees.

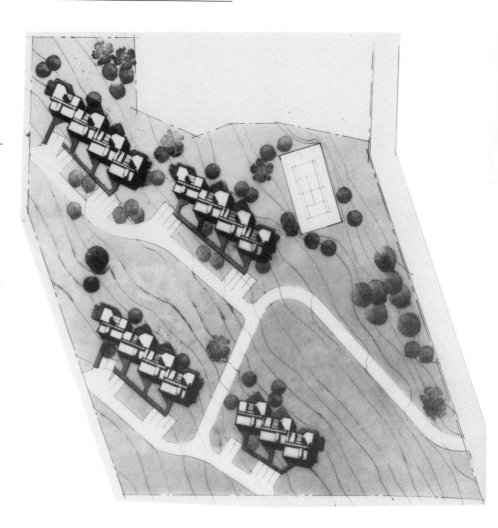

4.11   Site layout.

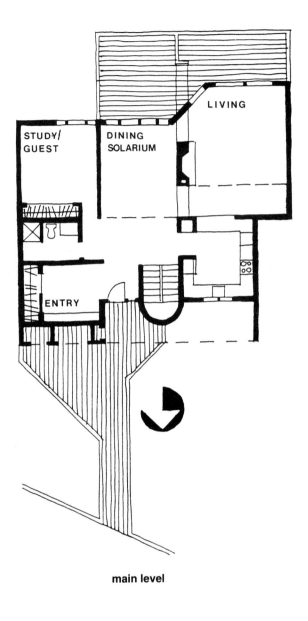

main level

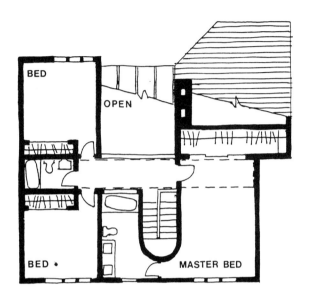

upper level

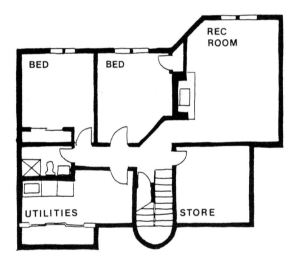

lower level

4.12 Dwelling plans.

constraints. They have, however, been arranged with the use of entry bridges and grouped in a staggered form to create a sense of individual identity and privacy from one dwelling to the next. (Fig 4.14).

The glass-roofed solarium is the central, dominant space in the house, contributing light and warmth to the rooms organized around it. A photocell controls the motorized insulating shade that operates in a winter mode, to maximize solar gain and prevent heat loss, and in a summer mode, to provide shade and reduce glare. The tile flooring and brick chimney store the sun's radiant heat and moderate temperature swings inside. Natural ventilation is provided by operating windows in the area above the solarium to create a chimney effect. The upper-level bedrooms are connected by a 'bridge' that overlooks the solarium. The space is capped by a continuous east-west skylight which creates a dramatic orientation to the sun and sky, while providing direct sunlight for the north and interior spaces (Fig 4.13).

Further reading
UPGRADE, W.L., 'Multi-family housing that's custom-fit to site', *Housing*, December 1980, pp. 50–3.

4.13 An east-west skylight provides direct sunlight for the north facing rooms and interior spaces.

4.14 Section looking west

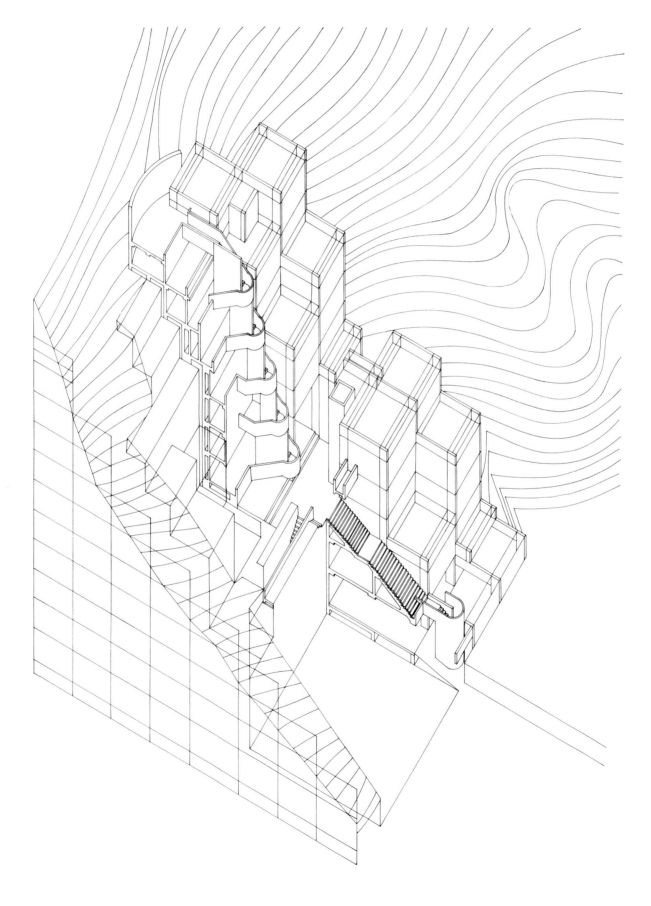

4.15   The 18 apartments are on ten levels.

Rokko Housing, Kobe, Japan

Architects:	Tadao Ando Architect and Associates
No. of dwellings:	18
Site area:	0.10 hectare (0.44 acre)
Density:	100 dwellings per hectare (40 dwellings per acre)
Size of dwellings:	1–4 bedrooms 83.5 sq m–139.2 sq m (893 sq ft–1,420 sq ft)
Parking/garages:	12 parking spaces underground garaging
Construction:	reinforced concrete roof; reinforced concrete on waterproof asphalt walls; exposed concrete (silicone sprayed); windows: aluminium sash.

Japan is a mountainous country and the cities are concentrated in the few small plains enclosed by steep hills, which have generally remained untouched. Some of these slopes are now being developed, as in the case of the Rokko Housing where the architect, Tadao Ando, has built on a 60 degree south-facing slope with distant views of the sea. The units, built in exposed concrete are set into the slope and integrated amongst the trees (Fig 4.16). The 18 'apartment' dwellings are on ten levels. Vertically, the building divides into three. Steep steps, climbing from the entrance culminate in a public courtyard space (Fig 4.15). The centrality of the courtyard's position in the composition is stressed by the strong plumb-line of the next set of stairs – spiral in form – which climb up another five storeys from the courtyard. The result is a striking composition of horizontal planes which blends well with nature. Each apartment comprises three or five units measuring 5.8 m by 4.8 m (19 ft by 15 ft 9 ins). The units are unusually proportioned, with plastered walls and carpeted floors. The windows and doors are enormous to take full advantage of the view (Fig 4.18).

4.16   The Rokko housing blends into its hillside site.

Further reading

KESTENBAUM, J.E., 'A series of planes cupped in the palm of a mountainside', *Architecture* (the AIA Journal), September 1984, vol. 73, no. 9, pp. 138–40.

POPHAM, P., 'Solo Artist', *Building Design*, 23 September 1983, no. 658, pp. 24–6.

4.17   The quality of the concrete finish is extremely high.

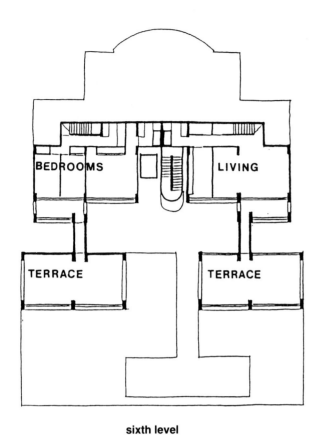

sixth level

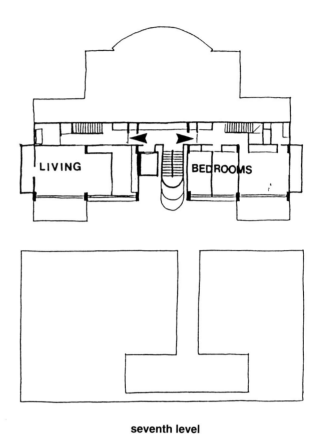

seventh level

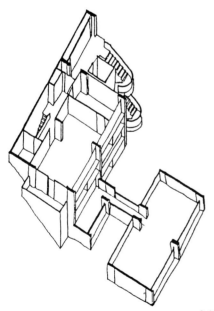

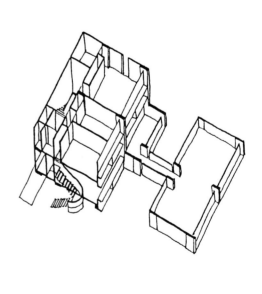

4.18   A selection from the numerous dwelling plans.

Albany Oaks, Albany, California, USA

Architect:	Edmund Burger
No. of dwellings:	9
Site area:	0.2 hectares (0.5 acre)
Density:	45 dwellings per hectare (18 dwellings per acre)
Size of dwellings:	139 sq m (1500 sq ft)
Parking/garaging:	16 car parking spaces
Construction:	concrete 'sonotube' formed columns, 'truss joist' plywood floor trusses, wood-framed walls and roof.

This project demonstrates a number of principles for building on a steeply sloping site which are not found in projects described earlier. Firstly, the construction of the dwellings is on stilts with the ground beneath remaining unchanged (Fig 4.19). Except for the car parking areas, there is little need for retaining walls. Access to all the dwellings is by an electrically powered, inclined elevator which runs alongside a series of walkways raised on stilts which wind their way around the existing trees on the site (Fig 4.20). Secondly, the housing has been arranged on the hillside to present a positive composition when viewed from a distance. This is enhanced by the skilful grouping of dwellings which enables the roof form to be continuous down the slope (Fig 4.21). The dwellings themselves are within a simple square with cut outs for external decks (Fig 4.22). The scheme blends superbly into the site and demonstrates so successfully how sensitive design can make the most from what would be so frequently a site that would be too steep to develop with grouped housing.

4.19 At Albany Oaks the hillside housing is constructed on stilts.

4.20   The continuous roof line follows the houses down the slope and raised timber walkways wind their way through the existing trees.

4.21   Albany Oaks viewed from a distance.

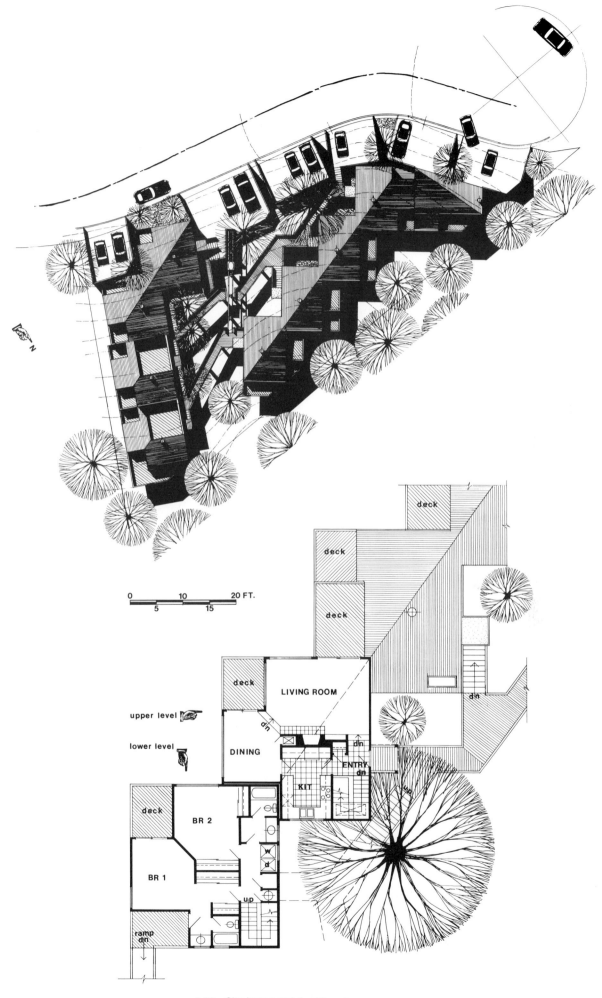

4.22 Site layout and dwelling plans.

Woodrun Place Condominiums II, Snowmass Village, Colorado, USA

Architect:	William Turnbull Associates
No. of dwellings:	62
Site area:	2.63 hectares (6.5 acres)
Density:	23.6 dwellings per hectare (9.5 dwellings per acre)
	62 persons per hectare (25 persons per acre)
Type of accommodation:	
townhouses	44
flats	12
employee units	6
Size of dwellings:	116 sq m average (1250 sq ft average)
Parking/garages:	80 car parking spaces
Construction:	timber-framed construction with steel post and laminated framing over concrete garages; the charcoal-grey concrete roof tile system was chosen for its technical advantages in a variable mountain climate; the architects describe the 'rusticated' pale grey stucco cladding as reinforcing the image of 'European masonry farmhouses'.

Located in a prime residential area on a steep north-facing slope, the site affords sweeping views and presented a remarkable challenge to the architects. The design intent was to create a pleasant village atmosphere against the rugged and spectacular mountain landscape within very complex brief and site requirements. The project includes 56 condominium dwellings, a conference centre, a 'recreational spa', and 56 covered car parking spaces. The dwellings are all within one continuous building which weaves around an upper octagonal plaza to the west and a lower entry 'turn around' to the east (Fig 4.23). A covered pedestrian arcade, important in the snowy winters, connects these areas by a grand staircase located in the central tower building. Vestibules off the arcade at the plaza level lead to one and two-bedroom town houses and to three-bedroom town houses above, which command extensive views. Vestibules at the east end provide access to two-bedroom town houses

above the covered car parking. These units have garden terraces to the south. The central tower accommodates the main lobby and conference area with three-bedroom flats above.

The massing of the buildings was dictated by the restrictive height and slope limitations (Fig 4.24). The buildings are organized in a way that prevents shadows on adjacent roads and homes. The dormered roof system and cantilevered decks not only add a sense of scale to the building, but also convey an individuality to each town house unit (Fig 4.25).

Further reading

'Colorado condominium that is complex in plan and form', *Architecture* (the AIA Journal), August 1984, vol. 73, no. 8, pp. 70, 71.

'An Alpine echo in the Rockies', *Architectural Record*, August 1984, pp. 96–9.

4.23   The building crowns the top of the hill.

4.25 The dormered roof system and cantilevered decks convey a certain individuality to each town house unit.

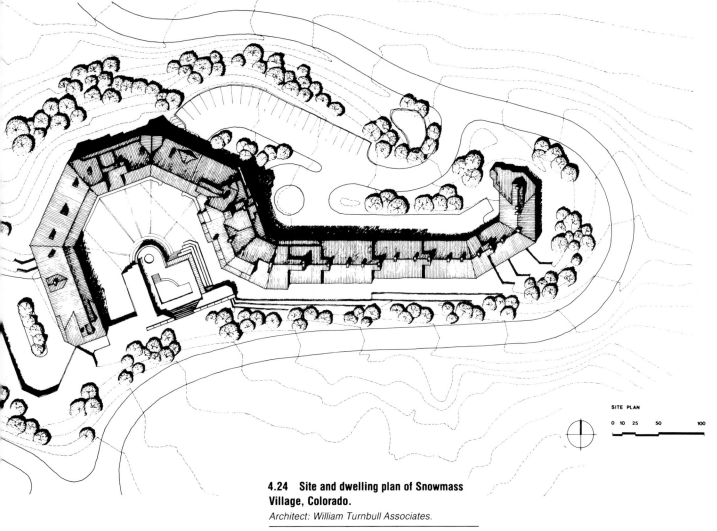

SITE PLAN

0 10 25   50   100

4.24 Site and dwelling plan of Snowmass Village, Colorado.

Architect: William Turnbull Associates.

Ramot Housing, Jerusalem, Israel

Architect:	Zvi Hecker
No. of dwellings:	724
Site area:	18 hectares (44.5 acres)
Density:	40 dwellings per hectare (16.1 dwellings per acre)
Type of accommodation:	
apartments	516
apartments specifically designed for elderly people	52
apartments for young couples	156
Size of dwellings:	
Typical apartment for 5–6 persons	150 sq m (1614.6 sq ft)
2-person apartments for elderly people	60 sq m (718 sq ft)
apartments for young couples	96 sq m (1033 sq ft)
Parking/garages:	700 car parking spaces
Construction:	*1st stage* – a completely prefabricated system of pre-cast concrete elements in which loads are carried by load bearing walls 14 cm (5.5 inches) thick, spaced 3.30 m (10 ft 10 ins) apart. The design of the scheme as a whole is based on the specific shapes of these elements: the dodecahedron, the cube and the combination of the two. The geometry of the cube provides the inside lattice of the subdivision into apartments, while the dodecahedron envelops the outer surface of the building, forming the typical unit of uncovered open terraces, and integrating the inside with the outside of the structure (Krafft 1980/1981) (Fig 4.27).
	Second stage – conventional construction; concrete load bearing walls with stone facing.

The project is located on a hillside some 4.5 kilometres from the centre of Jerusalem (Fig 4.26). Its layout resembles the shape of a 'leaf-like palm of a hand divided into five branch-like fingers' (Krafft 1980/1981) (Fig 4.28). In the centre of this 'palm' are the main shopping, administrative and other community buildings, a green, central open space, a kindergarten and nursery school. The dwellings are grouped along the five 'fingers' in 'V'-shaped terraces. The buildings conform to the two main planning principles in Jerusalem: nowhere are they higher than four storeys, and they are faced with stone in the form of strips cast into the external panels (Fig 4.29). Car parking is kept to the outside of the development, leaving the internal spaces entirely pedestrian and free for the location of children's playgrounds.

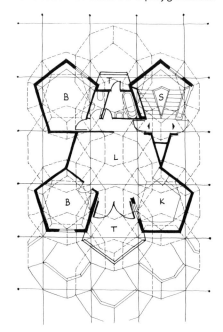

4.27   Dwelling plan.

4.26   Phase 1 elevations.

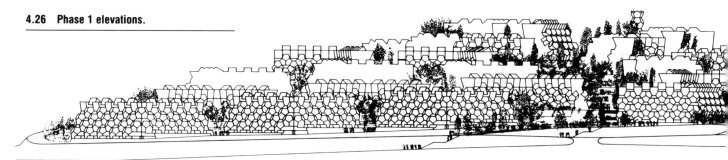

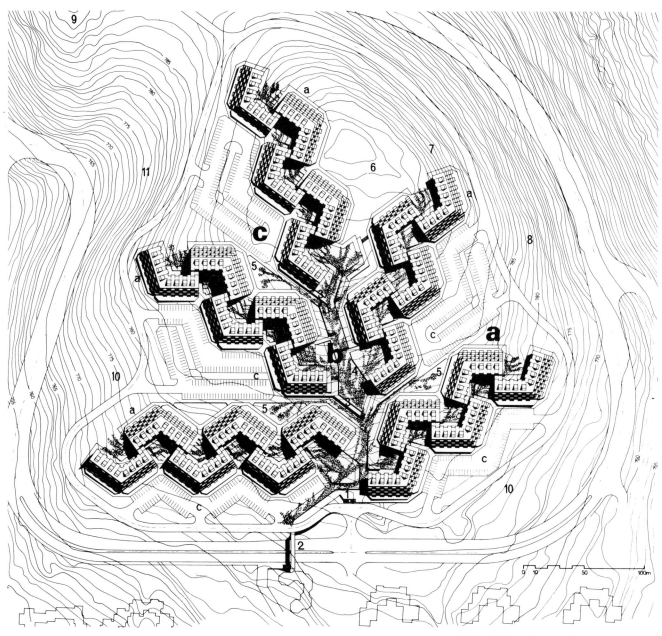

4.28 The layout resembles the leaf-like palm of a hand.

General layout

a Terraced V-shaped buildings
b Pedestrian access pathways
c Vehicular traffic, access and parking
1 Main access entrance to the housing complex
2 Overhang pedestrian bridge
3 Stores and commercial facilities
4 Green central open space, kindergarten & nursery school
5 Playgrounds for children
6 Most elevated tophill platform
7 Site for the local synagogue
8 Site for Yeshivat-Kolel-Polin for rabbinical studies
9 Site for elementary school
10&11 Recreational open space

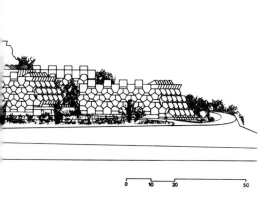

Each terrace comprises 27
apartments which contain two to four
bedrooms and an open terrace. The
14 types of apartment differ in size,
shape and internal layout. The layout
of each apartment is organized around
a central atrium courtyard off which
radiate the other rooms. These rooms
are larger than would be found in most
western housing because of the living
patterns of the occupants (Fig 4.27).

Ramot 2 is more conventional in
form and construction but is none the
less imposing on the site (Figs 4.30 to
4.32).

Further reading

DAVEY, P., 'An eye on Israel: work of Hecker',
Architectural Review, June 1979, vol. CLXV,
no. 988, pp. 355–8.

DOBERTI, R., (Zvi Hecker, la geometría
manifesta', *Summarcos – Geometra en al
espacio*, 30 April 1979, pp. 2–36.

'Hive of angular, prefabricated dwelling units',
Architecture, (the AIA Journal), mid-August
1982, vol. 71, no. 10, pp. 78–9.

'Ramot Housing, Jerusalem, Israel',
*Architecture Contemporaine/Contemporary
Architecture*, 1980–1981, Bibliothèque des
Arts, Paris and Lausanne, pp. 32–4.

**4.29   Phase 1: view of part of the
development.**

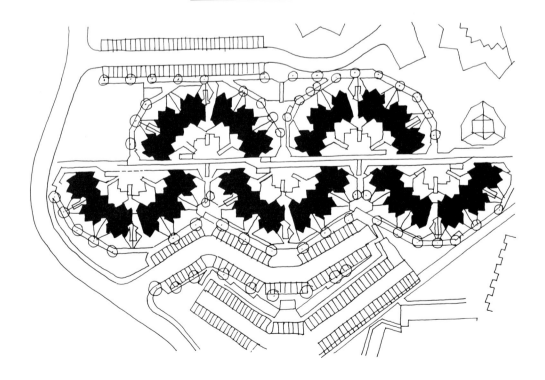

**4.30   Phase 2: grouping of dwellings – there
are 28 apartments in each of the 5 buildings.**

4.31 Phase 2: general view of the hillside.

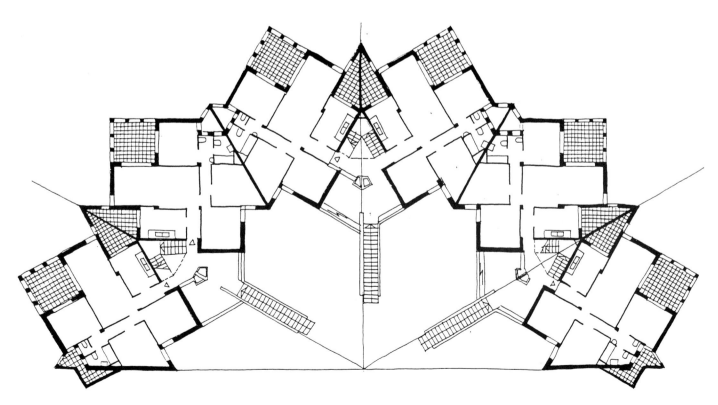

4.32 Phase 2: second-floor dwelling plans.

Giloh: A Satellite Township on the periphery of Jerusalem, Israel

Architect:	Ram Karmi

Type of accommodation:	percentage within project:
3-room apartments for young couples – these are organized to facilitate future expansion	70%
4–5-room apartments for larger, more established families	20%
2-room apartments for elderly or single people	10%

Construction:	reinforced concrete construction covered with bulky rock-like facing to comply with the policy that buildings in the Jerusalem area must have exterior stone finishes.

In the 1970s and 1980s, a number of satellite townships were designed on the periphery of Jerusalem. Ram Karmi was invited by the Ministry of Housing to join a team of architects designing one of these, Giloh, which is located to the south of the city, off the road to Bethlehem. The team was headed by architect Avram Yaski, who was responsible for the master plan of accommodating 37,000 people in 10,000 apartments, to be achieved in three phases of development (Fig 4.33). The overall plan divides the township into sub-zones, each for 700 to 1000 families and every sub-zone is surrounded by walls and parking. Ram Karmi considers that the main road network takes little account of the terrain and that this shapes the overall form of the development. However within the sub-zones the housing is designed around pedestrian streets with car parking kept outside the walls. In a personal description of the scheme, Karmi advises:

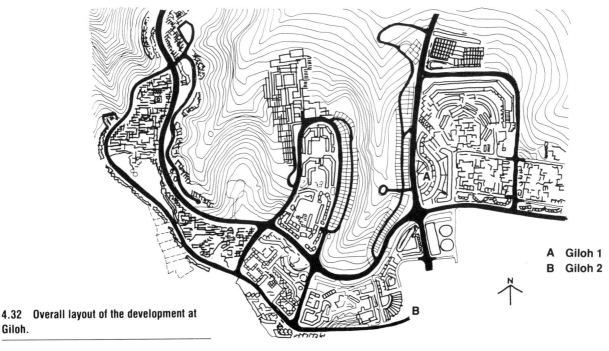

A Giloh 1
B Giloh 2

N

4.32 Overall layout of the development at Giloh.

4.34 Giloh 2.

Karmi attempts in his designs to create a series of pedestrian 'streets'. The formal organization of the dwellings and the character of the streets unfold according to a natural pattern relating to the hierarchy of activities.

One's progress through the street is punctuated through the use of subtle devices such as level changes, light changes, view changes, staircases which present themselves invitingly when they are needed. There are simple rules: let people see where they are going before they get there – any drastic changes in direction should be made by stairs and ramps which deliver them on to the next level facing the direction in which they want to go; always give an alternative route; make every sequence of spaces a rhythmical progression that invites processions. The tension that might develop between spaces can be extremely dramatic (Karmi 1983/ 1984)

Within the scheme there are town houses, terrace buildings with small parks, four-storey linear buildings (Fig 4.34), at least one-high-rise and a few one and two-storey houses.

The dwellings were designed to be individual and to offer the opportunity for adaptation and extension. Karmi writes that each dwelling should provide:

One of the big problems is to reconcile different scales of speed between the automobile and the pedestrian. I think that these two things are never complementary, they can never exist adjacent to one another, they can only meet at points . . . the straight line is exclusive to the pedestrian domain, and the generator of human activities that might be discovered along its length. The automobile might serve this line at points, it cannot go through, it goes round. Systems of mechanical transport must never be taken as initiators of urban design.

. . . its occupants with exclusive spaces – the porch and the covered terrace – where a measure of individuality might be realized. Inwardly, the unit must allow a realization of individual indentity; outwardly, the configuration of units of which it is a part, must lead to a gradual realization of the community. The spaces between each dwelling and its neighbours must encourage the common life and purpose of a neighbourhood. This is the private end of the process of socialization. (Karmi 1983/1984)

The architecture reflects a very specific urbanistic design philosophy on Karmi's part. Despite its monumental character, Karmi's philosophy tends towards the humane and the romantic. He seeks, through the use of a Mediterranean vernacular, to realize the intimate scale of the dwelling cluster, whose image and sense of place derive from the judicious design of pathway, staircase and entrance. To a vocabulary of flat roofs and simple rectilinear shapes, Karmi adds such vernacular features as arches, picturesque massing, and heavy, blank walls facing the street.

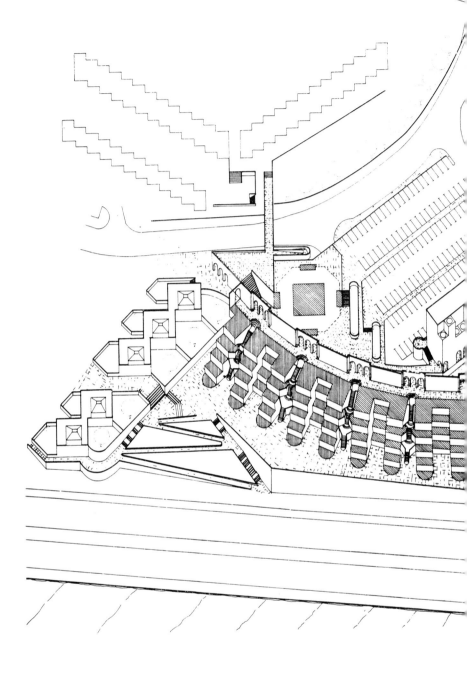

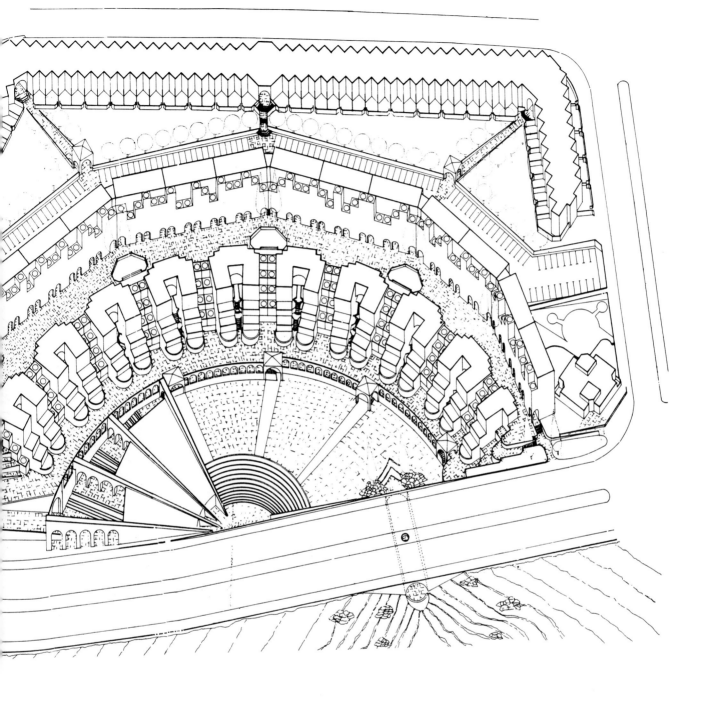

4.35   Giloh 1: isometric view.

A   Town houses
B   Arcade block
C   The Crescent
D   Piazza
E   Parking

4.35   Giloh 1: the crescent.

Giloh 1 – 400 dwellings (1979)

The entrance to Giloh 1 is through a piazza bordered by an 'S'-shaped housing complex that is separated into identical horseshoe-shaped buildings of four-storey terraced housing. Within each horseshoe, exterior walls climb upwards with landings on either side for apartment entrances (Fig 4.35). At the top of the stairway is a single long, curved and arcaded four–storey apartment building (Fig 4.36). Behind this structure comes parking, then a green, and finally, a continuous strip of town houses edging the street in a long zigzagging line.

Giloh 2 – 300 dwellings (1981)

The most striking feature of Giloh 2 is the narrow interior arcade, running length of the structure's axis (Fig 4.39), which is inside each of the four blocks of four–storey buildings that climb the hill in repeated 'V'-shapes (Figs 4.37, 4.38). On either side of this arcade landings with doors to two apartments are scooped out at regular intervals. Punctuating the centre of the passageway are seven skylighted, octagonal pods. The first, third and fifth contain stairs to upper units; the second, fourth and sixth have trees and other plantings (Fig 4.40). All bring in light and a touch of nature, and create a picturesque interior street (Fig 4.39).

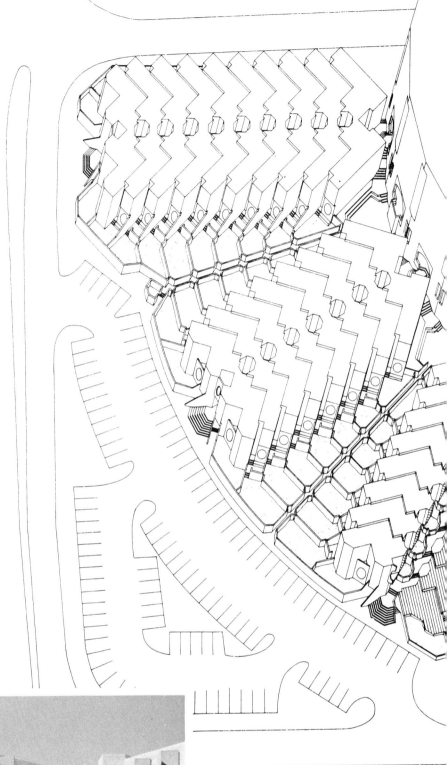

4.38   Giloh 2: four-storey buildings in 'V' shape buildings.

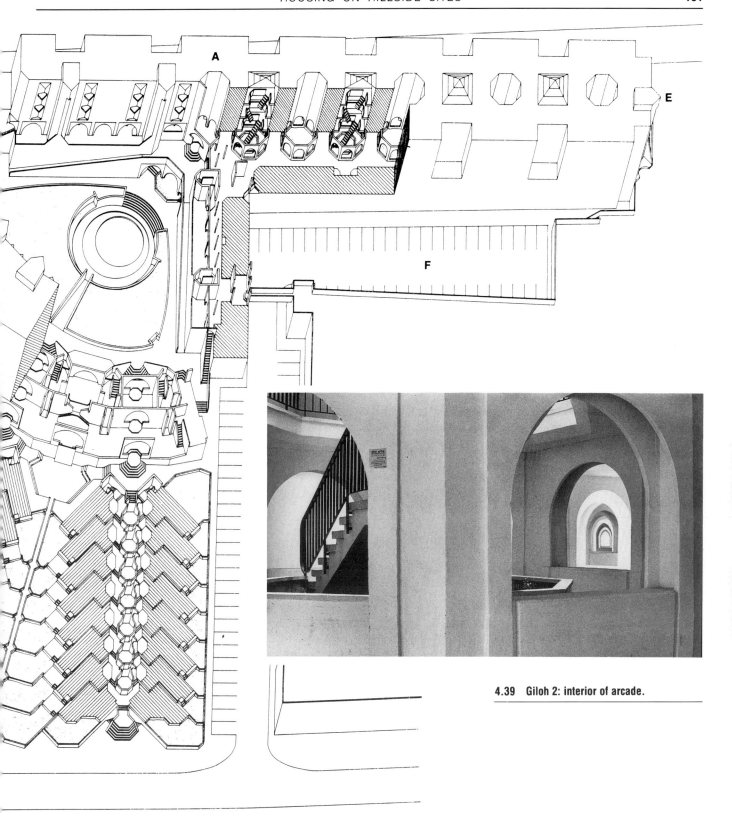

4.39 Giloh 2: interior of arcade.

4.37 Giloh 2: isometric view.

A Street block
B 'V' shaped housing
C Piazza
D Arcade block
E Main entrance
F Parking

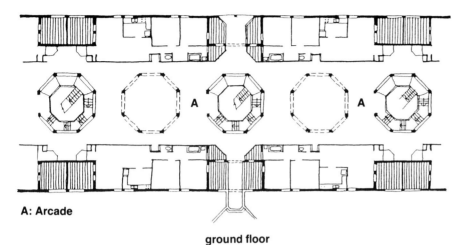

A: Arcade

ground floor

Further reading

KARMI, R., 'Giloh housing 1,2,3, Jerusalem, Israel', *Architecture Contemporaine/ Contemporary Architecture*, 1983–1984, Bibliothèque des Arts, Paris and Lausanne, pp. 46–53.

'Israel: Apartment Community melds modernism and regional influences', *Architecture* (the AIA Journal), mid-August 1982, vol. 71, no. 10, pp. 78, 79.

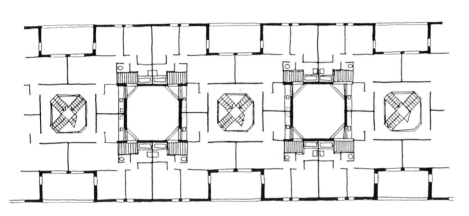

plans of street block   **typical floor**

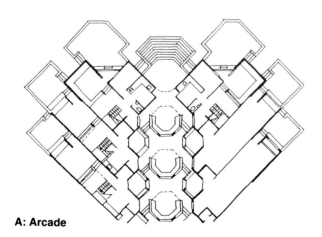

A: Arcade

ground floor

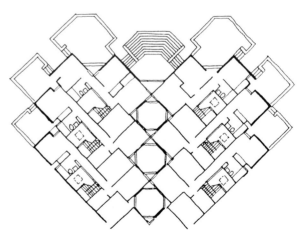

second floor

plans of the 'V'-shaped dwellings

4.39   Giloh 2: dwelling plans.

5 HOUSING FOR THE WHOLE COMMUNITY

THE structure of society in many countries is changing significantly. The trend is towards smaller households in terms of the size of families: there is a decrease in the proportion of traditional two-parent families, an increase in the proportion of elderly and single-person households and by desire disabled people to live as near to a normal life as possible amongst the community. The change that is taking place is so significant that the term usually adopted for anything other than family housing – 'special needs housing' – is inappropriate. The young and the elderly are in fact a large proportion of society, yet most housing built in Britain is designed for two generations: parents and children.

Housing for elderly people

In Britain the public sector has to date provided 94 per cent of the total amount of housing designed specially for elderly people. This figure does not include the large amount of ordinary housing which allows elderly people a high degree of mobility which was built in the past by local authorities and housing associations as part of their programme for providing general needs housing. The private sector has mainly concentrated on the upper end of the market; however, charitable organizations, such as the English Courtyard Association, have produced design solutions with a very fresh approach (Figs 1.12, 5.10 to 5.12).

In the USA, the elderly are recognized as the fastest growing segment of the population, but in a society that is generally more affluent than in Britain, elderly people are more able to purchase their own homes, and their preferences and needs have become important issues. These needs are frequently expressed in the form of retirement villages, comprising individual dwellings on their own plot of land, designed at low density. However, where the housing has been put together in the form of small groups, a high standard of design has frequently been achieved. The most common design solution is for the housing to be grouped around a central green and built in traditional materials to create recognizable qualities of home and security which offer comfort and pleasure to the residents (Fig 5.18).

However, as in Britain, there is a substantial sector of the population that is unable to afford the market rate for housing. In Santa Monica, California, attempts have been made to tackle this problem through the Community Corporation, founded in 1982. With funds from both private and public sources (principally a large low-interest loan from the Bank America Foundation), the Corporation constructs new dwellings for a mixed range of tenures, in which rents are limited to a fixed proportion of median income. The Corporation's success can be seen in the work of architects Hank Koning and Julie Eizenberg (Figs 5.1 and 5.2).

The important design criteria for housing the elderly are as follows.

1   The concept of grouping a maximum of 30 dwellings in a sheltered housing scheme, with its own warden and communal facilities which has long been understood by local authorities and Housing Associations in Britain.
2   The concept of special housing for elderly people is itself controversial; elderly people prefer to remain within their familiar surroundings for as long as possible. Developments of small numbers of ordinary housing on infill sites within the community, linked to mobile help when required, may well be the best solution to this need in most cases (Figs 5.33 to 5.35).
3   There is no substitute for reasonable space standards. Most elderly people will be moving from housing which is larger than they will expect to have in their new home and will have to give up many of their possessions. Moreover, elderly people generally require more space in rooms than younger people in order to move around comfortably. It could be all too easy to sacrifice this one essential ingredient of a satisfactory living environment in order to meet financial constraints.
4   The form of housing most preferred by elderly people is single-storey (Fig 5.3), or two-storey if this is not possible. Whilst few elderly people own a

5.1 Alternative living for elderly people, Santa Monica, California, USA.

Architects: Koning Eizenberg.

5.2 12/15th Street, Santa Monica.

Architects: Koning Eizenberg.

car at present, it is likely that in future there will be a much higher percentage who have been used to driving. It is not unreasonable, therefore, that in some instances parking provision should be higher than a minimum of one space per four dwellings.

5   There is a need for varying degrees of sheltered accommodation. This has been understood by the public sector

in Britain since the publication in 1969 of Circular 82/69 (Circular 84/69, Welsh Office) 'Accommodation specially designed for old people – Sheltered Housing'. This set out the requirements for two basic types of housing – Category 1 (Fig 5.4) which offers a high degree of independence to the resident with a considerable amount of supporting accommodation, such as meeting rooms, warden's house, guest accommodation, laundry, etc – and Category 2 housing which offers similar facilities but within a single building with heated corridors (Fig 5.29). In private sector schemes these principles

should be combined with the best ideas developed by organizations such as the English Courtyard Association, who provide houses designed for maximum adaptability as the residents' state of health changes. The downstairs bathroom may start as a cloakroom and then be converted to bath or shower room if circumstances dictate that the resident(s) of the cottage must live downstairs with a nurse or relative overhead

5.3 Housing designed for elderly people in Felbridge Surrey.

Architects: Trevor Dannatt and Partners.

(Fig 5.11). Their schemes also have a high level of insulation and double glazing and are designed to wheelchair standards.

6   Elderly people may feel disorientated and socially isolated in a new environment. Moving to sheltered housing can particularly cause depression, a loss of self-esteem, and a fear of losing contact with the outside world. These can be tackled by good management but design has a significant role to play.

The important design criteria for sheltered housing are smallness and familiarity. The design must create a homely atmosphere, particularly in the entrance and communal areas. It must also provide the opportunity for informal social interaction. The laundry is a meeting place as well as a room in which the washing is done; a hairdressing room is a place in which to gossip; some residents might enjoy the presence of a small bar. Corridors should be subtly lit, personalized and designed so that the residents know where they are within the building. Communal and individual rooms should have wall lighting and be decorated in a way that is familiar — e.g. with wallpaper and recognisable pictures. Familiarity is not normally achieved with double height rooms and fair-faced brick walls, but rather through the provision of cosy corners, conservatories, verandahs (Fig 5.31) and open fireplaces in the communal areas, as well as through a generous supply of bay windows and patios adjacent to individual dwellings. Window sills should be low so that passers-by can be

5.4   Raybell Court, Isleworth, Middlesex.
Architects: Manning Clamp and Partners.

seen by people sitting in their chairs or confined to their beds: windows into rooms overlooking corridors can help with social contact: sills should allow for the display of personal possessions. Even the choice of door knobs and casement stays are important elements in creating familiarity and this should be considered equally with convenience of use. This is an important point because it is all too easy to create unfamiliarity

through solving technical problems. Kitchens, for examples, need to look good as well as function properly. Elderly people enjoy walking, even short distances: outside areas should be designed to form a series of small spaces through which they can wander. The character of these should be that of the traditional cottage garden with a variety of quiet corners and seating areas situated both in sunny and shady locations.

**5.5   The Gables, Hambledon Street, Blyth,
Northumberland by Darbyshire Architects.**

5.6 Sheltered housing for the Nene Housing Society at Whittlesey, Cambridgeshire.
Architects: Mathew Robotham Associates.

5.7 Rygårdcentret nursing home and sheltered housing in Gentofte, Denmark.
Architects: Ejlers and Graversen.

7 The image that a project creates is important but it is essential not to mark it out as being different. Housing for elderly people should perhaps proclaim itself as simply another good housing project. In this respect the development must be appropriate for its site. In their projects at Isleworth and Whittlesey, Cambridgeshire, Manning Clamp and partners and Mathew Robotham Associates have created familiarity from the use of materials common to the area (Figs 5.4, 5.6). The grouping of

the dwellings reflects the best traditions of village architecture with variety of building height, provision of bay windows and porches and overhanging eaves, all of which are enjoyed by the residents. At Tuckers Yard, Peterborough, Mathew Robotham Associates have created a central access 'street' which was designed as an outside/inside space (Figs 5.21 to 5.25). Like the project at Blyth, Northumberland (Fig 5.6), it is an essentially urban form of development entirely suitable for its location.

At Poole, architects Smith, Hutton, Nichols have created an entirely different form. The individual dwellings have been grouped within a building envelope that resembles a large Edwardian house (Fig 5.26 and 5.27). All of these projects have recognized the need to relate to the surroundings, so the housing does not immediately indicate that it caters for specialist needs; all have created a sense of place that is unique to that project.

These principles are also well illustrated in examples from

Scandinavia as well as from Britain. In Denmark, sheltered housing can be private or owned by the local authority. Both private and public forms of sheltered housing are subject to inspections to ensure that standards are maintained. The occupants pay rent. Three types of dwellings for up to twenty-five per cent of their incomes for an economic elderly people are built: collective housing; sheltered housing and full care housing. Collective housing is often incorporated into an ordinary housing development with the addition of a contact and call system to the nearest institution. Sheltered housing (Fig 5.7) comprises one and two roomed apartments. Each dwelling has its own entrance, kitchen and bathroom; it is adapted for handicapped occupants and has a high

level of service and shelter. The full care dwelling is generally a single room except where two rooms are combined for the use of married couples. Each room must be not less than 15 sq m (162 sq ft) in size and must include a large toilet with shower facilities, an entrance hall with cupboard space and in some cases a mini-kitchenette. The level of service associated with full care housing is very high. Day centres are frequently provided for use by people living in other housing in the district as well, and these cater for physiotherapy, occupational therapy, and a wide range of social activities, films, games, hobbies, physical training, etc (Fig 5.8).

5.8   The ergotherapy room, Rygårdcentret.

Housing for Disabled People

There has been a great deal of research carried out into the design of housing for disabled people: however, the check-list approach, which has resulted in the adoption of standard approaches, particularly by local authorities and housing associations in Britain, needs to be developed into a broader appreciation of the problem by society as a whole. The best designs serve the individual disabilities of residents, but are not bound by them. The blind and the deaf, as well as those with mobility problems and mental illness, have specialist requirements which designers need to take into account in order to create aesthetic and innovative, as well as functional housing. The projects in Cambridge-shire (Figs 5.54, 5.55) and

Birmingham (5.56 to 5.58), which are illustrated, are amongst the few designed in Britain which have been designed specifically for disabled people: such they are a credit to the clients and architects alike.

Housing for young people

Another growth area is the increasing number of young people who are establishing their own home, yet the provision of new housing to meet this need is very small. Typical dwelling plans for purpose-built flats are illustrated in Fig 5.9. The project by Colquhoun, Miller and Partners, which accommodates up to 70 young people in a nine-storey block (Figs 5.48, 5.49), is particularly successful. Such a solution is made acceptable by the presence of a resident caretaker who is able to exercise some control over the entrance to the block.

In the USA, an awareness of this new market has produced innovative design solutions. There, developers have learned that not all two-income households are traditional families. Architects are designing units with twin baths and bedrooms, allowing an equal division of the space. Plans include private and communal areas, easy-care materials and professional amenities that include answering and other services. The duality of design features – in lieu of the family room – allows residents to share expenses while leading separate lives, even within shared space.

A similar concept of sharing space has been developed by the Housing Commission of the New South Wales Government in Australia for young people who have just left home (Figs 5.50 to 5.53). Clearly, an example has been set for other countries to follow.

5.9 Housing for young people at The Martindales, Clayton Green, Preston. Plans of one-bedroom and bed-sitting flats.
Architects: Tom Mellor and Partners.

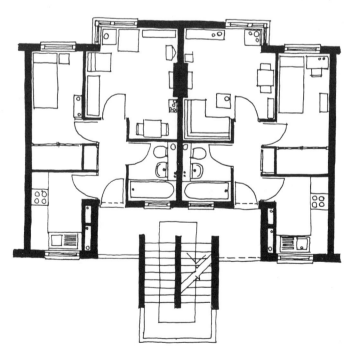

1-person, 1-bedroom flat

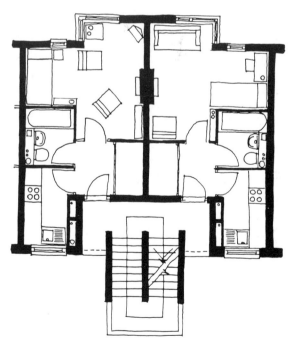

1-person bed-sitter

Cottages and Flats for sale to Retired People, Walpole Court, Puddletown, Dorset, England

Architects:	Sidell Gibson Partnership
No. of dwellings:	23 new cottages and flats
Site area:	0.8 hectare (2 acres)
Density:	28 dwellings per hectare (115 dwellings per acre)
Type of accommodation:	2 and 3–bedroom 'cottages' and flats for sale to elderly people
Size of dwellings:	
houses	100 sq m – 117 sq m (1,076 –1255 sq ft)
flats	79 sq m (850 sq ft)
Heating:	electric (night storage); a high level of insulation has been achieved throughout.

The scheme provides 23 two and three-bedroom houses and flats for sale to people over 55. The stated aims of the client, the English Courtyard Association, are 'to provide attractive comfortable housing to people who value their independence, but have reached a stage in life when the management of a home and garden is becoming a burden; to create a background of security against the worry of being alone or getting ill; and to protect fixed incomes and capital against inflation'.

The first phase is centred on the little courtyard formed by the former stables and garden cottages which have been converted into two and three-bedroom houses and flats. The second phase comprises new cottages and flats located on two sides of a garden courtyard (Fig 5.10),

5.11 Dwelling plans. Key to units:

1	sitting-room	9	front door
2	dining-room	10	hall
3	kitchen	11	back door
4	bedroom 1	12	French windows
5	bedroom 2		
6	bathroom/WC	13	wardrobe
7	shower/WC	14	cloak cupboard
8	ground-floor bedroom	15	airing cupboard
		16	private patio

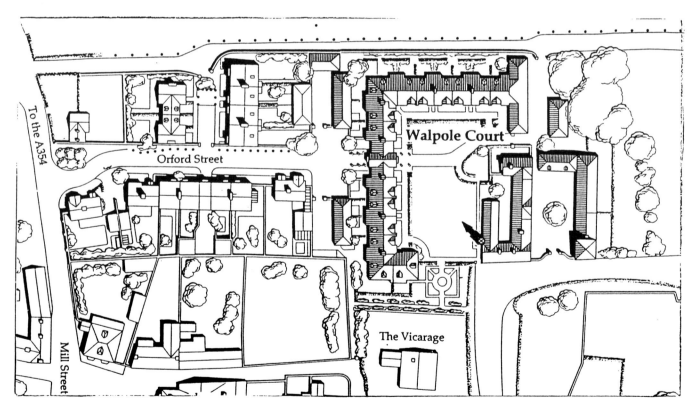

5.10 Walpole Court in its village setting.

ground floor

first floor

ground floor

first floor

ground floor

first floor

5.12   Courtyard housing at its best.

approached through an archway from
Orford Street. The third side of the
courtyard is formed by the stables and
cottages of phase 1. Each cottage is
on two storeys and comprises sitting-
room, dining-room and kitchen on the
ground floor and two double bedrooms
and a bathroom/WC on the first floor.
There is also a shower/WC on the
ground floor that can be adapted for
use as a cloakroom or bathroom to suit
individual requirements (Fig 5.11). If a
resident finds difficulty with the stairs
(although a stair lift can be fitted) the
house adapts into a ground-floor flat
of sitting-room, bedroom, kitchen
and bath or shower/WC. Two of the
cottages have three bedrooms. Every
dwelling has a garage. The grounds in
which the dwellings are situated are
very mature (Fig 5.12); however,
every cottage has a small private patio
where the residents can cultivate their
own plants. There is a resident
warden and a relief warden to answer
emergency calls 24 hours a day and all
dwellings have an alarm system. There
is a guest bedroom and a laundry
room.

Areas have been measured from plans
provided by the architects.

Further reading

BUCHANAN, P., 'Discipline of Alms',
Architectural Review, October 1985,
vol. CLXXVIII, no. 1064, pp. 56–61.

DOE, NHBC, RIBA, *Housing Design Awards
1987*, a *Building* publication, pp. 30, 31 and
34, 35.

VALINS, M., *Housing for Elderly People*, The
Architectural Press, London, 1988, pp. 44–7.

'Housing Design Awards 1987', *British
Architectural Design Awards 1987*, McMillan
Martin 1988, pp. 195, 198.

'Las Victorianas', Sacramento, California, USA

Architects:	Dreyfus and Blackford
No. and type of dwellings:	40 flats designed for 1 and 2 elderly people
	5 units are designed for handicapped people.
Site area:	0.35 hectares (0.86 acres)
Density:	114 dwellings per hectare (46 dwellings per acre)
Size of dwellings:	58 sq m (624 sq ft)
Construction:	timber-framed with lap boarding externally.

Alkali Flat is the oldest remaining residential area in Sacramento, dating back to the 1850s. This project has therefore been designed to blend in with the surroundings. Architectural details recall Victorian woodwork but are simplified to acknowledge present-day economics.

The small scale of the buildings is repeated in five separate structures, each housing eight one-bedroom apartments (Fig 5.13). Each apartment is designed for a single elderly tenant or a couple, and includes living and kitchen areas, one bedroom and a bathroom. The complex also provides a small recreation room with a kitchenette, adjacent to communal laundry and service facilities. Interior courtyards define private outdoor sitting areas and preserve the existing trees of the site. This is traditional architecture at its best (Fig 5.14).

5.13 Ground floor plans of 'Las Victorianas'.

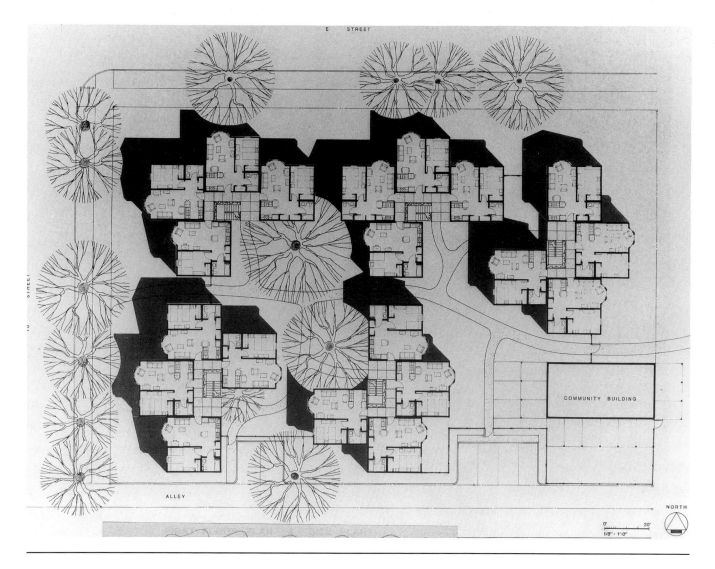

5.14 Traditional American architecture.

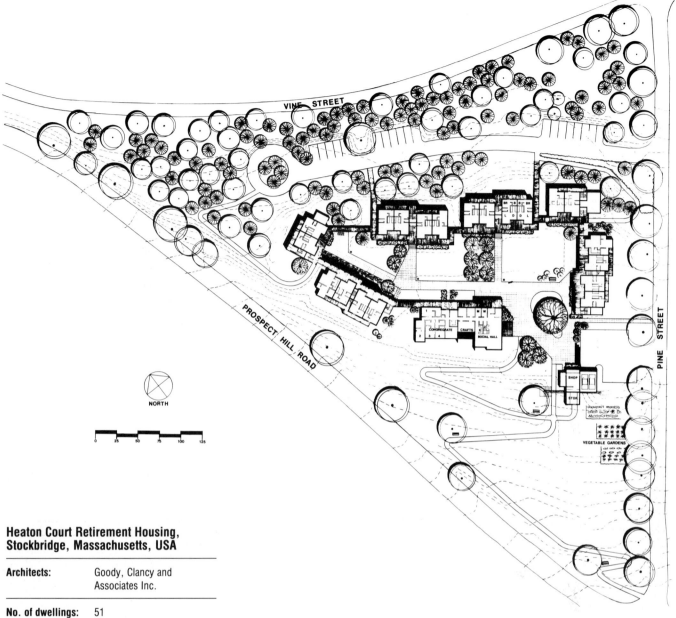

NORTH

0 25 50 75 100 125

5.15   Site layout of Heaton Court.

Heaton Court Retirement Housing, Stockbridge, Massachusetts, USA

Architects:	Goody, Clancy and Associates Inc.
No. of dwellings:	51
Site area:	2.8 hectares (7 acres)
Density:	18.2 dwellings per hectare (7.3 dwellings per acre)
Type of accommodation: flats	51
	all dwellings are designed for elderly people; 4 contain facilities for handicapped people
Size of dwellings: 1-bedroom, 1 or 2-person dwellings	46.45 sq m (500 sq ft)
Parking/garages: car parking space:	25
Construction & materials:	timber-framed construction with plywood sheathing, clapboard covering externally; timber roof trusses covered with asphalt shingles.

Located on a site previously occupied by a rambling resort hotel, this low-income, government-subsidized housing for elderly people fits in well with its small town neighbourhood. The dwellings are clustered around a courtyard (Fig 5.15) and are linked by continuous porches and galleries, providing covered passages and level walking surfaces for the residents. The entrances, living-rooms and dining areas all face the porches on the active, court side giving everyone – even those who are housebound – a view of activity. Bedrooms and bathrooms are on the quieter side, away from the court (Fig 5.16).

Car parking is provided on the top side of the site on a level with the

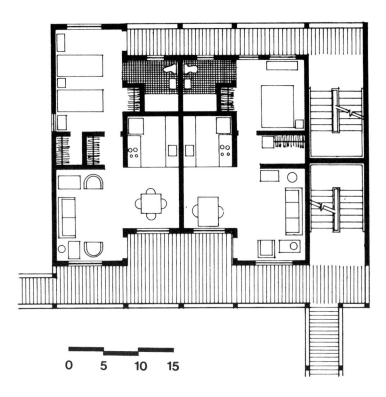

0   5   10   15

5.16   Typical dwelling plans.

second floor of the development (Fig 5.17). At this level, bridges connect the porches and galleries, permitting the three-storey buildings on the north side to have units that are only one flight up or down. The one-storey buildings on the south side of the development are low enough to allow sunshine to penetrate the courtyard and to open the development to the superb views of the Berkshire Mountains. All the community buildings have been designed to allow full access to the less able residents.

The four dwellings designed specifically for disabled people are located close to the car parking and the better views. All the dwellings are designed to allow through ventilation and thereby eliminate the need for air-conditioning. The amenities include raised planters to enable the residents to look after their own plants without undue bending, a vegetable garden and park-like walks. The architecture takes its form from the local tradition (Fig 5.18).

Further reading
'Calm excellence in a retirement housing complex', *Architecture* (the AIA Journal), mid-May 1980, vol. 69, no. 6, pp. 220–2.

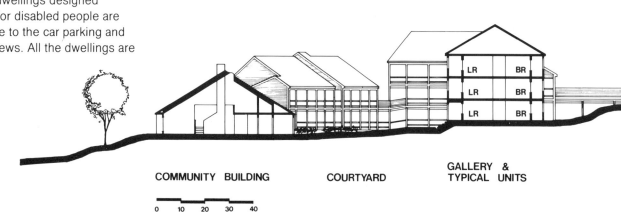

COMMUNITY BUILDING   COURTYARD   GALLERY &
                                                                    TYPICAL UNITS

0   10   20   30   40

5.18 The internal courtyard.

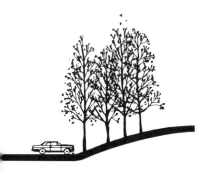

PARKING

5.17 Section through the site showing the principles of pedestrian access to the dwellings.

Noble Horizons, Community for Elderly People: Salisbury, Connecticut, USA

Architects:	Jeter, Cook and Jepson
No. of dwellings:	47
Site area:	26.71 hectares (66 acres)
Density:	1.75 dwellings per hectare (4.3 dwellings per acre)
	5.75 persons per hectare (14.2 persons per acre)

Size and no. of dwellings and ancillary accommodation:

1-bedroom cottages	69.2 sq m (745 sq ft)	19
2-bedroom cottages	92.9 sq m (1,000 sq ft)	25
home for elderly people	1,301.07 sq m (total) (14,005 sq ft)	1
intermediate care facility	1,510.54 sq m (total) (16,172 sq ft)	1
skilled nursing facility	967.53 sq m (total) (10,415 sq ft)	1
chapel	111.48 sq m (1,200 sq ft)	
community dining/recreation facility	649.02 sq m (6,986 sq ft)	

A chapel and community dining/recreation facility are included.

Parking/garages:	101 car parking spaces, including 57 open spaces
	15 car ports providing 44 spaces
Heating:	electric baseboards
Construction:	the larger, multi unit buildings are arranged in a modified cruciform shape and are of steel construction with masonry and cedar external wall finishes; the individual dwellings are of timber-framed construction with cedar cladding.

This rural village for elderly people was built on a 66-acre site near the centre of Salisbury (Fig 5.19). The community provides for both the well and the infirm, allowing continuity and familiar surroundings through various levels of care. The image that the development presents is that of a small New England settlement nestling into the trees, with chestnut-stained cedar cottages arranged in clusters (Fig 5.20). The single-storey clusters for ambulent elderly people are connected by walkways and open green spaces. The one-bedroom dwellings are located near the entrance and the two-bedroom dwellings around a cul-de-sac.

There are three levels of care provided: for those requiring modest assistance in housekeeping and personal care, there is a 25-bedroom home; for residents requiring nursing supervison, there is the intermediate care unit and for those requiring total nursing, the nursing home provides 24-hour care. A community centre provides a visual focus to the development. It is linked by a covered bridge to the nursing home across the road, and connected by an administrative area to the home for elderly people.

Further reading
'A continuum of care', *Architecture* (the AIA Journal), October 1983, vol. 72, no. 10, p. 55.

5.19   Site plan of Noble Horizons, Salisbury, Connecticut.

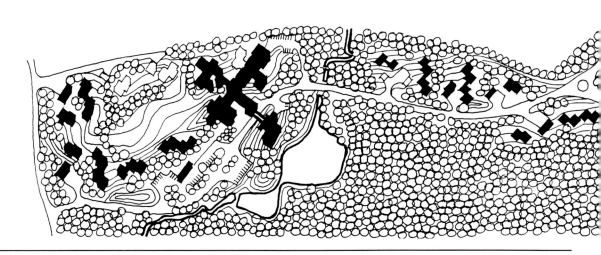

5.20 The chestnut-stained cedar cottages
are arranged in clusters.

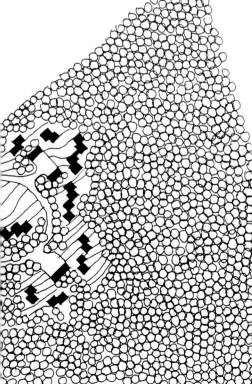

Tuckers Court, Tuckers Yard, South Street, Stanground, Peterborough, England

Architect:	Mathew Robotham Associates	
No. of dwellings:	41	
Site area:	0.417 hectares (1.03 acres)	
Density:	98.3 dwellings per hectare (39 dwellings per acre)	
	184.6 persons per hectare (74 persons per acre)	
Size and no. of dwellings:		
5-person house	95 sq m (1023 sq ft)	1
1 and 2–person flats for elderly people	32 sq m (344 sq ft) and 44 sq m (474 sq ft)	34
2 and 3 person bugalows for elderly people	44 sq m (747 sq ft) and 65 sq m (700 sq ft)	6
Parking/garages:	10 car parking spaces	
Construction:	traditional construction using trench filled concrete foundations; screeded concrete ground-floor slabs; load bearing concrete block insulated cavity walls; pre-cast concrete plank intermediate floors; floating chipboard floors on polystyrene slabs; insulated dry linings; trussed rafters with natural red clay pantiles at 40° pitch; external walls rendered; stained hardwood double-glazed windows and screens; wood-stained boarding to gables; floor finishes – brick to street; carpet in communal areas and vinyl tiles in flats; roads finished in concrete blockwork; paths in brick and gravel.	

The project is planned around a linear internal 'street' onto which all the dwellings open (Figs 5.21, 5.22). The upper-floor flats have their own stairs leading to a front door on the 'street' (Fig 5.25), which is fully glazed where it passes a series of small landscaped courts, each given its own distinctive character by the particular planting design.

5.21   Site layout of Tuckers Court.

The architects were anxious that their project should make a positive contribution to the existing street scene. They have replaced the demolished nineteenth-century terrace-houses on South Street, built back the enclosure of the street and improved and enclosed the small, unpaved road called Tuckers Yard, which penetrates the site on the south

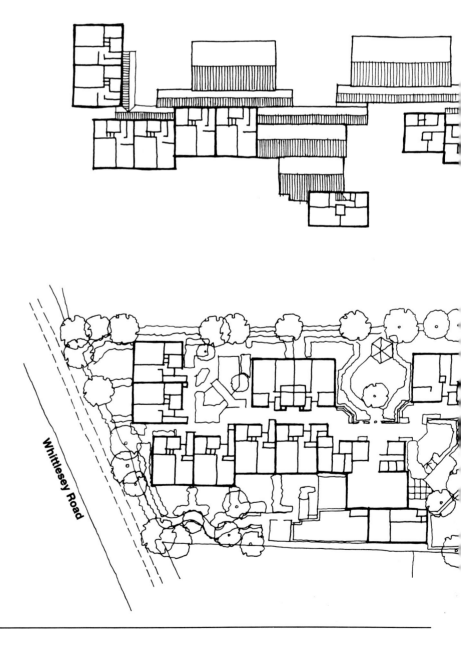

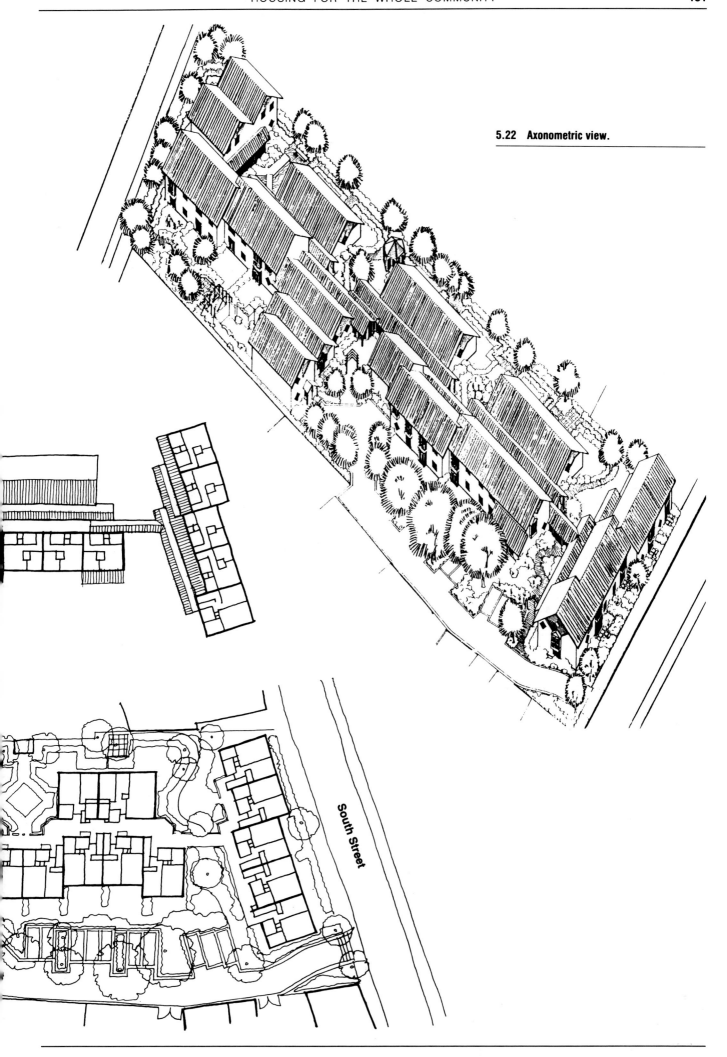

5.22 Axonometric view.

South Street

side. At the terminal focus of Tuckers Yard lies the main entrance to the project and the common-room.

The materials used echo the vernacular tradition that is common in the English Fenlands. The white rendering matches the nearby thatched Post Office and the 1930s cottage-type houses. The red clay pantiles are typical of the area (Figs 5.23, 5.24).

Further reading

DOE, NHBC, RIBA, *Housing Design Awards 1989*, a *Building* publication, pp. 50, 51.

VALINS, M., *Housing for Elderly People*, The Architectural Press, London, 1988, p. 22.

PERKINS, G., 'Sheltered Street, Tuckers Court, South Street, Stanground, Peterborough, *Concrete Quarterly* (the journal of the Cement and Concrete Association) January–March 1986, no. 148, pp. 27–9.

5.23   View showing the covered walkways and spine corridors.

**2-person flat
ground floor (A)**

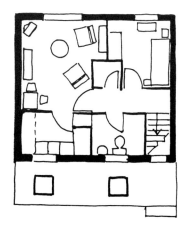

**1-person flat
first floor (B)**

**section:
1 person flat
over 2 person flat**

5.24 Gable ends.

entrance at ground
level for first floor
flat

2-person flat
first floor (C)

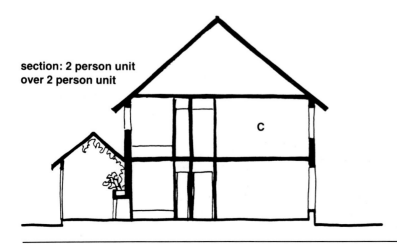

section: 2 person unit
over 2 person unit

5.25 Dwelling plans and section through the
scheme showing the covered walkways and
spine corridors.

St Peter's Vicarage, Poole, Dorset, England

Architects:	Smith, Hutton, Nichols
No. of dwellings:	23
Site area:	0.147 hectares (0.36 acres)
Density:	156 dwellings per hectare (63 dwellings per acre)
	204 persons per hectare (83 persons per acre)
Size and no. of dwellings:	
5-person house	88 sq m (947 sq ft) 1
1 and 2-person dwellings for the elderly	32.6 sq m (344 sq ft) and 47.5 sq m (511 sq ft) 22
Parking/Garages:	5 spaces
Construction:	concrete frame and load bearing brickwork: cavity brick external walls; timber roof; concrete floors; stained tilt and turn windows.

Vicarage Court is an area of Parkstone, Poole, which consists traditionally of large detached Edwardian villas. The site is on a corner, formerly occupied by one such villa, the vicarage of St Peter's Church. For both these reasons it seemed sensible to the architects that the built form should be in the same position on the site and should have the same massing and volume as an Edwardian villa (Fig 5.26). A square plan of each floor, divided into nine further squares, allowed the use of the central square for circulation and the middle square on the north side for the lift, stairs and services (Fig 5.27). The remaining seven squares each contain a flat which enjoys east, north or west orientations. This basic concept is modified on the ground floor by the use of one of the squares for entry and another square extended with a bay window (on the south-west corner) as a common-room. The top floor, which fits under the complex geometry of a pitched roof with dormers, accommodates three flats and a guest

room. The central core of the building is given natural daylighting from a light-well which passes through the building to a conical rooflight directly above the central square on the ground floor.

5.26 The St Peter's Vicarage building reflects the Edwardian villa which formerly stood on the site.

Further reading

WILLIAMS, A. and PARTNERS, 'Domestic Feel', *Building*, 25 September 1981, vol. CCXLI, no. 39, pp. 31–8.

DOE, NHBC, RIBA, 'Vicarage Court, St Peters Road, Parkstone, Poole, Dorset', *Housing Design Awards 1983*, Housing Awards Steering Committee, p. 74.

5.27   Site layout, floor plans and section.

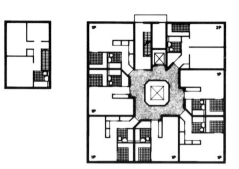
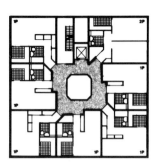

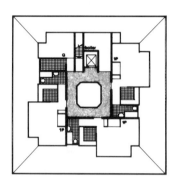

ground floor

third floor

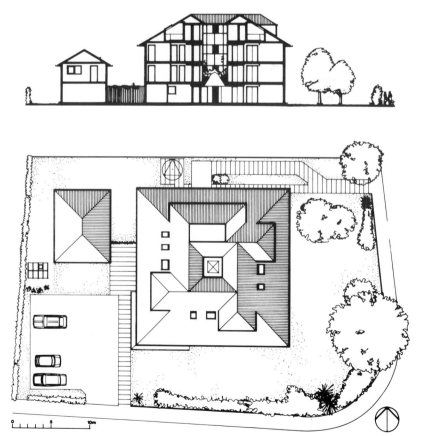

Housing for Elderly and Disabled People, Greenwich, London, England

Architects:	Trevor Dannatt and Partners, with John Shaw, in association with J.M. Moore, Borough Architect, London Borough of Greenwich
No. of dwellings:	45
Site area:	0.3 hectares (0.74 acres) (excluding area used for branch library and day centre)
Density:	150 dwellings per hectare (61 dwellings per acre)
Type of accommodation:	bed-sitting-rooms and 1–bedroom dwellings for 1 and 2 persons respectively
	5 and 2–person family units designed specifically for wheelchair use
	4–person, 3–bedroom flat on 2 floors for the warden, adjacent to the control room and visitors' suite
	social suite with direct access to the garden
Construction:	trench-filled foundations; load bearing walls and partitions; reinforced concrete floor slabs and roofs; asphalt waterproofing, with solar reflecting finish, applied to roofs and parapets; walls are London stock facing bricks; windows are standard steel casements; 8-person passenger lift is fitted with a stretcher extension at the back of the car.

The housing is located in an area of large nineteenth-century houses. The plan form results from the shape of the site, its aspect and its trees (Fig 5.28). The use of angled plans and splayed walls enables all main rooms to gain some southerly aspect. The internal corridors are designed to avoid long vistas and uninterrupted wall surfaces, while side lighting comes from indents at two points. Entrance doors to the flats are recessed to provide a greater degree of privacy to people entering. The accommodation consists of bed-sitting-rooms and one-bedroom dwellings for one and two people respectively. In addition there are five two-person dwellings designed for wheelchair use. The warden has a four-person, three-bedroom flat on two floors, which is adjacent to the visitors' accommodation and the control room. The communal rooms can be used independently of the living accommodation and have direct access to the garden. The planning of the accommodation creates an architectural form that relates well in scale and appearance to its surroundings (Fig 5.29).

Areas have been measured from plans provided by the architects.

Further reading

'O. P. housing, Greenwich', *The Architectural Review*, December 1978, vol. CLXIV, no. 982, pp. 374–6.

DANNAT, T., 'Hourglass or quartz crystal', *The Architectural Review*, December 1978, vol. CLXIV, no. 982, pp. 374–6.

5.28 The view from Langton Way – the two-storey wing on the left incorporates two flats for families with disabled people.

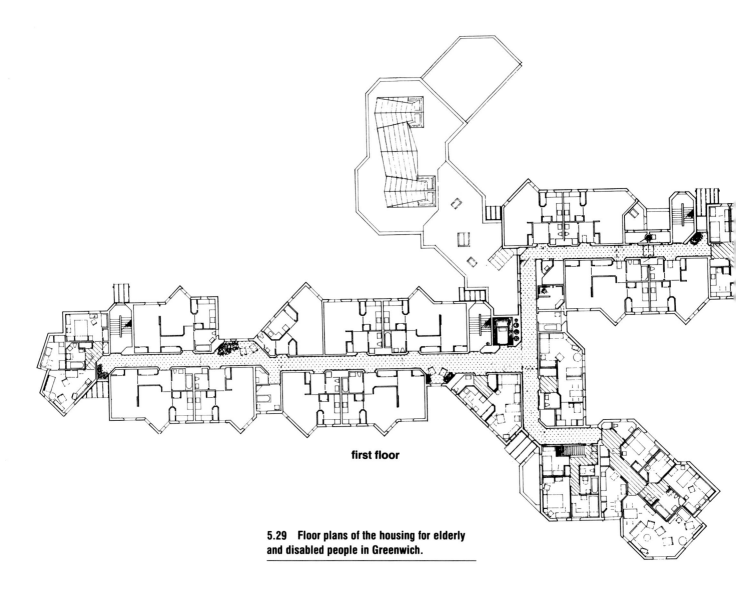

first floor

5.29 Floor plans of the housing for elderly and disabled people in Greenwich.

ground floor

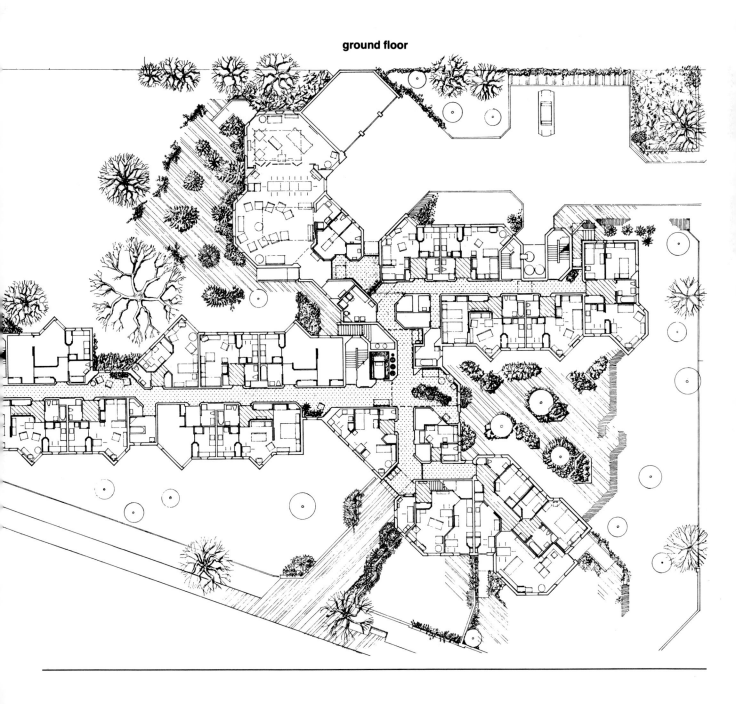

Sheltered Housing for the Architects' Benevolent Society, Claverton Court, Chester, England

Architects:	Brock, Carmichael Associates with BCA Landscape
No. of dwellings	8/1–person, bed-sitting-room flats
	2/2–person, 1–bedroom flats
	1/1–bedroom flat for the warden
	1 guest flat
Size of dwellings: 1-bedroom flats	41 sq m (445 sq ft)
2-bedroom flats	54 sq m (578 sq ft)
Construction:	load bearing construction; external walls brick; the roof is finished with natural slates; external joinery is dark stained hardwood.

Claverton Court is located in an established residential area containing several mature trees (Fig 5.30). The scheme includes eight single-person bed-sitting-room flats and two-person one-bedroom flats, with a warden's flat, communal accommodation plus a special guest flat for visiting friends or relatives (Fig 5.32). Although residents would not necessarily have physical disabilities, wheelchair access throughout was required. It is possible to expand the scheme by 100 per cent.

Each resident's flat is completely self-contained with its own well-equipped kitchen and bathroom, and is fitted with a bell alarm system to summon assistance should it ever be needed. All flats look outwards towards the road on the boundary of the site and inward through the conservatory to the rear gardens. The south-facing conservatory is designed as an all-weather, landscaped social space and is very attractively planted

5.30   A view of Claverton Court looking towards the south-facing conservatory.

and popular with the residents
(Fig 5.31). There is a small communal
lounge next to the dining-room: also a
utility and washing room, and a special
treatment room are provided. A paved
forecourt is the focus for all pedestrian
and vehicular movement and provides
further interest, as the residents can
observe from the dining-room and
conservatory the movements of
deliveries and visitors.

Areas of dwelling units have been measured
from plans provided by the architects.

Further reading

DOE, NHBC, RIBA, *Housing Design Awards
1985*, Sabrecrown Publishing, pp. 80, 81.

VALINS, M., *Housing for Elderly People*, The
Architectural Press, London, 1988, pp. 123,
124.

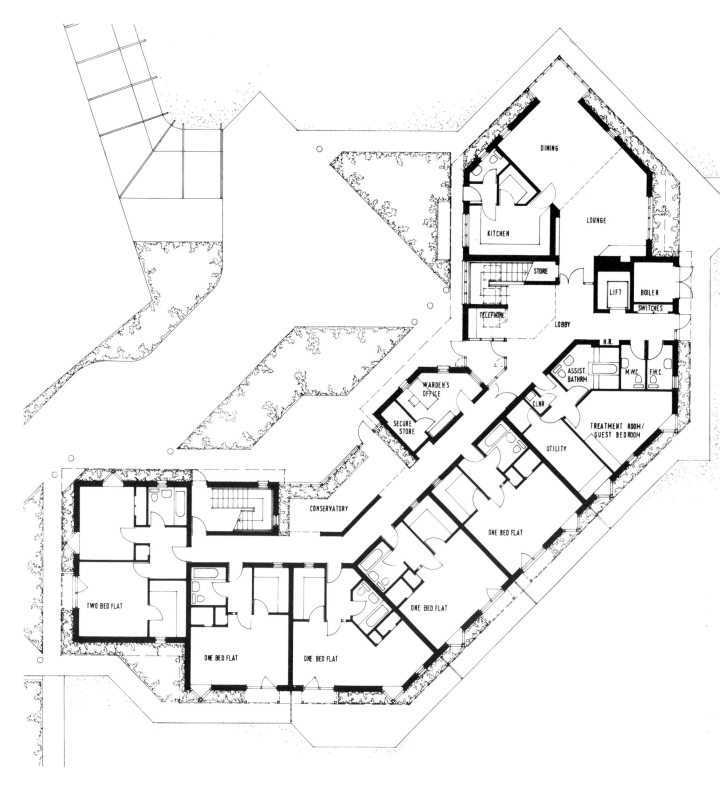

ground floor

5.32   Floor plans.

first floor

Templars, Place, Marlow, Bucks, England

Architect:	Broadway Malyan
No. of dwellings:	9
Site area:	0.17 hectares (0.42 acres)
Density:	47 houses per hectare (10 houses per acre)
Type of accommodation:	2 and 3–storey houses

Size of dwellings:

3-bedroom house	101 sq m (1087 sq ft)
4-bedroom house	142.5 sq m (1534 sq ft)
Construction:	emphasis was placed on low-energy consumption with fibreglass insulated cavity wall construction and chipboard flooring on extruded polystyrene to the ground floor; multi-red stock facings and red engineering plinths, copings and soldier courses complemented the knapped flints which are laid against an outer skin of concrete block; stained feather-edge boarding and softwood double-glazed windows contrast with the masonry.

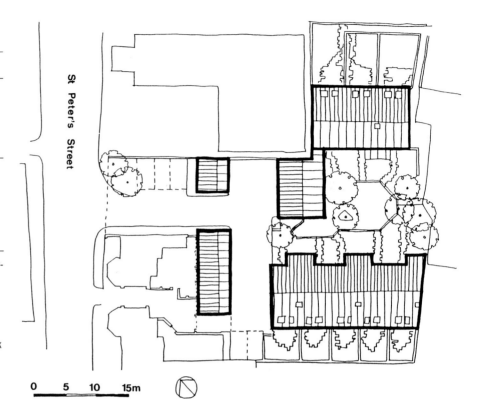

St Peter's Street

0   5   10   15m

5.33   Site layout of Templars Road.

The project is located on a site in Marlow which is set back from St Peter's Street on land formerly occupied by a Church of England infant school. Situated in a conservation area, the site called for a special courtyard approach to the design. The client's brief was to provide small, high-quality houses for elderly people trading down. The result was the design of 3-storey mews housing with small, walled gardens (Fig 5.33). The vehicular approach to the houses maintains a continuity with the courtyard through the use of identical surface materials and the quality of the planting. The constrictions of the small site, and the attempt to make the scheme sympathetic to the historic neighbourhood, largely dictated the character and methods of construction, with material and detail design creating their own character rather than imitating any particular style. The use of knapped flint-stone on the external walls of the dwellings

is of particular merit (Fig 5.34). Each house has two bathrooms, and a high standard of fitting out including the provision of all appliances in the kitchens (Fig 5.35). Dog grate fireplaces with facing brick surrounds, raised hearths and built-in niches and log boxes are provided in the living-rooms.

Further reading
DOE, NHBC, RIBA, 'Housing Design Awards 1985', Sabrecrown Publishing, pp. 18, 19.

5.34   The delightful use of knapped flintwork.

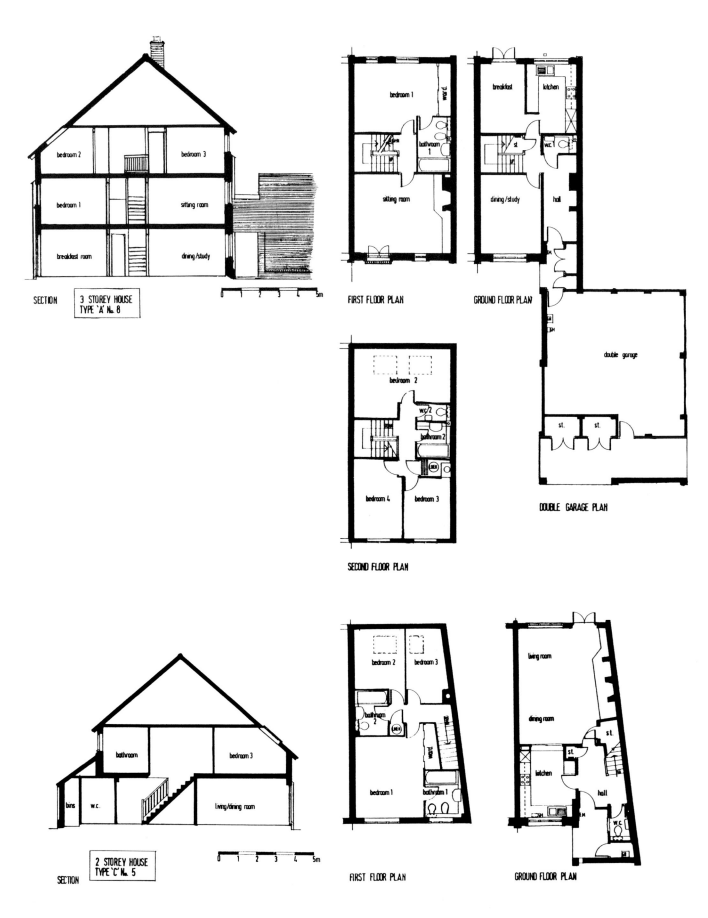

5.35 Dwelling plans.

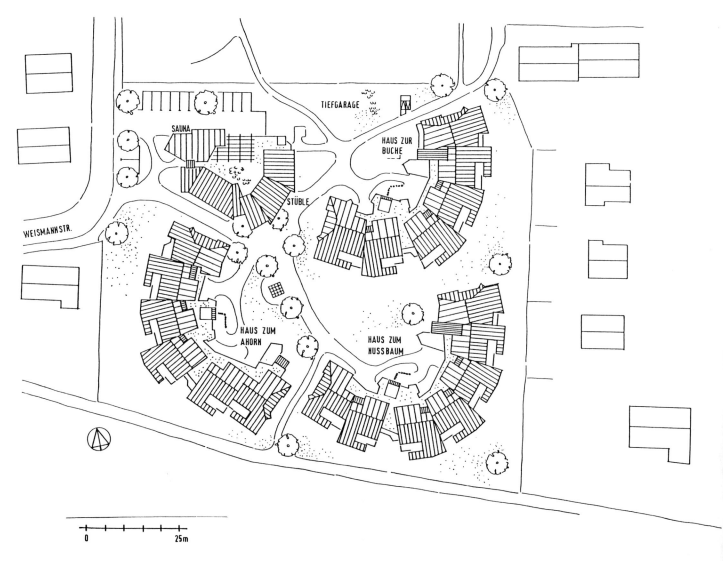

TIEFGARAGE

HAUS ZUR BUCHE

SAUNA

STÜBLE

WEISMANNSTR.

HAUS ZUM AHORN

HAUS ZUM NUSSBAUM

0   25m

Altenwohnanlage, 'Laubenhof', Freiburg, Germany

Architect:	Rolf Disch
No. of dwellings:	89
Site area:	1.1 hectare (2.7 acres)
Density:	80.9 dwellings per hectare (33 dwellings per acre)

Type of accommodation:

flats for 4-person families	10
flats for elderly people	79

The scheme also includes communal meeting facilities and sauna.

Size of dwellings (dwellings illustrated in plans):

flats for families	84.6 sq m (911 sq ft)
bed-sitting flats for elderly people	58.5 sq m (630 sq ft)

The scheme comprises three crescents of three-storey housing which enclose landscaped pedestrian courts (Fig 5.36). A communal meeting room is located at the entrance to the scheme, together with the majority of the car parking. The wedge-shaped dwellings for the elderly are in bed-sitting room form, but are ingeniously designed to provide maximum living space (Fig 5.37). The larger, family dwellings are contained within the shell of two elderly persons' dwellings. Bathrooms are internal and form a buffer between living spaces. Large balconies and loggias abound to give each dwelling its own particular character (Fig 5.38). The common galleries leading to the entrances of the upper-floor dwellings (Fig 5.39) are designed to create a feeling of spaciousness. The kitchen windows project into the galleries and the front doors are recessed. The quality of these areas is so much higher than would normally be achieved in Britain.

5.36 Site layout of the housing for elderly people in Freiburg.

Further reading
'Laubenhof – Altenwohnanlage "Im Haltinger" Freiburg in Breisgau', *Deutsche Bauzeitung*, 2 February, 1984, vol. 118, pp. 38–42.

5.37   Dwelling plans.

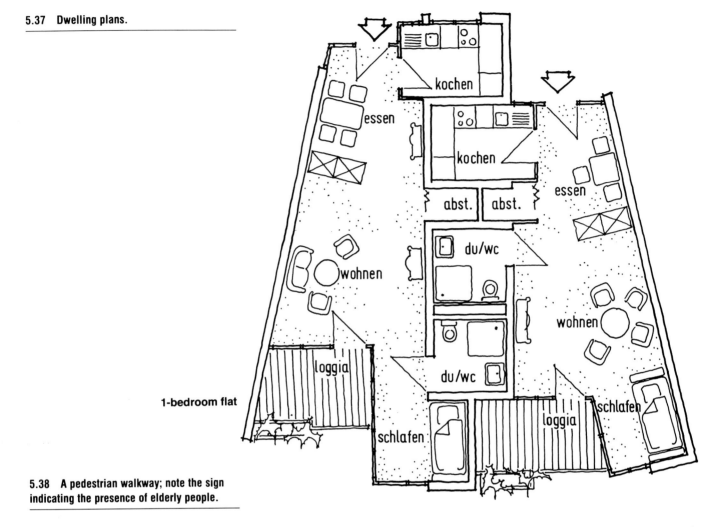

kochen

essen

kochen

abst.   abst.

du/wc

wohnen

wohnen

du/wc

loggia

1-bedroom flat

schlafen

loggia

schlafen

5.38   A pedestrian walkway; note the sign indicating the presence of elderly people.

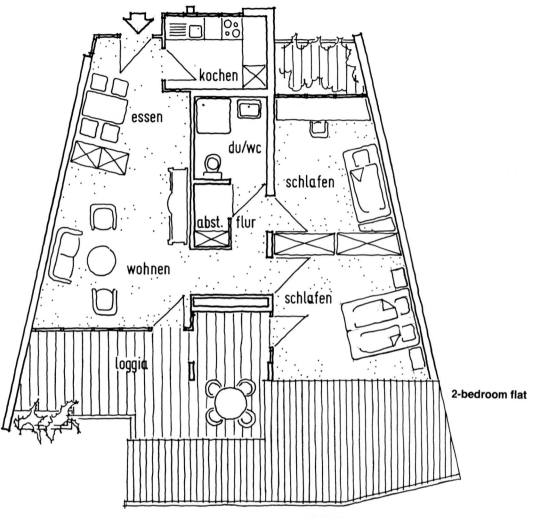

kochen

essen

du/wc

schlafen

abst. flur

wohnen

schlafen

loggia

2-bedroom flat

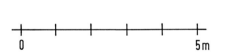

0   5m

5.39 An upper walkway demonstrates that such access to upper-floor dwellings can be successfully designed.

Møllegården Care Centre, Gladsaxe, Copenhagen, Denmark

Architects:	Erik Ejlers and Henning Graversen
Site area:	6 hectares (14.8 acres)
No. of dwellings:	106 dwellings for elderly people
Density:	35 dwellings per hectare (14.3 dwellings per acre)
Type of accommodation:	
	56 'nursing care units' for people who can no longer take care of themselves
	50 'protected dwellings', units for people who need extra services but can lead a normal life otherwise
Size of dwellings: protected dwellings	46 sq m (496 sq ft)
Nursing care units	26.5 sq m (285.6 sq ft)
Parking/garages:	84 car parking spaces in a large single area
Construction:	concrete post and beam construction; façades are light, wood-clad elements; the roofing material is black corrugated translite.

5.41   The nursing home and day centre as seen from the square.

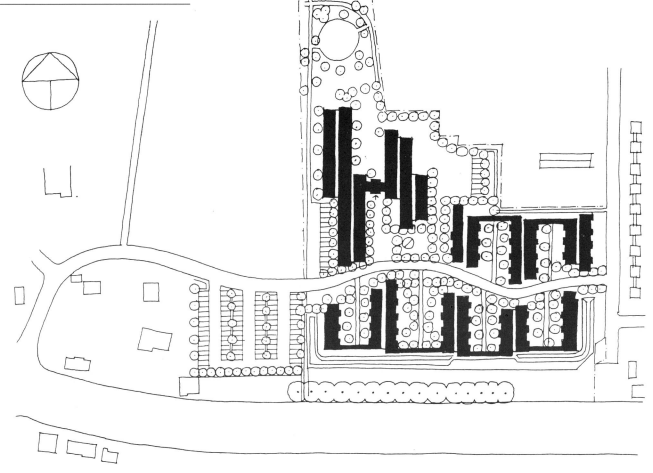

5.40   The site layout of Møllegården Care Centre for elderly people.

The site lies on the outskirts of Copenhagen and borders on to green areas and a lake. The project comprises dwellings for elderly people with different care needs (Fig 5.40). It includes a day centre which offers service and treatment to the residents and to elderly people living in the neighbourhood (Fig 5.41). The architects were anxious to avoid an institutional atmosphere and therefore designed the project in a dense/low-rise form of one and two-storeys. The 'protected' dwellings are grouped along covered pedestrian streets. The streets of dwellings are arranged around green courtyards and outdoor recreation spaces.

The day centre and the 'nursing care units' are located in 2 two-storey wings. The units are one-room apartments with bath, tea-kitchen, and a small terrace. On the floors above are communal living-rooms and observation rooms, doctors' offices, etc. The ground floor of the day centre contains activity areas and a living-room, while the first floor is reserved for therapy, doctors' offices and administration uses. The protected dwellings are identical two-room apartments, each with their own entrance and small garden (Fig 5.42). The bay window in the living-room visually connects the apartment to the small garden and the garden court. The paving materials and planting emphasize the domestic character of the project. The different functions of the outdoor areas are marked by changes in the character and colour of the paving, rather than indicating the differences by curbs and other changes of level (Fig 5.43).

Areas have been measured from plans provided by the architects.

Further reading

'Omsorycentret Møllegärden, Gladsaxe', *Arkitektur DK*, June 1978, vol. 22, no. 6, pp. 226

L'Industria delle Costruzioni, March 1983, no. 137, p. 33.

5.43   A pedestrian street runs through the development: this connecting link draws people to the centre.

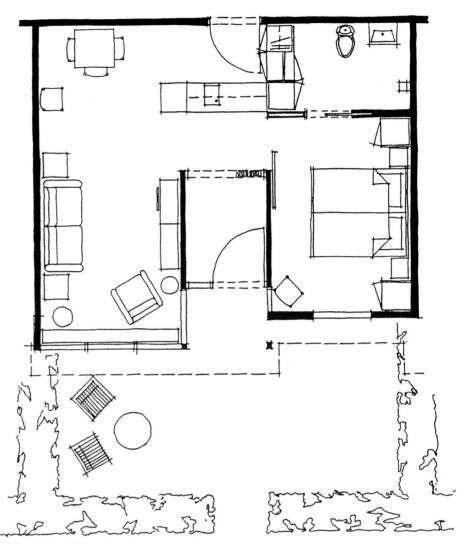

5.42   Plan of sheltered dwelling.

Old People's Home, Savela, Finland

Architects:	A. Konsultit
No. of dwellings:	72
Site area:	2.4 hectares (5.9 acres)
Density:	171 dwellings per hectare (69 dwellings per acre)
	185 persons per hectare (75 persons per acre)
Type of accommodation: flats	designed specifically for elderly people
Size of dwellings:	62 1–room flats 28 sq m (301 sq ft); 10 2–room flats 42 sq m (452 sq ft)
Parking/garages:	12 car parking spaces
Heating:	district heating to radiators in rooms
Construction:	timber-framed

The care of elderly people is taken very seriously in Finland and this scheme is an excellent example of a design which fits the need (Fig 5.44). In addition to the individual small flats (Fig 5.45), the scheme comprises communal facilities which include meeting and hobbies rooms (Fig 5.46). Of particular merit is the complete lack of any feeling of institutionalism, made possible by the grouping of the flats into a number of houses, and the very domestic quality of the architecture (Fig 5.47).

Further reading

DI LUZIO, C., 'Residenze per anziani in Europa, 1982, Eurostructpress Award – Finlandia, Finland, *L'Industria delle Costruzioni*, March 1983, no. 137, pp. 34, 35.

5.44 The view across an internal garden in the elderly people's housing at Savela, Finland.

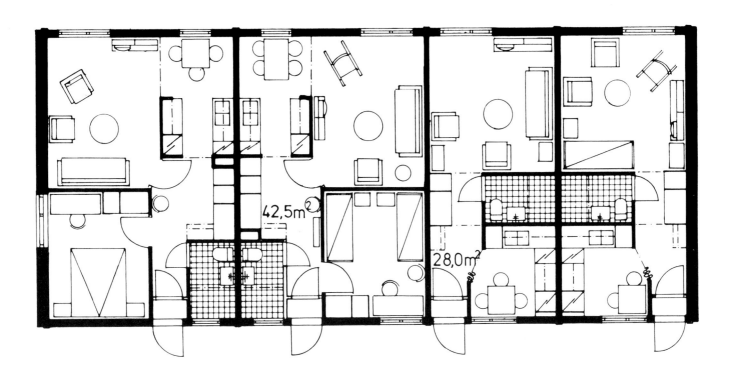

42,5m²

28,0m²

5.44 Plans of one-bedroom flats and bed-sitting-rooms.

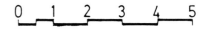

0   1   2   3   4   5

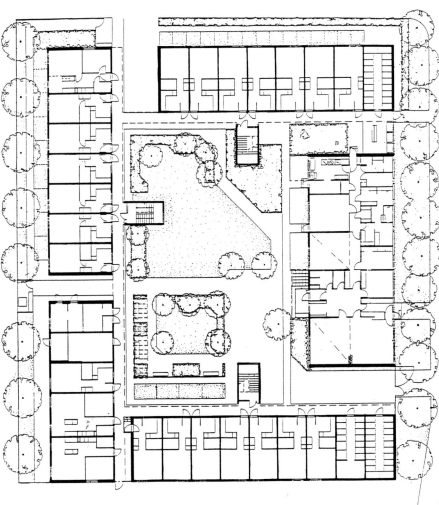

5.46 Dwellings and facilities are grouped around an internal garden.

5.47 A domestic quality has been achieved in a very Finnish manner.

Single-Person Flats, Haringey, London, England

Architects:	Colquhoun, Miller and Partners	
No. of dwellings:	37	
Site area:	0.115 hectares (0.28 acres)	
Density:	321 dwellings per hectare (132 dwellings per acre)	
	616 persons per hectare (253 persons per acre)	
Size and no. of accommodation:		
2-person units	48 sq m (517 sq ft)	34
1-person units	28 sq m (302 sq ft)	2
4-person caretaker's dwelling		1
Construction:	calculated load bearing brick cross walls and piers, with reinforced concrete floors and roof slab; external finishes are facing brick piers and flank walls and brick soldier courses of floor slab levels; windows are high-performance stained timber opening casements, with spandrel panels of glass blocks.	

5.48   Front elevations of the flats for single young people in Haringey, London.

Architects, Colquhoun, Miller and Partners have demonstrated in this project for the London Borough of Haringey, that housing for single people in an urban environment can be economically and satisfactorily provided in a nine-storey block of flats (Fig 5.48). There are four flats to a floor, and each two-person flat comprises a living-room, bedroom, small kitchen and bathroom. The single-person flats are located on the ground floor and comprise a bed-sitting-room, small kitchen and bathroom (Fig 5.49). There is a caretaker's flat, together with laundry, common–room and kitchen, porter's office and ancillary plant room.

Further reading

LECUYER, A., 'Housing Links', *The Architects' Journal*, 9 September 1981, vol. 174, no. 36, pp. 480–4.

'London Now – single person flats, Garton House, 119 Hornsea Lane N6', *RIBA London Region Year Book*, 1981, p. 103.

'Single person flats', *A + U*, April 1982, no. 139, pp. 95–7.

'*Young people's housing by Colquhoun and Miller*'. *Arquitectura*, Feburary 1983, pp. 44–8.

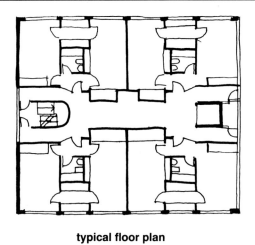

typical floor plan

entrance floor plan

5.49 Floor plans.

Youth Houses in Sydney, Australia

Architects:	Bruce Rickard and Associates Pty Ltd
Type of accommodation:	4 houses, each comprising 8 bedrooms for young people and 1 unit for house parents
Size of dwellings:	the area of the accommodation is from a total of 323 sq m (3477 sq ft) to a total of 349 sq m (3757 sq ft).
Parking/garages:	1 or 2 parking spaces usually 1 garage for house parents
Construction:	all the houses have concrete floors, brick walls, some are painted externally; timber-framed roofs; aluminum door and window-frames; steel columns support the roof members over large floor to ceiling glass doors and panels.

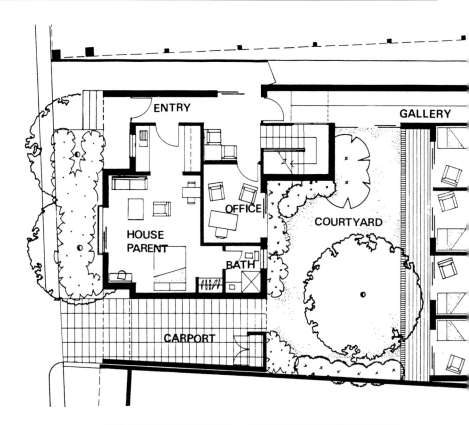

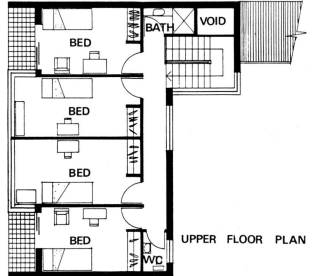

These four houses are the first of the youth housing to be built under the New South Wales Singles Housing Programme which provides accommodation in the following forms.

1　Singles apartments providing housing on a long-term basis for single people over 18 years of age.
2　Youth housing providing purpose-built, transitional supportive accommodation for male and female young people between the ages of 12 and 18 who have left home, and seek refuge from difficult home circumstances.

5.50 Plans of youth housing at Baldwin Street.

5.51 Kitchens are large so the young people can cook for themselves.

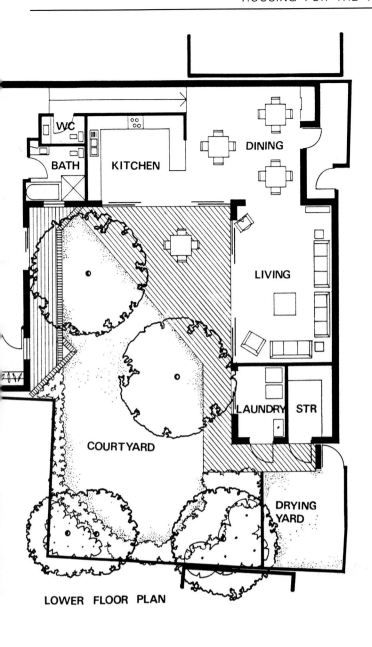

WC
BATH KITCHEN
DINING
LIVING
COURTYARD
LAUNDRY STR
DRYING YARD

LOWER FLOOR PLAN

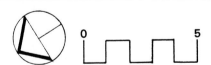

0   5

The four houses built so far are located in Erskinville, Camperdown and Stanmore, in built-up streets generally of terrace-type housing. The brief called for houses that would look and feel like a home, provide a comfortable residence for young people and integrate with the neighbourhood (Fig 5.50). The houses accommodate eight young people in single bedrooms with shared bath and shower rooms, a bed-sitting-room for a house parent, a common living-room, dining-room, kitchen and laundry (Figs 5.51, 5.52).

Bedrooms, where possible, open directly onto a terrace or balcony. The house parent's accommodation is located close to the front door. A garage or car port for one car is provided on the site. The houses are planned around internal courtyards. Kitchens are arranged so that a group of young people can cook and receive cooking lessons from the house parent at one time (Fig 5.51).

The dining-rooms allow for meals to be taken round a large family table or for smaller groups to be formed. There is an office on the ground floor for the house-parent who has a living/bedroom with kitchenette, and a wc/shower room.

The general aim of the design was to fit each house into the pattern of its street. The major problem on all sites was how to create, on a double frontage, a big house that was of a similar scale to the adjacent, mainly smaller houses, on single frontages. In addition, the two-storey houses adjacent to some of the new houses have very high ceilings, which created the problem of how to retain the scale of these older houses in the new houses with much lower ceilings (Fig 5.52). Another objective was to obtain optimum climatic benefit by procuring northern exposure to all communal rooms and most bedrooms. A further objective was to give importance and spatial interest to the communal living, dining and kitchen areas. This was achieved by placing these areas in single-storey situations so that the ceilings would follow the roof pitch.

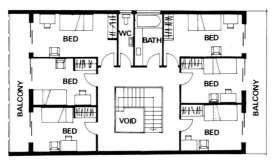

UPPER FLOOR PLAN

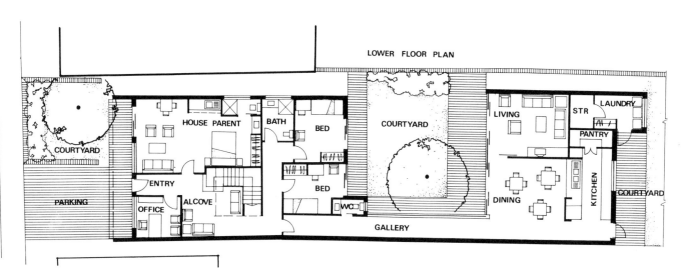

LOWER FLOOR PLAN

5.52   Plans of youth housing at Knight Road.

Further reading
'Youth Housing', *Architecture Australia* July
1988, vol. 77, no. 5, pp. 78–83.

**5.53   The Knight Road housing has been
designed to fit into its surroundings.**

33 Dwellings for Disabled People, 'Southbrook Field', Church Lane, Papworth Everard, Cambridge, England

Architects:	Mathew Robotham, Associates
No. of dwellings:	33
Site area:	1.24 hectares (3.0 acres)
Density:	26.61 dwellings per hectare (10.7 dwellings per acre)
	33.06 persons per hectare (13.4 persons per acre)

Size and no. of dwellings:

flats	42 sq m (452 sq ft)	2
single-storey dwellings (bungalows)	42 sq m and 55 sq m (592 sq ft)	31
Parking/garages:	4 parking spaces; 16 car ports	

Heating:	underfloor off-peak electric heating with top-up electric wall panel heaters
Construction:	trench-filled concrete foundations; insulated concrete blockwork; cavity walls; trussed rafters to cloisters; farmhouse orange concrete roof tiles; rendered walls in cloisters and undulating bands of timber boarding and 'stock' brickwork on the garden side; concrete pipes form structural columns; dry lining to all walls; softwood high performance windows; sill timber stained.

Papworth Village Settlement is a charity and housing association whose objects are the rehabilitation, training, employment and housing of physically handicapped people and their families. It was established 65 years ago, and over the years has grown into a thriving community, where physically disabled and fit people are fully integrated. The fit members of disabled people's families and key fit employees ensure both social and economic viability.

The scheme (Fig 5.54) has been designed to meet the needs of 33 single physically disabled people, including some elderly people, who may be confined to wheelchairs. It has been designed to provide independence and privacy, but with warden care when needed. Maximum

5.54   Site layout of the housing for disabled people at Papworth Everard.

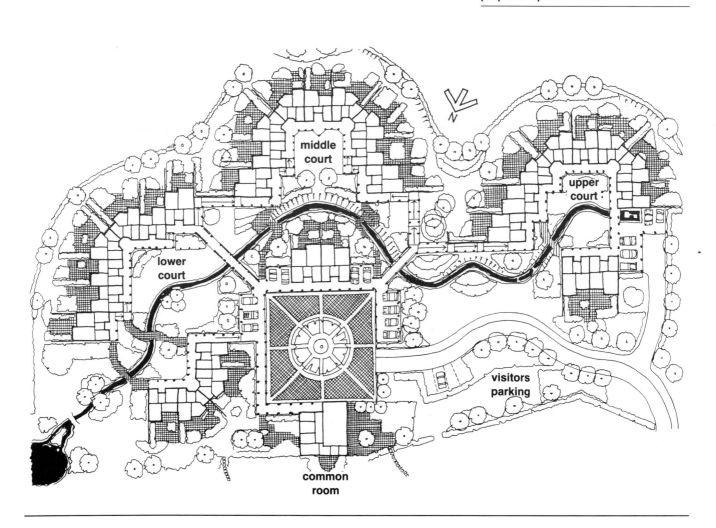

**5.55   Pitched roofs and tiles create a very
domestic atmosphere.**

flexibility within single-person
accommodation was an important
element of the brief, including the
possibility that some residents may
wish to marry while in residence. The
main dwelling type is a self-contained
single-person flat with separate
sitting-room, bedroom and bathroom.
Eight of the flats will be provided with
a double bedroom. Because of the
relatively high number of wheelchair
occupants, single-storey
accommodation with minimum
access gradients was necessary. A
common-room with warden's office,
kitchen, laundry, and guest bedroom
has been sited centrally.

Sixteen car ports have been
provided, with covered access to the
dwellings through the 'cloisters'
(Fig 5.55).

Housing for Disabled People, Bristol Road, Birmingham, England

Architects:	Birmingham City Architect's Department; William Reed, City Architect	
No of dwellings:	17	
Site area:	0.2 hectares (0.5 acres)	
Density:	85 dwellings per hectare (34 dwellings per acre)	
	135 persons per hectare (54 persons per acre)	
Size and no. of dwellings:		
1-bedroom 1-person flat for disabled person	46.6 sq m (502 sq ft)	4
1-bedroom 2-person bungalow for disabled people (type A)	54 sq m (581 sq ft)	1
1-bedroom 2-person flat for disabled people (type B)	65.8 sq m (708 sq ft)	4
2-bedroom 3-person maisonette	73.5 sq m (791 sq ft)	8
Construction:	all blocks are constructed with load bearing brick/block insulated cavity walls on reinforced concrete raft foundations, with pre-cast concrete first floors and prefabricated trussed rafter roofs, clad in slates or concrete tiles.	

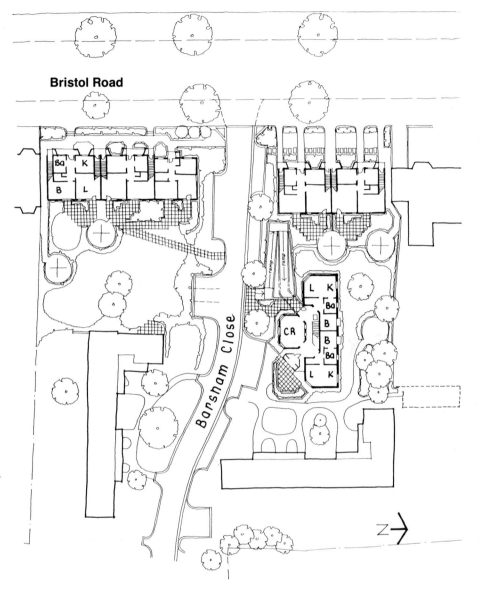

Bristol Road

Barsham Close

Z →

5.56 Site layout of the housing for disabled people, Bristol Road, Birmingham, for the Birmingham City Council Housing Management Committee.

The site is situated 1.5 miles (2.4 kilometres) south of the city centre, on a busy trunk road, in an area comprising a mixture of old and new residential property. The scheme is the third phase of Birmingham City Council's housing development on the site, and comprises 17 dwellings contained in two three-storey blocks, one two-storey block and one bungalow (Fig 5.56). The project adjoins a warden service housing scheme, built in 1978 as a second phase of the development, and is bisected by an unadopted informal cul-de-sac shared by vehicular and pedestrian traffic. The site frontage is flanked by listed two-storey houses built around 1840 which have strongly modelled rendered frontages. The two new frontage blocks are three storeys high to maintain the roof line of the neighbouring Victorian houses and are designed to match them as closely as possible in scale and facing materials. To this end external walls are rendered and painted, windows have heavy concrete cills and raised surrounds, and the roofs are clad in asbestos cement slates.

5.57   Ramps lead up to the upper-floor flats.

A single-storey dwelling has been included at the end of one of these blocks to repeat the visual rhythm of the existing frontage properties.

As traffic noise levels are high, habitable rooms are generally situated at the rear of these blocks, and windows on the front elevation are double-glazed for sound insulation.

The ground-floor disabled dwellings have paved terraces giving wheelchair access to clothes drying areas with rotary dryers, adjustable for height, screened by circular, painted walls. The two-storey block contains four flats and a common-room, and is intended to provide short term accommodation for disabled people making the transition from a sheltered life at home or in residential care, to an independent life in the community (Fig 5.57). While staying here for a few weeks or months, they can experience the physical and psychological problems and benefits of living on their own with minimal outside assistance, their needs can be assessed, and suitable permanent accommodation

can be arranged. The flats have been designed to serve a range of disabilities (Fig 5.58). Two of them have baths, two have showers, and one has an overhead hoist from bedroom to bathroom. A wheelchair lift has been installed and site levels have been exploited to provide a ramped approach (and fire exit) for the first floor flats (Fig 5.59).

There is a paved terrace at ground level and a balcony on the first floor for sitting out. This block has external facing brick walls and profiled red roof tiles to match the adjacent warden service scheme. Disabled dwellings in all three blocks are linked via an alarm call system to a central control, manned day and night by the City Housing Department.

Further reading

DOE, NHBC, RIBA, *Housing Design Awards 1985*, Sabrecrown Publishing, p. 46.

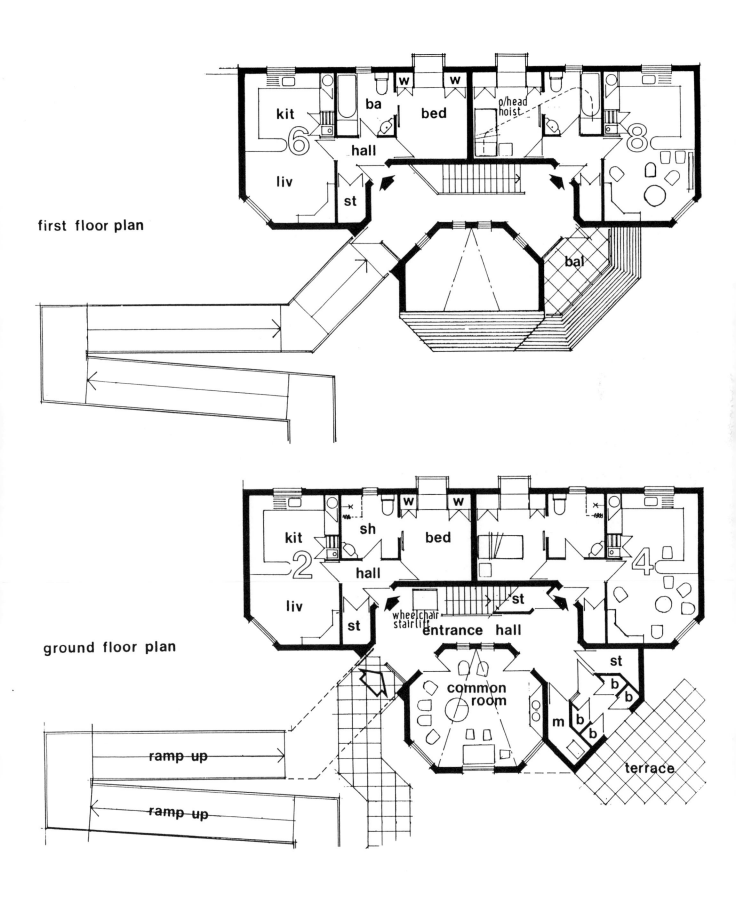

first floor plan

ground floor plan

5.58 Dwelling plans: wheelchair and common room.

5.59   A stair-lift enables easy access for
disabled people to the upper-floor
accommodation.

6 PARTICIPATORY HOUSING

THIS chapter considers the involvement of the eventual occupants in the design of their housing. The process varies from mere consultation at one level to total involvement at the other (i.e. the architect works for the occupants). This is in contrast to the usual situation in which the architect works for a developer, a local authority or any other client organization. The ultimate form of participatory housing is self-build where the occupants build their houses themselves (Fig 6.6). Participatory housing is frequently linked with the term 'community architecture' but the two should not be confused. The true definition of 'community' architecture is where the architect lives amongst the community for which he/she is designing. Living amongst the people can be beneficial but is not the only criterion for serving the needs of a community: professional knowledge and experience are still the most important requirements of an architect. In her article on community architecture in the USA, Mary C. Comerio commented that most community design centres 'were staffed by young inexperienced professionals whose ideology was stronger than their technical skills' (Comerio 1987:16). Special skills are, however, essential, particularly a willingness to listen, understand and communicate. Colin Ward summed up the requirement by saying, 'I have come to the conclusion that it is this personal service element that is more important to these new-style clients than anything that

resembles the activity as a creative designer that is supposed to be the mark of an architect'. He goes on to say that 'when potential residents actually *are* in control of the planning of their future homes they almost invariably make choices which reflect not only their immediate needs but other people's future needs (Ward 1987:12). Tom Woolley, community architect and Professor of Architecture at Queens University School of Architecture, Belfast, has studied dweller satisfaction in three tenant co-operatives and this has convinced him that architects have a lot to learn about the techniques of participatory design. In his community architecture paper, given at the Institute of Community Studies Housing Co-ops Research Seminar in 1986, he made the following point:

> User satisfaction was related more strongly to the degree of control which the clients exercised over the projects. In the most successful case . . . the tenants had taken the initiative, had control of the direction and the management of the project and were willing to take on and fight all comers to ensure a successful completion. This created a general sense of solidarity and common purpose among the co-operative members which I am convinced is reflected in higher levels of satisfaction. (quoted in Ward 1987:13)

Woolley considers that, 'the credit for the success of such projects should

go much more to the clients and the way they organized themselves rather than to the architects in view of the limited nature of the design participation activities'. He also makes the very important point that 'architecture is not necessarily the central concern of a community group – the control, location or funding of the development, whether housing or community buildings, may be much more vital'.

The process of participatory design of housing can be time consuming and far from easy. It is not, therefore, a cheap method of procuring housing. There is a particular problem in the early stages of a project when the feasibility of building the houses requires architectural input and there is no guarantee of the project proceeding. These problems were highlighted in *The Architects' Journal*:

> First, the public costs of housing co-operative education to achieve full client participation must be seen as a sound investment in empowering local communities on regenerate and develop self-sustaining economies . . . second, the desperate need
> for effective co-ordination of government departmental activities must be a reality . . . third, the scale of pump priming public expenditure for feasibility studies and land reclamation must be recognised. The private sector cannot and will not risk such large resources up front. (*Architects' Journal*, March, 1988:5)

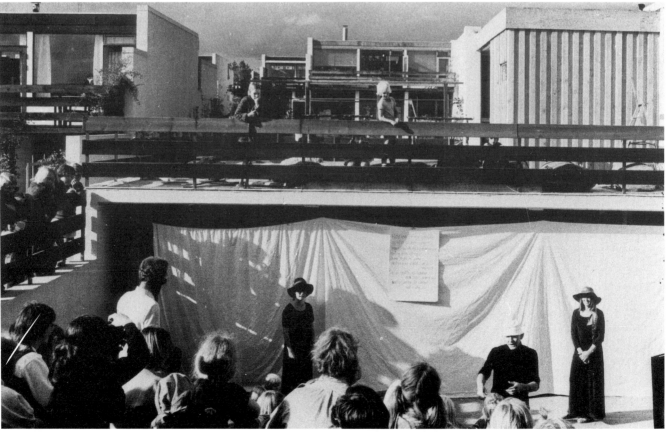

Most examples of participatory housing in Britain primarily involve architects working with groups of future occupants on re-establishing options within the standard approach to housing (Fig 6.1). Co-operative developments in the Netherlands and Denmark have gone far beyond the British examples: in these countries the concept of groups of people living together as a community is highly developed.

In the Netherlands a prime exponent of participatory housing is Herman Hertzberger, whose major intention has always been to translate into reality the social theories that he and others believe in. He has achieved this conversion of theory to built form in three projects:

1 eight experimental houses type 'Diagoon' at Gebbenbaan, Delft (1971) (Figs 6.8 to 6.10);
2 city renewal, 'Haarlemmer Houttuinen' in Amsterdam (1982) (Figs 6.11, 6.12);
3 'Kassel-Dönche' Heinrich Schutzalle, Kassel, Germany (1985) (Figs 6.13 to 6.16).

This can also be seen in his housing built as part of the international housing exhibition in Berlin (1987) (Fig 2.15). For Herman Hertzberger, the participation of the occupants in the design of housing includes not only the initial planning, but means a continual relationship between building and user when the projects are occupied. This relationship arises from his treatment of public, semi-public and private spaces in which he deliberately plans for social contact at differing levels. In this way the occupants themselves are actually contributing to the exhancement of his work.

6.1 Co-operative housing in Grafton Street, Liverpool.
Architects: Brock Carmichael Associates with BCA Landscape.

6.2 Skraplanet: an early co-operative housing development in Denmark.
Architect: Jan Gudmund-Høyer.

In Denmark, co-operative housing has taken on new architectural forms in recent years: high density low-rise accommodation has become the norm, and distinction between private and public space is agreed upon by the residents rather than predetermined by design beforehand. Each family has its own dwelling, but all share the common facilities which include meeting rooms, play areas for children, laundry, library, sewing and television room. All residents share in the co-operative duties, such as cleaning, and cooking meals to be taken by everyone living in the project. They purchase items together which they could not acquire individually and they help to cultivate communal

6.3 The standardization of building components enabled this housing at Tinggården, Herfølge, Denmark, to be highly economic to construct.
Architects: Tegnestuen Vandkunsten.

gardens in which space is provided both for growing vegetables and for the community to relax and play together. The co-operatives are managed on the basis of regular meetings which everyone is obliged to attend. The pioneers of this kind of housing are young professionals with one or two children.

Among the first examples of co-operative housing was Jan Gudmund-Høyer's *Skraplanet* (Fig 6.2) in which the houses are arranged on the hillside site so as to allow unrestricted views across the roofs of the dwellings below. The first housing scheme of this kind to be sponsored by the state was Tinggärden by architects Tegnestuen Vandkunsten which was completed in 1976 (Fig 6.3). Numerous schemes followed. The formula was different to that of the multi-storey blocks of the 1960s: settlements were no longer large; they comprise buildings of one, two or a maximum of three storeys. This is closer to the traditional lifestyle in Denmark where the majority of people live in detached houses. The effect common to the schemes was to avoid the sad lack of variety which so often happens in conventional housing. The aim was to achieve, at reasonable cost, a form of 'controlled variety' in the types of home offered within an overall cohesion.

The architectural practice Tegnestuen Vandkunsten has linked this change to its aim for a collective society – the individual family living in a community. The vision of the architects 'has strong overtones of William Morris's ideal of an egalitarian yet modestly affluent society living in close contact with nature' (Davey 1988:78). All of their schemes (Figs 6.17 to 6.27) seem to adopt familiar patterns. Cars are kept to the outside which allows for the creation of a hierarchy of pedestrian spaces and communal greens leading from private gardens at the rear of dwellings. The housing itself is constructed using materials that are often more common in industrial and agricultural buildings, and is built in a way that maximizes the potential for standardization of

components. This cheap construction enables the housing to be as accessible as possible to the residents in financial terms.

Dorit Fromm explains how much people enjoy living in such housing. They feel safe, surrounded by friends, and they can always get help and support. However, not everyone feels the same:

A few find living in common housing too social for their taste. Some find group decisions too tiresome to achieve, or weighted towards couples with children. Single people find an unequal distribution in common house payments which are often divided by household and not

6.4 'Seldwyla', Zurich.
Architect: Rolf Keller.

on an individual basis. But there are people who feel the design and layout are not communal enough, that the units are too large and are too separated from the common space. (Fromm 1985:67)

The pioneering work in the Netherlands and Denmark is taken even further in Switzerland by Rolf Keller, who along with *Atelier 5* is perhaps the most influential architect in his country. His housing at Seldwyla (Figs 6.4, 6.28, 6.29), on the outskirts of Zurich, was designed by himself together with other architects, with the close participation of all the future occupants. He prepared the overall concept and the other architects designed their own houses and houses for some of the future residents. Rolf Keller now lives in the development where he also has his office. The result is a harmonious development that appears to have been designed by only one person, such was the strength of Keller's beliefs and the confidence of the other architects and residents in him.

The criticism that all participative housing receives is that, despite all the collaboration, the inhabitants have not had a perceptible effect on the architecture. In other words, the designer's ideas have been predominant. It is, however, frequently commented that where the residents have had the upper hand the quality of design is poor, and that no architecture of quality has come from participation. E.M. Farelly counters these criticisms by commenting that the most successful architects working with communities – Erskine (Fig 6.5) and Hertzberger, for example, 'listen but still care deeply, passionately for architecture as an art.' Their schemes bear unmistakably the 'signature of [their] architect. Participatory perhaps, but there can be no doubt as to who really designed the building.' This comment is perhaps also true of the examples from Austria which are illustrated. Farelly's article refers to Walter Segal's self-build housing in Lewisham (Fig 6.6), commenting that he,

beloved by many for his personal

6.5 Ralph Erskine at Byker, Newcastle upon Tyne.

magnetism and ingenious building system, encouraged the self-builder, but allowed participation in *design* only within the very tight constraints of the system he invented and stamped indelibly, despite a lifetime of denials, with his own personal *style*. (Farelly 1987:31)

Mary C. Comerio perhaps offers the best guidance when she says:
participation provides the feedback that improves the function of the scheme. Should pedestrians pass through a communal space? Where should parking be located? Should kitchens be open plan? These

6.6 'Segal Close', Lewisham.
Architect: Walter Segal.

functions clearly affect the design but they do not necessarily imply that the inhabitants need to control the materials, mood and rhythm of the design. (Comerio 1987:19)

Self-build housing has existed as a form of procurement for many years, but in Britain it has mainly been in the form of sites being divided into plots for individual people to build their own homes. The concept of groups of people joining together to do this on a communal basis is relatively new. Walter Segal successfully demonstrated in Lewisham that with the right kind of support, groups of people can work together (Fig 6.6). However, what has never been explained so far is the enabling role played by the local authority and its architects' department, without which the project would not have succeeded. It is perhaps sufficient to conclude that Walter Segal's ideas are now being furthered by the architects who worked for Lewisham Borough Council at the time.

The collaboration of groups of people in self-build housing schemes is not a straightforward process. In a description of Oksval III and IV (Figs 6.35 to 6.37), the Norwegian architect Jan Hille gives a first-hand account of the difficulties that arise when involving future residents in the design and construction of their own homes. He draws attention to the need for a clear understanding of the responsibilities of supervision, time schedules, co-ordination, and the need for the goodwill of any contractor involved. In the case of his project, the extent of the work to be done by the occupants was fixed beforehand on an optional basis and was limited to the following: partition walls and fittings of basement and attic plans; floor and wall finishes; outdoor construction and landscaping. In his description of Oksval III and IV, Jan Hille advises:

the benefit of users participating in the design and building process is not one of economy as planning and co-ordination is more time consuming. Rather more important is the fact that the inhabitants had the possibility to influence and to some extent shape their own environment, and hereby establishing a feeling of responsibility and belonging. The housing scheme is and has been from the start socially very stable.

6.7 Participatory housing at Graz-Neufeldweg, Austria: the balconies and open frame are designed for future extensions as required by the occupants.
Architect: Gunther Domenig.

The projects from Austria (Figs 6.7, 6.38 to 6.45) are unquestionably of the present day and reflect the confidence which society in that country has for its young architects. Perhaps these projects, more than any of the others illustrated in this chapter, demonstrate that architecture of the highest quality can be created when there is complete trust between architect and client. The project from Stockholm (Figs 6.46, 6.47) which concludes the chapter extends the principle of self-build in a different direction, as it identifies a method in which the public sector and an individual group of people can work together in a partnership in terms of both the financing of the project and its implementation from inception to completion.

The major criticism usually levelled at participatory housing is that it is only applicable to small-scale development and does not provide an answer to the need to construct new housing in large quantities. These criticisms can ony be responded to by architects being prepared to re-examine their role in housing. When large numbers of

houses were built by public bodies in most western countries, the architect's role was paramount, but this role has since declined. It is only recently that the private sector in Britain has started employing architects to design its housing, and this, in the main, is the provision of only a partial service which does not include supervision. There is no contact with the eventual occupant either beforehand or afterwards. Architects are no longer involved in research and development to any significant extent, as those in the public and government sectors were in the 1960s. Nick Wates predicted the problem now facing the profession as a whole when he said that 'unless architects get directly to grips with environmental problems of ordinary citizens, they will become an obsolete and irrelevant profession' (Wates 1985:60). If his warning is not heeded, the result may be that architects in the future will have little or no direct involvement in housing. User-participation in design is therefore a new force which architects must harness.

Participatory Housing in The Netherlands and Germany

Architect:	Herman Hertberger

Diagoon Housing, Delft

No. of dwellings:	8
Site area:	0.38 hectares (0.9 acres)
Density:	13.3 dwellings per hectare (5 dwellings per acre)

Size of dwellings (including integral garage):	171.4 m² (1845 sq ft)

Haarlemmer Houttuinen, Amsterdam

No. of dwellings:	76
Site area:	0.65 hectares (1.6 acres)
Density:	117 dwellings per hectare (47 dwellings per acre)

Type of accommodation:	
2-storey, 3-bedroom maisonettes	60
1-person bed-sitting-room apartments	16

Size of dwellings:	
1-person bed-sitting-room apartment (located at the ends of the terraces)	46.3 hectares (502 sq ft)
lower 3–bedroom maisonettes	83.68 sq m (901 sq ft)
upper-3-bedroom maisonettes	95.4 sq m (1027 sq ft)

Kassel-Dönche, Germany

No. of dwellings:	15

Type of accommodation:	2-bedroom flats
Size of dwellings:	84.4 sq m (904 sq ft)

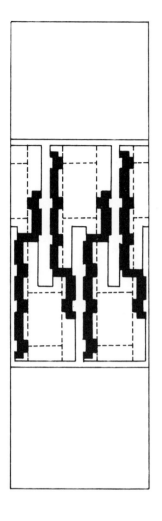

Herman Hertzberger's work throughout, aims to create a sense of neighbourliness by exploiting the potential to merge public and private spaces. To a considerable extent, this ideal echoes the Dutch habit of not closing living–room curtains at night to save giving offence, and bringing chairs and tables into the street so as to eat outside in hot weather.

Hertzberger's 'Diagoon' housing at Delft (built in the 1970s) was a test case for his theories (Fig 6.8). The plan of the dwellings exploits the split-level form which allows extensive views from one level to another (Fig 6.10). It also provides the opportunity for upper-level semi-private outdoor areas which increases the sense of space in the dwellings (Fig 6.9).

The 'Haarlemmer Houttuinen' housing is located between a busy main road to the north and a pedestrian street to the south. The

plan for the area envisaged that the street would be the social focus for the area, so all entrances were located this side of the dwellings, and the balconies overlook it. The four-storey terrace contains two levels of maisonettes (Fig 6.11). The lower-level maisonettes are entered through a small front garden, while the upper ones are approached firstly via a straight flight entrance beneath their balcony. This leads to the entrance to the maisonette at first-floor level, from which an internal staircase leads to the main living accommodation on the second floor. Projecting piers with balconies give rhythm to the street and a high sense of individuality to the dwellings in what could otherwise have been a monotonous terrace. The arrangement is

> typical of Hertzberger ... there is a complex and many layered overlapping of public and private realms [Fig 6.12] and of indoor and outdoor space creating possibilities for multitudes of subtly different uses and interpretations. (Buchanan 1985:27)

6.8   A diagram showing the grouping potential of 'Diagoon' housing.

6.9   The building form creates the opportunity for semi-private outdoor areas at each level.

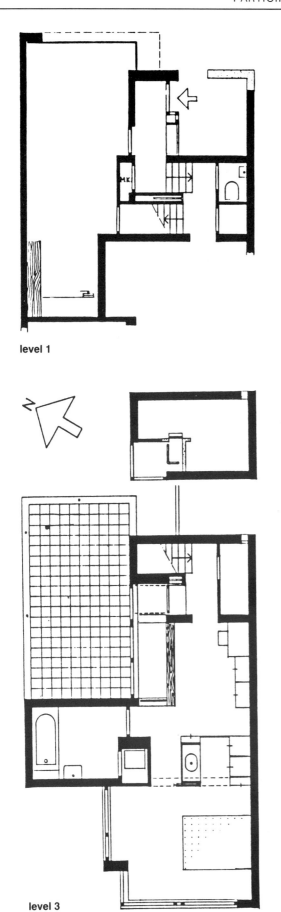

level 1

level 3

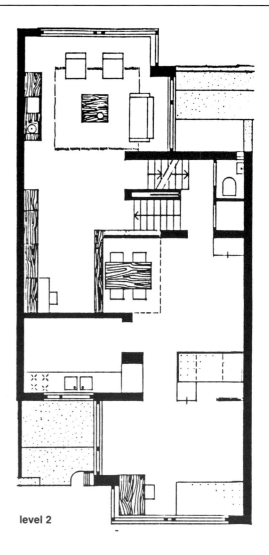

level 2

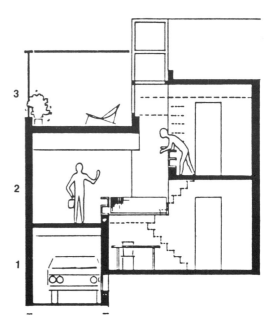

6.10 Diagoon housing: the split-level form of the dwellings allow extensive views from one level to another.

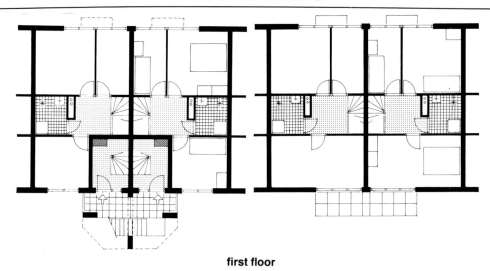

first floor

ground floor

6.11   Haarlemmer Houffuinen. Dwelling plans.

6.12   Projecting balconies and piers provide rhythm to the pedestrian street below.

**6.14   Kassel-Dönche: a stairway with a
projecting common room above.**

The project at Kassel, built 1979–82,
comprises two short segments of a
serpentine block (Fig 6.13), the form
of which had already been determined,
and its length divided between a
number of architects for detailed
consideration (which is a totally
unheard of practice in Britain, but one
that has much to recommend it if
variety within a terrace is to be
achieved). Hertzberger decided that
the approach best suited to the
fulfilment of his social vision was to
exploit the design of the staircase
which provides access both to his
dwellings and to the adjoining flats
designed by other architects
(Fig 6.14).

His design solution continues to
show just how far even the most
commonplace of housing types, in this
case walk-up flats paired about a
shared stair, can be reworked to be
dramatically enriching. Instead of
occupying the usual dark, dirty and
sometimes dangerous slot between
flats, the stair has been opened up to

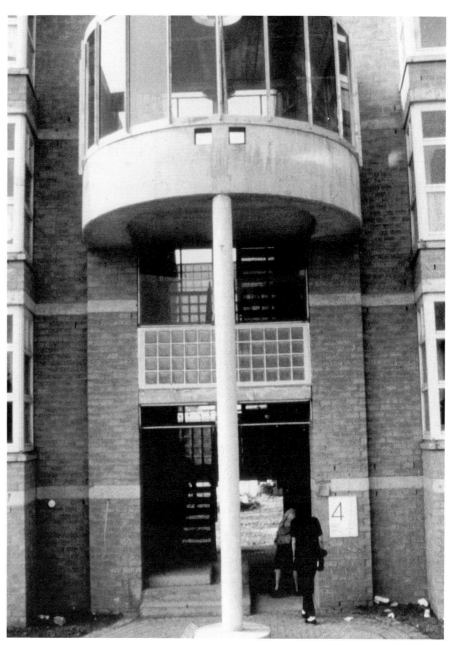

**6.13   Site plan of Kassel Dönche –
Hertzberger's flats are shaded.**

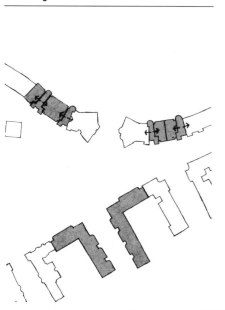

**6.15   Kassel Dönche: dwelling plans,
communal stairways and balconies.**

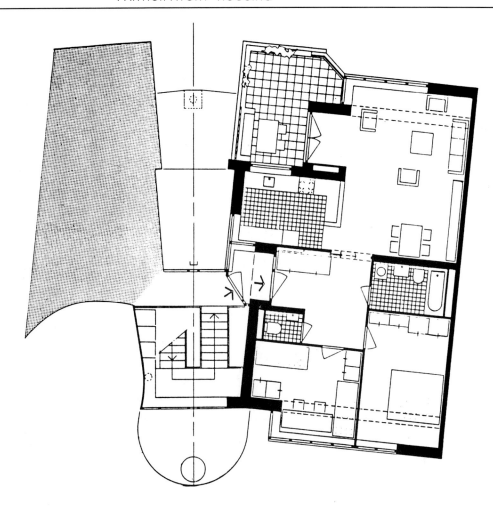

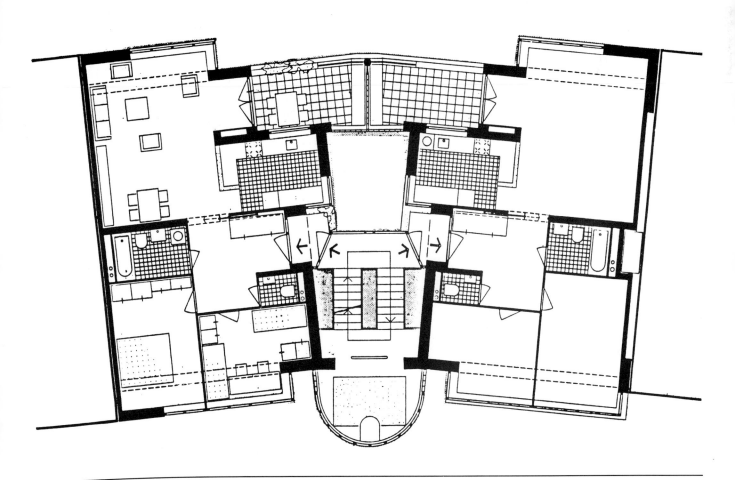

be lit from both ends and above. This well-lit, pleasant stair has been further elaborated to accommodate various functions so that it is thoroughly overlooked and safe. An upper landing on each stair projects out as a communal space (Fig 6.15) and play room. These areas appear to be well-used and, although part of the semi-public domain, have been furnished and decorated with plants by the residents. Children play on the stairs in safety as they can be seen from the kitchens of the adjoining dwellings.

As well as exploiting the staircases for all they are worth, Hertzberger has also used the balconies on the opposite side of the building to create public and private spaces (Fig 6.16). Off each living-room and kitchen is a balcony large enough to hold a dining table. In addition, on alternate floors, these balconies project either forward from the face of the building or towards each other: in this way part of each balcony is private from neighbours, while another part can be seen from two storeys, thus providing an opportunity for social exchange.

Hertzberger has created a housing project which goes against today's trend for an increasing withdrawal into the individual suburban home. The success of the scheme at Kassel arises from his skilful handling of the communal and private external spaces, which provide the opportunity for social interaction, whilst ensuring maximum privacy.

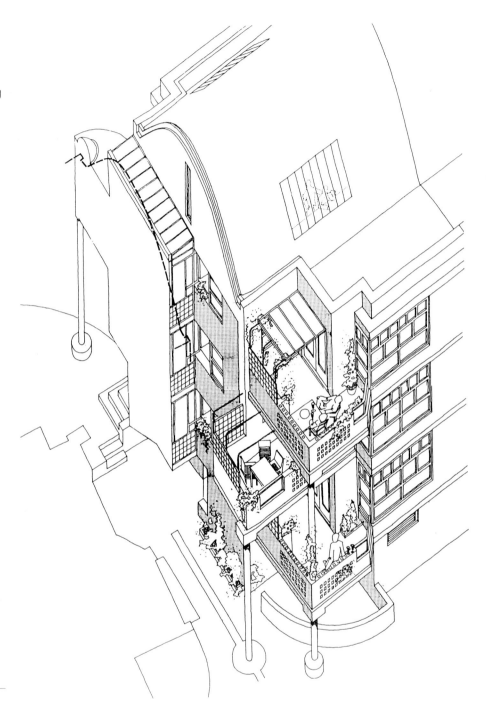

Areas have been measured from plans provided by the architect.

Further reading

BUCHANAN, P., 'New Amsterdam School: Herman Hertzberger', *Architectural Review*, January 1985, vol. CLXXVII, no. 1055,. pp. 25–7.

'Kassel Lesson', *Architectural Review*, October 1985, vol. CLXXVIII, no. 1064, pp. 43–5.

'Une une-habitation à Amsterdam', *L'Architecture d'aujourd'hui*, February 1983, no. 225, pp. 56–9.

'Drei Wohnquartiere – Kassel-Dönche', *Baumeister*, July 1983, no. 7, pp. 655–63.

6.16 Balconies create a variety of public and private outdoor areas.

Tinggården, Herfølge, South of Copenhagen, Denmark

Architects:	Tegnestuen Vandkunsten
No. of dwellings:	130
Site area:	2.38 hectares (5.88 acres)
Density:	55 dwellings per hectare (22 dwellings per acre).

Size of dwellings: 5 basic house types	basic dwellings of 45 sq m (48 sq ft) and 66 sq m (710 sq ft) which are extended by the addition of supplementary rooms of between 12.7 sq m (137 sq ft) and 16.9 sq m (182 sq ft)
communal house	125 sq m (136 sq ft)

Construction:	masonry is of mottled red brick; non-load bearing walls are fibre board; external cladding of Swedish red boarding; sloping ceilings in the all-purpose rooms are clad in timber boarding; floors are bleached ash parquet; roofs of of grey, corrugated asbestos cement sheeting.

Tinggärden in Herfølge (Fig 6.17) was one of the first non-profit-making housing projects to be built in Denmark during the 1970s. It was also one of the first in which the residents had a say regarding the design. The idea that occupants should have a wide degree of freedom in deciding the layout of their own homes was a new concept at the time, but with the support of the Danish Building Research Institute, the architects contacted a number of families who had expressed interest in helping to plan their own housing development.

The residents were originally more concerned with organization than with the physical design aspect. They wanted a mixture of owner-occupied and rented dwellings; they wanted a larger share of the building area devoted to common facilities than usual – even though this meant a reduction in the size of the individual dwelling (Fig 6.18). By employing a large number of dwelling types in six groups of 12–15 dwellings, it was possible to design the project with a

6.17 A varied, visually interesting community is created at Tinggården, Herfølge.

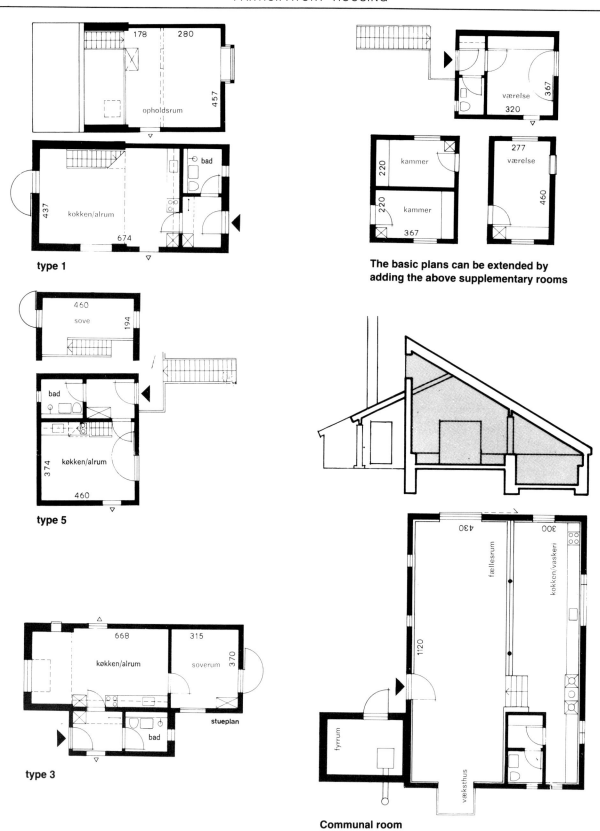

type 1

The basic plans can be extended by adding the above supplementary rooms

type 5

type 3

Communal room

6.20   The project contains five basic dwelling types (three of which are illustrated), which can be extended by adding supplementary rooms. The communal room is illustrated in the bottom right corner.

6.18   Site layout: 1   meeting house
2   communal house

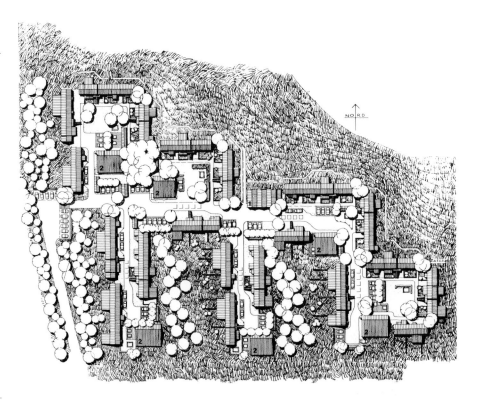

larger share of the building area devoted to common facilities than usual – even though this meant a reduction in the size of the individual dwelling (Fig 6.18). By employing a large number of dwelling types in six groups of 12–15 dwellings, it was possible to design the project with a view to subsequently combining individual dwellings to form new units, if the residents found this desirable. The houses differ widely, both in design and materials (Fig 6.20) and are thus an illustration of how it can be possible, in a new, carefully planned development, deliberately to incorporate 'accidental' character and surprises (Fig 6.19).

Further reading

FROMM, S., 'Living-together Housing', *The Architectural Review*, April 1985, vol. CLXXVII, no. 1058, pp. 63–71.

HANSEN, P. and LARSEN, F.A. (eds.), 'How the Danes Live', a special edition of the *Danish Journal*, The Royal Danish Ministry of Foreign Affairs, Copenhagen, 1981, pp. 17, 18.

'Modi di abitare', *Abitare*, April 1980, vol. 36, no. 183, pp. 8–13.

'Boligbebyggelsen Tinggården, Herfølge', *Arkitektur DK*, June 1979, no. 6, pp. 249–59.

'Tinggården', *Arkitektur*, March 1980, no. 2, p. 26.

'Tinggården Herfølge', *Arkitektur*, April 1982, no. 3, pp. 16–18 and 38.

6.19   There is immense elevational variety.

Scale 1:1500

Hedelyngen, Herlev, Denmark

Architect:	Tegnestuen Vandkunsten
No. of dwelings:	132
Site area:	5.1 hectares (12.6 acres)
Density:	25 dwellings per hectare (10.3 dwellings per acre)

Size of dwellings:

A1 single-storey	80 sq m (861 sq ft)
A2 single-storey	65 sq m (700 sq ft)
B one-and-a-half-storey	87 sq m (936 sq ft)
C one-and-a-half-storey	94 sq m (1012 sq ft) and supplementary room 21 sq m (226 sq ft)
D two-storey (not illustrated)	106.5 sq m (1146 sq ft)

Construction:	a combination of heavy and lightweight construction; the walls are of concrete panels, faced on the outside with brickwork and waterproof plywood; the ceilings and internal walls are of prefabricated timber panels covered with plywood; the roofs are covered with concrete tiles.

The development consists of 142 dwellings grouped around a common green with a community house in the centre (Fig 6.21). The buildings are greatly diversified, designed in one or two storey form with bays, indentations and exterior stairways. The emphasis of the design has been placed on creating a strong community feeling. Each cluster of dwellings is grouped around a common play area and car parking is kept to the perimeter of the site (Fig .22). There are four basic dwelling types: one of one storey; two of one and a half storeys, and one of two storeys (Fig 6.23). The roofs are designed so that the total volume of the interior can be enjoyed and this adds considerably to the sense of space (Fig 6.24). Supplementary rooms and one-room flats can be added later to the basic dwellings. The community house contains party rooms, meeting rooms and hobby rooms as well as the public laundry. (See also Fig 1.5.)

6.22   The view across the green.

6.21   Site layout of Hedelyngen, Herlev:
1   community house
2   existing house
3   kindergarten

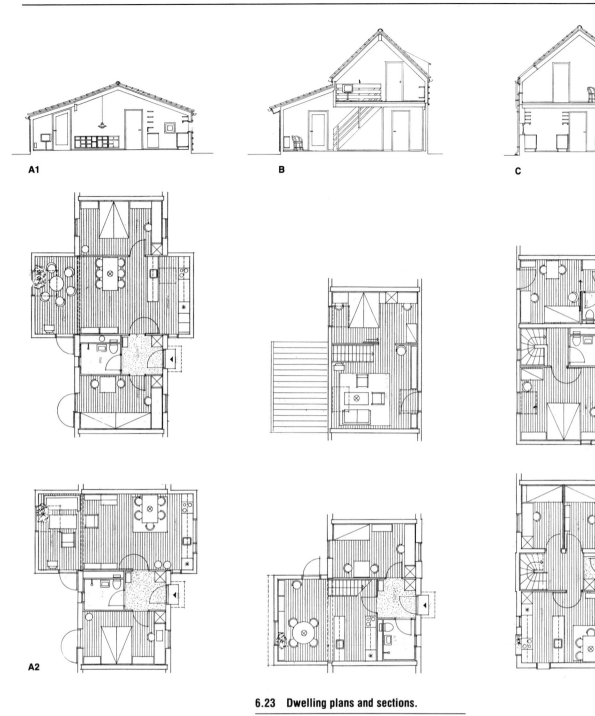

A1

B

C

A2

6.23 Dwelling plans and sections.

6.24 The interiors are finished to a very high standard.

Jystrup Sawmill, Zealand, Denmark

Architects:	Tegnestuen Vandkunsten
No. of dwellings:	21
Site area:	1.6 hectares (2.9 acres)
Density:	13.1 dwellings per hectare (7.2 dwellings per acre)
Type of accommodation:	houses and bungalows
Size of dwellings:	93 sq m–140 sq m (1000–1500 sq ft)

The Vandkunten group's ideas of
collective housing have been
developed even further in their project
in Jystrup on Zealand in which
privately owned dwellings and
common areas are under one roof.
The building form takes the shape of
an 'L' (Fig 6.25), with dwellings on
either side of a glazed pedestrian
access area which provides warmth
and shelter in the winter and a play
area for children (Fig 6.26). The
dwellings on the outer wall of the 'L'
are two storey whilst those on the
inner side are single-storey, dropping
down in level to the central green.
This allows the roof to fall over the
whole development in such a way as
to allow sunlight to penetrate into the
central access area and the upper
level of the two-storey houses. The
communal facilities are located at the
junction of the two arms, containing
cooking and dining facilities downstairs
and a living-room, sewing room and
children's playroom upstairs
(Fig 6.27).

Most of the living units are small and
the common-rooms are not luxurious
in order to keep costs to the minimum:
much of the finishing work was done
by the residents.

Areas have been measured from plans
provided by the architects.

Further reading

FROMM, S., 'Living-together housing',
Architectural Review, April 1985, vol. CLXXVII,
no. 1058, pp. 63–71.

'Energy saving prototype for low rise housing
in an urban setting', *Architecture* (the AIA
Journal), mid-August 1982, vol. 71, no 10,
pp. 88, 89.

**6.25   An overall view of Jystrup Sawmill,
Zealand, Denmark.**

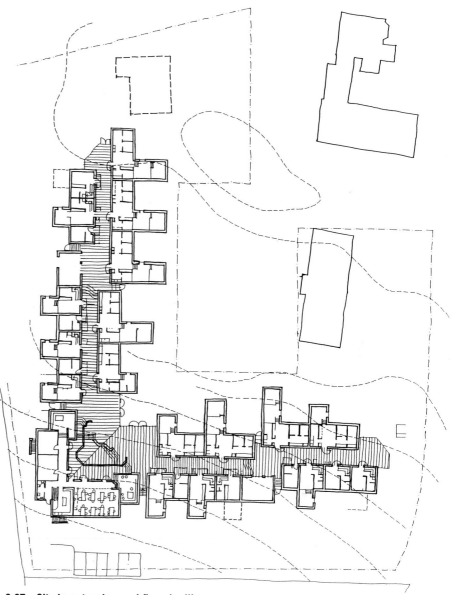

6.27   Site layout and ground-floor dwelling plans.

6.26   The internal covered way provides shelter all year round as well as being a play area for children.

Seldwyla, Zumikon, Zurich, Switzerland

Architects:	Rolf Keller (15 houses) Rudolf and Esther Guyer (2 houses) Guhi, Lerchner, Philipp (7 houses) Manuel Pauli (2 houses) Fritz Schwartz (2 houses)
No. of dwellings:	40
Site area:	0.8 hectares (1.9 acres)
Density:	50 dwellings per hectare (20 dwellings per acre)
Type of accommodation:	2-storey houses of various sizes

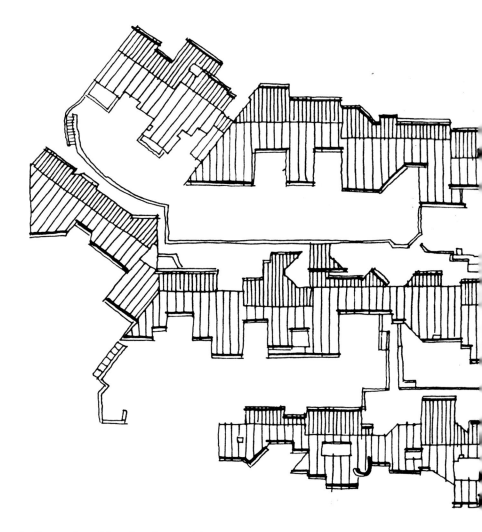

Rolf Keller is a most important figure in Swiss architecture. He has campaigned for many years against the way in which modern developments of all kinds have spoiled the environment (see Keller 1973).

His architecture at Seldwyla is a built expression of his dream. Built on a south-facing hillside, the development houses 40 families (Fig 6.28). He established a co-operative of future inhabitants which included five other architect members who designed some of the dwellings within his overall concept. His overall plan indicated routes, communal elements and plot boundaries, and he also determined building lines, roof pitches, materials, etc. The detailed design was left to the individual architects, and it is to Keller's credit that this policy has resulted in astonishing variety within a completely harmonious architectural whole

In the centre of the development is a village square and a community room, together with Keller's own office (Fig 6.29). Car parking is located underground. The materials used are soft: the walls are finished in white render and the stout, circular columns (Fig 6.4) and exposed, untreated sawn timber are capped with long roofs of orange tiles. The result is a development with an appearance of great maturity.

6.29   The village square and community room.

6.28 Seldwyla, Zurich: roof plan and site layout.

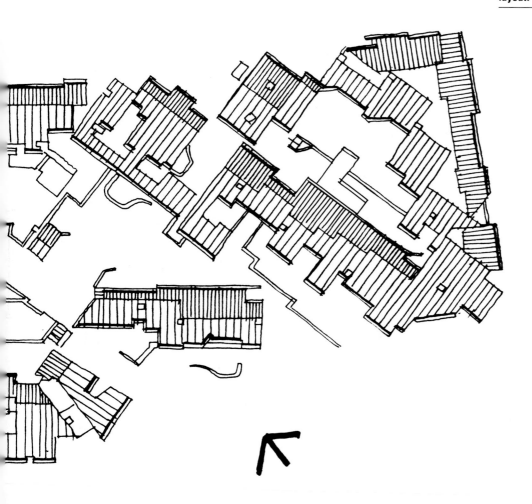

Areas have been measured from plans
provided by the architect.

Further reading

BLUNDELL-JONES, P., 'Keller in context'.
Architectural Review, June 1985, vol. CLXXVII,
no. 1060, pp. 66–75.

'Chriesmatt', *Deutsche Bauzeitung*,
April 1984, pp. 15–19.

'Dubendorf CH', *Baumeister*, April 1984,
pp. 44–9.

Chriesmatt, Dubendorf, Zurich, Switzerland

Architect:	Rolf Keller
No. of dwellings:	117
Site area:	2.5 hectares (6.2 acres)
Density:	46.8 dwellings per hectare (19 dwellings per acre)
Type of accommodation:	flats and terraced family houses
Size of dwellings:	83.2 sq m to 126 sq m (895 to 1356 sq ft)

6.31   The central pedestrian route with staircase access to the upper gallery.

Keller's other major project illustrated is entirely different from Seldwyla and comprises 92 flats and 25 terraced family houses. The development was financed partly by Keller's family, who owned the land, and partly by the pension fund of the food firm, Migros. Most of the family houses were sold to their occupants. The dwellings were skilfully grouped along both sides of a central pedestrian street (Figs 6.30, 6.31).

6.30   Chriesmatt, Zurich-Dubendorf: the site layout is full of the movement and interest that characterizes Keller's architecture.

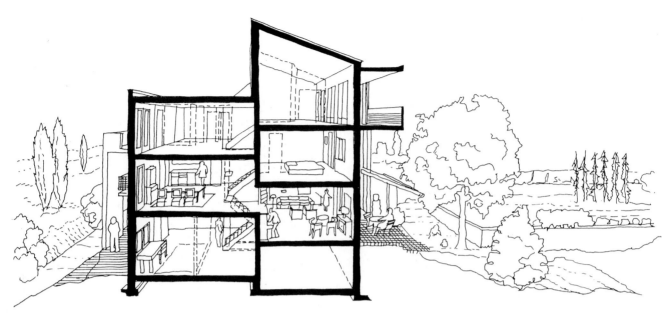

section through maisonettes

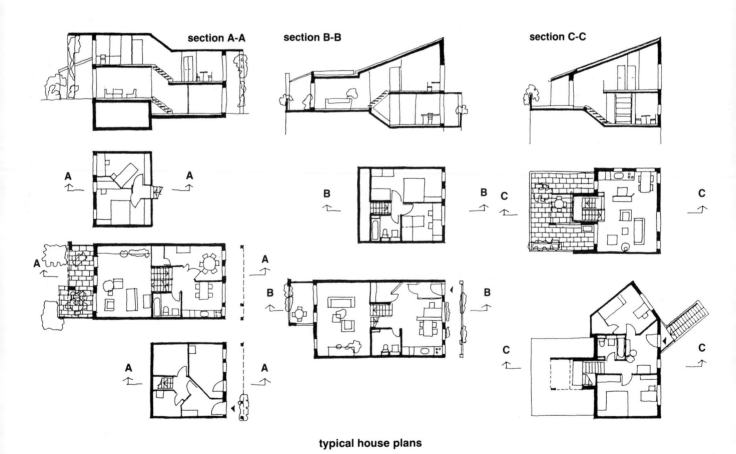

section A-A   section B-B   section C-C

typical house plans

6.32 Section through the dwellings and floor plans.

6.33   A variety of balconies, oriel windows and archways create a sense of individuality.

6.34   A lake was created where a road was planned.

Access to the upper-floor dwellings overlooking this street is via highly sculptural staircases and balconies (Fig 6.31) which provide covered, arcaded entrances to the dwellings below. The houses curve away from the central street and all have gardens. Within a strict architectural concept there is much variety. This comes from the use of a large number of dwelling types (Fig 6.32) and through the use of various kinds of windows, oriels, balconies, etc. (Fig 6.33) Car parking is underneath the buildings which is a typical feature of so much recently constructed grouped housing in Switzerland. At one end of the site Keller has developed an ecological pond (Fig 6.34): he takes great pride in demonstrating that this is in the place of a planned highway going from nowhere to nowhere. His efforts have gone far beyond those of most architects, and his achievement at Chriesmatt is considerable.

Areas have been from plans provided by the Architect.

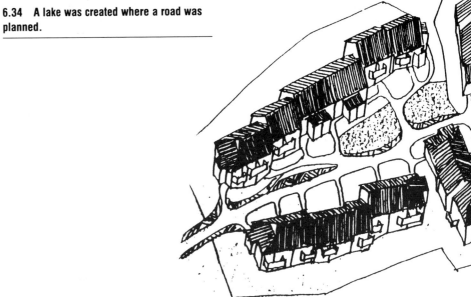

Oksval III–IV, A Local Housing Co-operation Project, Oslo, Norway

Architect:	Roslands Arkitektkontor AS
No. of dwellings:	260
Site area:	5 hectares (12.4 acres)
Density:	52 dwellings per hectare (21 dwellings per acre)

Type of accommodation:	
houses	198
flats	62

Size of dwellings:	
houses for 1–7 people	116.36 sq m (1254 sq ft)
flats for 1–5 people	72.6 sq m (782 sq ft)
communal facilities	(total areas) 782 sq m (8428 sq ft)

Parking/garages:	190 car parking spaces; 122 garages
Heating:	electric heating with solid fuel fireplace in living-room.

The aims behind the design of this scheme were to protect the natural characteristics and vegetation of the site and to involve the future residents in the design and, to some extent, in the building process. The site is steeply sloping, long and narrow, and faces east with a view over Oslo Fjord. The overall plan is made up of clusters of houses with a pedestrian route running through the groups (Fig 6.35). Public activity is concentrated along this spine (Fig 6.36) as all entrance gates are connected to it. Within each cluster of housing is a public space for sitting and childrens play. Each cluster is made up of approximately 25 units built as terrace-houses of four to eight units in a row. A kindergarten and community house are located centrally.

There are three basic dwelling types, different in size, adaptability and number of storeys (one to three (Fig 6.37). From this basis, 32 plans were developed to meet the special needs of the occupants as determined during the design period. To obtain the best orientation and aspect, the main level of all dwellings was designed as open-plan, with the living area, dining and kitchen spaces running from one outer wall to another. The kitchen, bathroom and staircase were standardized in all plans.

Further reading
'Oskral III and IV, Oslo', *Arkitektur*, September 1982, no. 7, pp. 22, 23, 38.

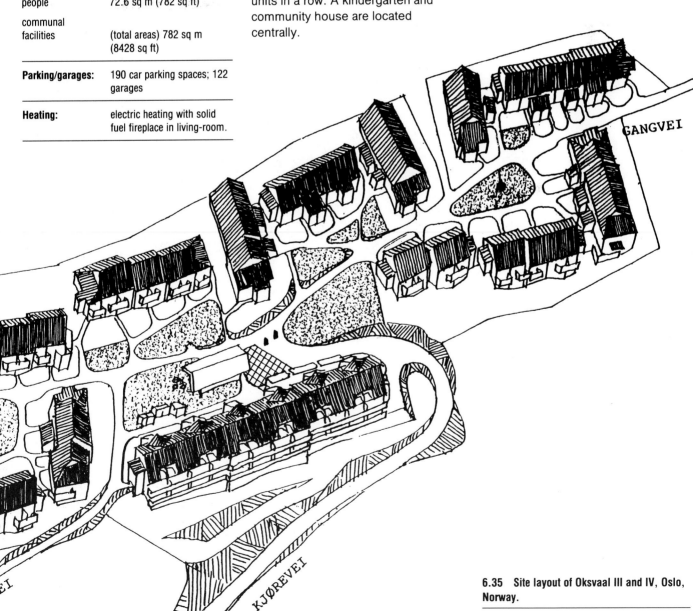

6.35 Site layout of Oksvaal III and IV, Oslo, Norway.

6.36   General views of the housing.

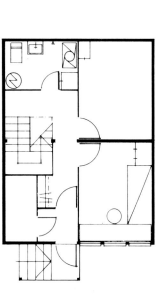

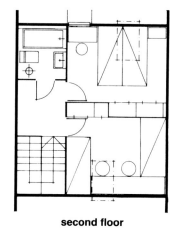

section

first floor

ground floor

second floor

6.37   Floor plans and section through two/three-storey houses.

Graz-Puntigam, Austria

Architect:	Eilfred Huth
No. of dwelings:	66
Site area:	2.3 hectares (0.93 acres)
Density:	28.7 dwellings per hectare (11.6 dwellings per acre)
	120 persons per hectare (49 persons per acre)
Type of accommodation: houses	66
dwellings designed for disabled people	10
Size of dwellings:	180 sq m (average) (2000 sq ft)
Parking/garages:	70 car parking spaces
Construction:	blockwork finished with coloured render; concrete floors; metal sheet roofing.

Eilfreid Huth considers that architecture should be the expression of a social process involving a high degree of participation of the future occupants in the design stages. He believes that people should be allowed to display their own taste in their houses, rather than dominating them entirely with his own (Fig 6.38). At Graz-Puntigam he has designed terraced housing in which there are, within a strict geometric layout form a wide variety of plans (Fig 6.39), fenestration and colour as desired by the occupants. The dwellings are designed with 7 m (23 ft) frontages of masonry construction covered with render.

The result is most striking as every dwelling has its own individual identity, a fact greatly enjoyed by the occupants (Fig 6.40). The process of design with co-operation and participation relates to the educational level and ability of the prospective residents. Eilfred Huth said that,

individual decision making and individual performance, which have become important aspects of dwelling construction, give rise to new forms, and thus to a different appearance. It expresses the concept of variety, of individual divergence from the norm. Generally, it results in a significant and highly perceptible differentiation from the bland monotony of normal housing. (quoted in Blundell-Jones 1988:81)

6.38 Graz-Puntigam, Austria: there is individual expression throughout.

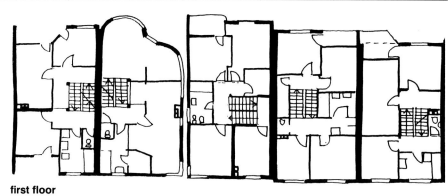

first floor

6.39   The participation process resulted in a wide variety of house plans.

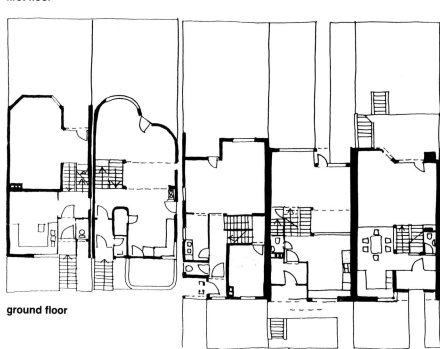

ground floor

6.40   The process also resulted in a large number of elevational variations.

Graz-Algersdorf, Austria

Architect:	Eilfred Huth
No. of dwellings:	26
Site area:	0.32 hectares (0.8 acres)
Density:	80 dwellings per hectare (32 dwellings per acre)
Type of accommodation: flats	26
dwellings designed specially for disabled people	18
Parking/garages:	30 car parking spaces

The project at Graz-Algersdorf (Fig 6.41) by Eilfred Huth was part of a large development comprising a home for handicapped people and 80 flats designed by three architects. Huth's contribution was a three and four-storey block containing 26 flats designed in the form of a crescent (Fig 6.42). The project is more uniform in its design that Graz-Puntigam, but there is still great diversity in the plans of the individual dwellings and communal staircases which resulted from the total involvement of the future occupants in the design process. The single lift in the round tower provides access to two flats at each level of the four-storey part of the block. Staircases at each end provide access to flats in the three-storey parts, whilst other dwellings, in between those served by the lift and staircases, are served by a short gallery at second-floor level which provides access to flats on the levels above and below.

Further reading

BLUNDELL-JONES, P., 'Participative Huth', *The Architectural Review*, December 1988, vol. CLXXXIV, no. 1102, pp. 80–3.

6.41 At Graz-Algersdorf three-storeys of split-level flats abut on to the four-storey block.

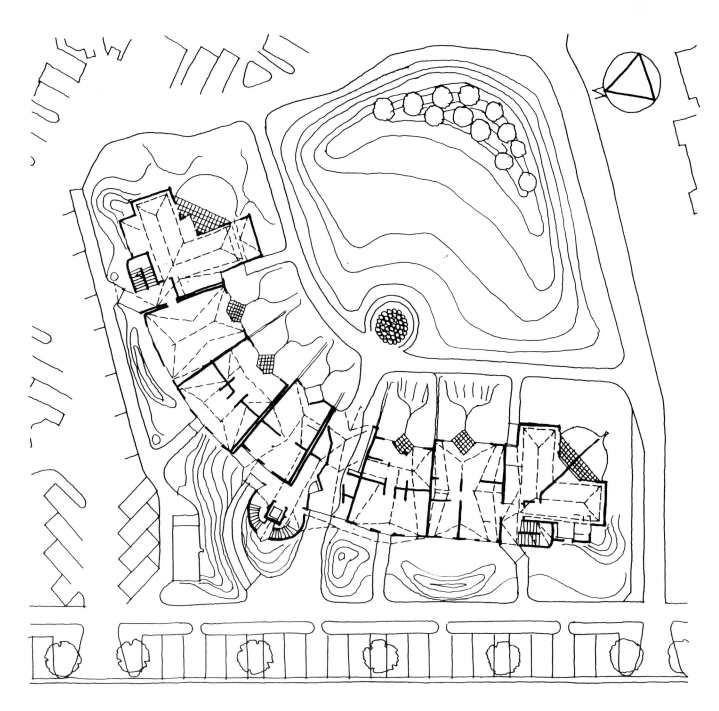

6.42 Graz-Algersdorf: the curved block looks on to a communal garden.

Participatory Housing at Eisbach, Rein, Austria

Architects:	Michael Szyszkowitz and Karla Kowalski-Szyszkowitz

No. of dwellings:	24
Site area:	0.69 hectares (1.7 acres)
Density:	34 dwellings per hectare (13.8 dwellings per acre)

Type of accommodation:	
maisonettes	24

Size of dwellings:	
3-person	70–80 sq m (753–861 sq ft)
4–5-person	80–100 sq m (861–1076 sq ft)
5-person	100–110 sq m (1076–1184 sq ft)
5 + people	100–130 sq m (1184–1399 sq ft)

6.43   An aerial view of Eisbach-Rein, near Graz.

The project involved extensive participation by the prospective residents. Initially they invited seven firms of architects to take part in a limited competition which they accessed with a specialist jury. The partnership Szyszkowitz-Kowalski was awarded the scheme and the designs were then produced through a full participative process. The dwellings are grouped in a continuous U-shaped block around an open communal garden (Figs 6.43, 6.44) containing a children's play area (Fig 6.45). Small gardens are provided to the front and rear. The dwellings are split-level maisonettes grouped one above the other. Access to the upper floor dwellings is via common staircases serving two dwellings per floor. The dwelling plans vary considerably, reflecting the architects' highly inventive and three-dimensional approach to design.

Further reading

BLUNDELL-JONES, P., 'Graz – sectional Szyszkowitz-Kowalski' *The Architectural Review*, December 1988, vol. CLXXXIV, no. 1102, pp. 66–72.

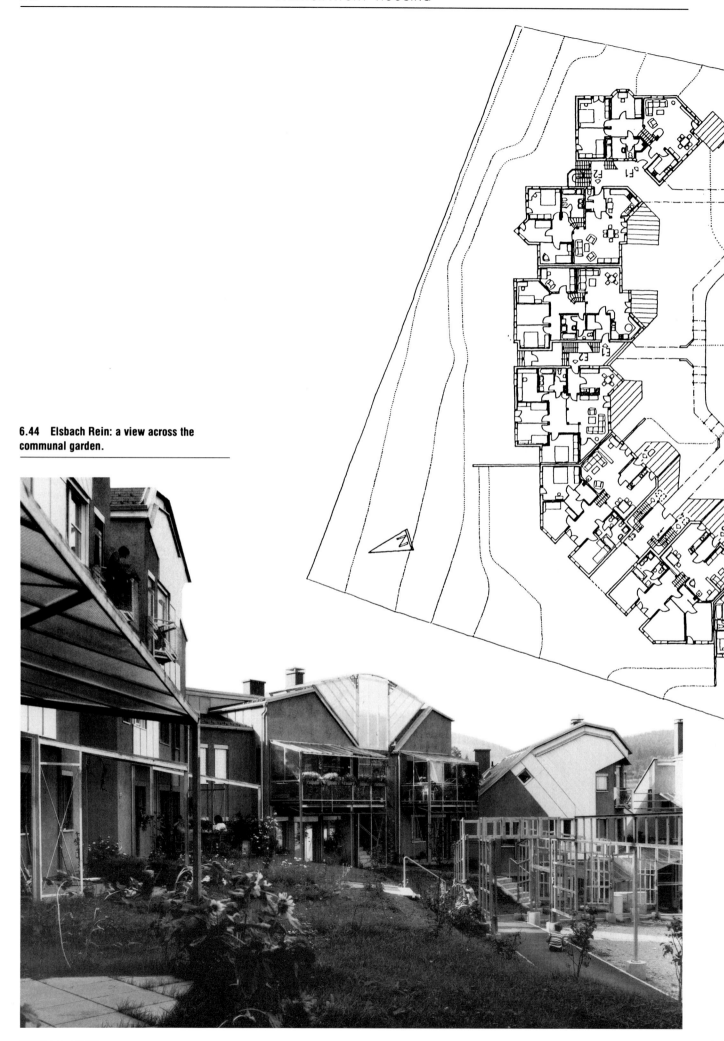

6.44 Elsbach Rein: a view across the communal garden.

6.45 Site plan showing the 'U'-shaped block of dwellings designed around a communal garden – car parking is kept to one side of the garden.

Self-build Houses at Bromsten, Stockholm

Architects:	Sodergruppen Arkitektkontor
No. of dwellings:	38
Site area:	1 hectare (2.5 acres)
Density:	38 dwellings per hectare (15 dwellings per acre)
Type of accommodation:	family houses
Size of dwellings: 3-bedroom house (illustrated)	118 sq m + 21.7 sq m garage (1272 sq ft + 234 sq ft)
3-bedroom split level house	129 sq m (1390 sq ft)
Construction:	'do-it-yourself' construction using timber-framing and a high level of insulation as seen on the architect's construction drawings.

This small group of self-build houses epitomizes what is best in traditional Swedish domestic architecture (Fig 6.46). Two dwelling types have been used, one of narrow frontage (Fig 6.47) and one of split-level form with living-room, kitchen, bedroom and bathroom on the upper level and two bedrooms, large hall and second bathrooms on the lower level.

The project was constructed within the self-build programme organized by 'SMAA' which is the abbreviation of 'smahusavdelningen', translatable as the Department for Single-Family Housing, a department within the Stockholm Real Estate and Housing Office. Development with SMAA takes the following course.

1   A local authority allots an area to SMAA for developing.

2   SMAA works out the basis for a building plan. This work is carried out in consultation with the Municipal Architect's Office.
3   SMAA works out tender documents for foundations, roads and other ground construction works, heating/hot water, drainage, sanitation and electrical installation.
4   SMAA organizes the mortgages. This includes estimating the cost of all the superstructure materials, fees and the cost of SMAA's own work.
5   The building of the foundations, roads, etc., is supervised by SMAA's controllers.
6   The occupants then build the superstructures in their leisure time.

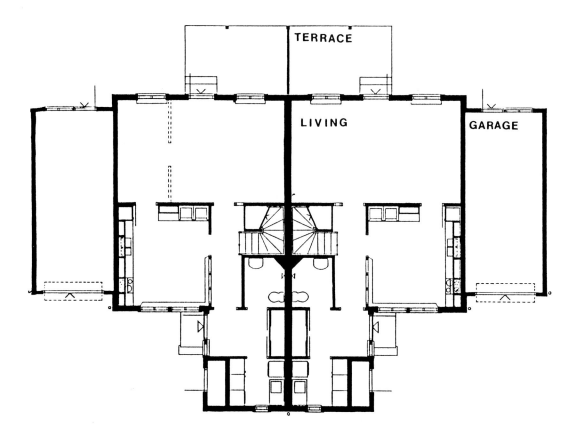

ground floor

The benefits of this type of organization are that housing is ten to fifteen per cent cheaper than conventional housing and that people become more attached to their house. The building operation is simplified and demands fewer constructional skills because prefabricated elements are used and the number of different types of houses in any one group of houses is limited. However, within these limitations the self-builder is given full freedom, and even advice, to choose such things as paints, wallboards, flooring and plants and trees for the garden. Ten houses in one group is considered enough to achieve a sound economic result, but groups of fifty or more have been developed at any one time.

Further reading
'Självbyggeri Bromsten, Stockholm'
Arkitektur, June 1984, pp. 26–8.

6.47   Elevations

6.46   Self-build houses at Bromsten, Stockholm: narrow fronted house type.

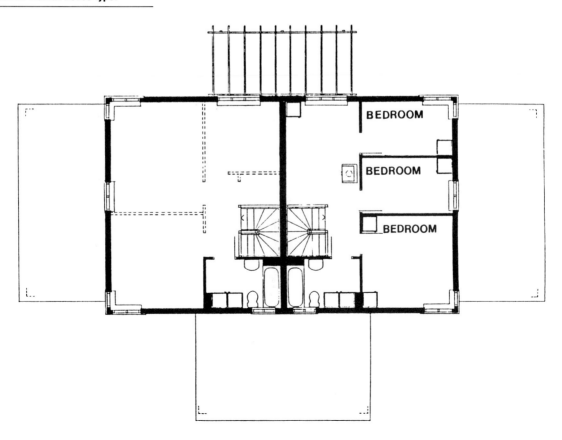

BEDROOM

BEDROOM

BEDROOM

upper floor

REFERENCES

BLUNDELL-JONES, P., 'Graz – Participative Huth', *Architectural Review*, December 1988, vol. CLXXXIV, no. 1102, pp. 80–3.

BROWNE, K., 'Connecting Vision', *Architectural Review*, March 1979, vol. CLXV, no. 985, pp. 165–77.

BUCHANAN, P., 'New Amsterdam School: Herman Hertzberger', *Architectural Review*, January 1985, vol. CLXXVII, no. 1055, p. 25–7.

CLELLAND, D., 'West Berlin 1984, The Milestone and the Millstone', *Architectural Review*, September 1984, vol. CLXXVI, no. 1051, pp. 18–114.
'Housing Lindenstrasse', *Architectural Review*, April 1987, vol. CLXXXI, no. 1982, pp. 57–9.

CLELLAND, D., and DAVEY, P., 'Berlin, origins to IBA', *Architectural Review*, April 1987, vol. CLXXXI, no. 1083, pp. 23–105.

COMERIO, M. C., 'Design and Empowerment: 20 years of Community Architecture', *Built Environment*, 1987, vol. 13, no. 1.

DAVEY, P., 'Danish Idealism', *Architectural Review*, May 1988, vol. CLXXXIII, no. 1095.
'Three on the water-front' *Architectural Review*, April 1989, vol. CLXXXV, no. 1106, pp. 46–54.

DEPARTMENT OF THE ENVIRONMENT and CENTRAL OFFICE OF INFORMATION, 'Rayment's and Bell's Almshouses, Linkfield Road Isleworth, Middlesex', *Awards for Good Design in Housing 1978*, HMSO, p. 24.

DEVENISH, J., 'Woolloomooloo Townscape – an exercise in controlled diversity', *Architecture Australia*, September 1981, vol. 70, no. 4, pp. 55–63.

ELLIS, C., 'Housing function follows form', *Architectural Review*, December 1986, vol. CLXXX, no. 1078, pp. 63–6.

FARELLY, E. M., 'Community Architecture, Contradiction in Terms?', *Architectural Review*, March 1987, vol. CLXXXI, no. 1081.

FROMM, D., 'Living-together housing', *Architectural Review*, April 1985, vol. CLXXVII, no. 1058, pp. 63–72.

GOUGH, P., 'Town Krier', *Architects' Journal*, 15 August 1984, vol. 180, no. 33, pp. 32–41.

HANNAY, P., 'Rauchstrasse 9', *Architectural Review*, March 1986, vol. CLXXIX, no. 1069, pp. 64–9.

HANSEN, P., and LARSEN, F. A. (eds), 'How the Danes Live', a special issue of the *Danish Journal*, Royal Danish Ministry of Foreign Affairs, Copenhagen, 1981.

JOHNSON, J., *A Guide to Green Buildings*, Ecology Unit, 1991.

KARMI, R., 'Giloh housing 1,2,3, Jerusalem, Israel', *Architecture Contemporaine/ Contemporary Architecture*, Bibliothèque des Arts, Paris and Lausanne, 1983–1984, pp. 46–53.

KELLER, R., *Bauen als Umweltzerstörung*, ('Building as Environmental Destruction'), 1973, Gestaltung Otmar Buchner, Zurich.

KRAFFT, A. (ed.), 'Ramot Housing, Jerusalem, Israel', *Architecture Contemporaine/ Contemporary Architecture*, Bibliothèque des Arts, Paris and Lausanne, 1980–1981, pp. 31, 32.

KRIER, R., *Stadtraum in Theorie und Praxis* ('Urban Space'), Academy Editions, London, 1979.

MORGAN, A. L. and NAYLOR, C. (eds), *Contemporary Architects*, St James Press, Chicago and London, 1987.

PALLASMA, J., 'Tradition and Modernity – the Feasibility of Regional Architecture in Postmodern Society', *Architectural Review*, May 1988, vol. CLXXXIII, no. 1095, pp. 27–34.

PERKINS, G., 'Woolloomooloo and a surf club' and 'Swansea Docks transformed – Swansea maritime quarter', *Concrete Quarterly*, October-December 1986, no. 151.

UPDEGRAVE, W., 'How to put the home-shopper survey to work', *Housing*, December 1980, pp. 49–53.

WARD, C., 'What a time it took for the penny to drop', *Built Environment*, 1987, vol. 13, no. 1.

WATES, N., 'Co-op Consolidation', *Architectural Review*, April 1985, vol. CLXXVII, no. 1058, pp. 57–60.

WILLIAMS, A. and Partners, 'Ferrara Quay, Swansea', *Building*, 8 April 1988, vol. CCLIII, no. 7540, pp. 75–60.

Architects' Journal, 23 March 1988, vol. 187, no. 12, 'Bandwagon jumping in Liverpool', p. 5.

Baumeister, July 1983, no. 7, 'Drei Wohnquartiere – Berlin, Ritterstrasse', pp. 664–7.

Techniques et Architecture, December 1983– January 1984, no. 315, 'Ilot 31 à Berlin Kreuzberg', pp. 120–2.

INDEX